The 18 Challenges of Leadership

THE

Challenges
of
Leadership

A Practical, Structured Way to Develop Your Leadership Talent

Trevor Waldock &
Shenaz Kelly-Rawat

PEARSON
Prentice Hall
BUSINESS

London • New York • Toronto • Sydney • Tokyo • Singapore • Hong Kong
Cape Town • New Delhi • Madrid • Paris • Amsterdam • Munich • Milan

PEARSON EDUCATION LIMITED

Edinburgh Gate
Harlow CM20 2JE
Tel: +44 (0)1279 623623
Fax: +44 (0)1279 431059
Website: www.pearsoned.co.uk

First published in Great Britain in 2004

ISBN 0 273 68810 3

British Library Cataloguing-in-Publication Data
A catalogue record for this book can be obtained from the British Library.

Library of Congress Cataloging-in-Publication Data
Waldock, Trevor.
    The 18 challenges of leadership : a practical, structured way to develop your
leadership talent / Trevor Waldock and Shenaz Kelly-Rawat.
        p.   cm.
    ISBN 0–273–68810–3 (alk. paper)
        1. Leadership, 2. Executives—Training of. I. Title: Eighteen challenges of
leadership. II. Kelly-Rawat, Shenaz. III. Title.

HD57.7.W337 2004
658.4′092—dc22
                                                                    2004044480

ARP Impression 98

Typeset in 11.5 pt Minion by 70
Printed in Great Britain by Clays Ltd, St Ives plc

The publishers' policy is to use paper manufactured from sustainable forests.

To Anne, Sam & Jonathan – the wisest and most supportive team a person could belong to

To Jogin, Adam & Nadia who encourage me to believe, each in their unique way, that anything is possible!

Contents

Acknowledgements

By Trevor

Eddie Vass, Peter Wiegand, Lutz Ketwig, Bill Hybels and Rob Poole – more mentors in leadership than a person has a right to, who all taught me something original about leadership.

Trevor, Rob, Carol, Howard, Hilary, Maggie and Lindsay – they taught me the secret of community in a leadership team.

By Shenaz

My mentors, George O'Connor and Sean Brophy, for generously sharing their insights and for inspiring me to appreciate the wisdom of Personal Construct Psychology.

My parents for giving me such a good start in life.

Trevor, my co-author, whose commitment and hard work made this book possible.

By both of us

Rachael Stock at Pearson who had the vision to back the idea and the patience to see it through to this book.

Jan Brand who makes everything happen for The Executive Coach.

Sharon Anderson worked her magic in editing the chapters into something we feel proud of.

David Kearney for giving Trevor and Shenaz the chance to meet each other and to learn so much that is implicit in this book.

To our clients, past and present, who allow us the privilege of sharing their working lives in the context of Executive Coaching.

Foreword

More words have been written on the subject of leadership than most other aspects of business, but a glance at the business media on any day reveals that little has been learned. Business failures abound, the doors continue to revolve on the corporate top floors, and the ethics and values of business seem to be in terminal decline. So where do we look to find good leaders today? Certainly not in the political arena, where untruths are regarded as best practice and spins are intentional. Religious leaders too either seem unable to keep the fanatics in check, or are themselves the fanatics. The public sector perhaps? Many would say, don't go there either, and I won't.

The truth is that there are sadly few role models of great leadership to be found in the traditional corridors of power. Those that we admire are usually mavericks such as Ricardo Semler, supported by a certain amount of hot air such as Branson or dead such as Ghandi. They are or were exceptional people before they were leaders so where did their leadership come from? Not from business schools or from academic tomes, but from inside themselves.

The authors of this book have struck a perfect balance between the necessary outer leadership skills, without which no one will follow, and inner leadership upon which all leadership really depends. How can one lead or manage others if one cannot lead or manage oneself? Leadership can be learned or evoked from within, but it cannot be taught from without. Trevor Waldock and Shenaz Kelly-Rawat are expert executive coaches who know how to provoke thought and insight and to challenge the reader to look deeply within.

The 18 well chosen challenges are addressed in a very logical sequence. Each one is explained clearly, supported by simple examples and then a series of provocative coaching questions are posed to the reader - often calling for a numerical self-assessment. And then ways forward are proposed. Since each challenge and the way forward is relatively self-contained, it is not necessary to read the book all the way through at a sitting. Rather it is one of those books that one can dip in and out of to select the issue of the day. I suggest that many people who have not previously seen themselves to be leadership material, will after reading this book reconsider their roles, and raise their sights.

This book comes at a time when the old power hierarchy model is revealing all its flaws, and the information explosion is encouraging all of us to demand more say in our lives and our world. All of us can benefit from enhancing our leadership skills and welcoming more choice, as we recognise that no one but ourselves can lead us to the promised land.

Sir John Whitmore
March 2004

Introduction

Organisations today are looking for more than effective managers. They are looking for engaged people who can think and see and plan. They want people who can create something that doesn't yet exist, not just manage what already exists. They are looking for leaders, at every level.

The difference between management and leadership is significant. There is something about the label or identity of 'management' or 'manager' that locks people into what is, what has always been, what is sitting in their in-tray or in-box, organising the current situation or the current resources, reacting and having a short-term focus – looking down at their feet. Conversely there is something about leadership that lifts up managers' heads, that engages them in a bigger story, that creates a sense of believing they can make a difference, that gets them realising they can think strategically, that they can behave more influentially.

When was the last time you lifted up your head? It is so easy to go through life looking down at your feet, watching for the next pothole, avoiding the potential hazards that lie ahead; too busy to look up, too pressured to raise the eyes beyond the immediate. There are hundreds of definitions of leadership (Warren Bennis said in the *Financial Times* recently that there were nearly 300 textbook definitions already!), but our definition is that *leadership is about lifting up your head and the heads of others*. The real challenge of leadership is to lead yourself across your life and career, in order to effectively lead others.

Being an effective leader enhances your career prospects and your job satisfaction. Working at developing your leadership potential is possibly the greatest investment you could make. This book is a structured and practical framework for developing your leadership talent – whatever your level in the organisation.

In our experience of developing leadership in organisations we have found that the commonality amongst our clients over the years is that they all face similar challenges which are steeped in the reality of the workplace. These challenges span from what are often called 'hard' business-focused issues like Vision and Strategy, to 'soft' personal challenges like Personality and Confidence. The 18 Challenges of Leadership have been distilled from the real challenges leaders face in their daily work. It invites you to examine how well equipped you are as a person to deal with each of these challenges. In essence *The 18 Challenges of Leadership* offers a number of benefits:

1. An education on the challenges of leadership distilled from hundreds of hours of practical experience underpinned by extensive reading, research and theory.

2. A fast and sound way of assessing your response to the challenges you face as a leader in your current role.

3. By the very process of assessing yourself you will discover that the 18 Challenges offer you a structured, reflective process that is guaranteed to raise your self-awareness and give you insight into your leadership. All research recognises that this is the foundation stone of leadership development.

4. The assessment creates an agenda for your leadership development.

5. The book then provides a practical step-by-step process to guide you through your development as a leader in response to each of the challenges.

Our aim for you is that this book will provide a space for you to continue to grow to your full leadership potential.

Two key concepts lie at the heart of this book and are woven into the whole of the 18 Challenges. First, we believe that if you are to lift up your head and the heads of others then awareness of the fundamental concept of Emotional Intelligence is important (see the work of Daniel Goleman and the Insight Challenge in Chapter 7). This is about our ability to understand and make sense of our emotions *intra-personally* (within oneself) and *inter-personally* (between oneself and others) so we can choose the right responses in our working life. The second concept is best known as the Inner Game (see the work of Tim Gallwey). Leadership has an internal theatre where a performance is taking place in which you may play all the parts of your drama: the internalised voices of your own perceptions, your family, your advocates, your enemies, your fears, your irrational beliefs. More obviously, leadership also has an external theatre. This is the outer dimension that everyone gets to see, in other words, your actual performance. In the words of Wimbledon Champion Venus Williams, 'most times when we lose, we defeat ourselves'. Our own inner theatre gets in the way of our external effectiveness, or, to put it another way, we usually get in the way of ourselves. Throughout this book we keep our eye on what is interfering with your performance and how to move on with inner and outer games.

About this book

Each chapter is structured in three sections

For ease of reading each chapter is broken down into three sections. Section A, is there to deepen your understanding of each challenge. Section B, is there to help you assess where you think you are in relation to each challenge. The third section, section C, provides a practical process for developing your ability to respond to that particular leadership challenge. Each chapter ends with exactly the same question, 'What are you going to do now?' We have provided keys in Appendix 1 to help you with action planning.

Engage in a leadership conversation

In our experience leadership development requires that you are engaged in each challenge, have a desire to change, have focus, openness, raised awareness and many other things, but at the heart of it all is a conversation between you and someone who is investing in your development. So we have sought to engage you and help you get focused by writing the book in such a way that you can hold conversations with yourself about each of the challenges that you need to focus on right now. There is a lot of talk about Executive Coaching these days, but our definition of Executive Coaching is simply this: 'it is the leadership conversation'.

So you need to make time

In working through this leadership development process you will be having a conversation with yourself. The reason why so many people get caught being a manager rather than a leader is that they simply don't make the time to go through this reflective process. While we have sought to model a conversation in the book to make the process as easy as possible, the one thing we have no control over is ensuring that you take some time out to invest in your own development as a leader. So you need to set aside manageable chunks of time in your diary (along with a notebook and pen by your side!) or invite a small group of people to invest in this process together.

Leadership development fits together like a puzzle

This book, built around The 18 Challenges of Leadership™, comes out of people's experience and is backed by our own extensive reading in this field. We are aiming to provide a picture of leadership that covers the 'harder' issues of strategy, the foundational issues of influence and proactivity, the important issues of wisdom, the personality, the life stages, the personal baggage everyone has and the need to create balance to sustain effective performance. As you dig into one challenge you will find yourself overlapping with another challenge. As you work through the Wisdom Challenge you may find yourself confronted with the Influence Challenge or the Proactive Challenge. This shouldn't be surprising because all the data comes from all kinds of people who are trying to make sense of coming to work and responding to leadership challenges in their daily situations. People's work lives as they live them are messy, integrated experiences. They are not divided up into six or nine or even eighteen neat segments. It is only in deconstructing the experience that each of the 18 Challenges emerge, but the actual lived experience is a unity. And while, in an individual's whole life or career perspective, some challenges may be more relevant than others at a point in time, a wise leader has them all on his or her radar screen. With this in mind, please note that these 18 Challenges are not written in order of importance, but simply in what we felt was a logical sequence.

The uniqueness of this book lies in how it integrates the whole spectrum of challenges faced by leaders, and we hope it guides you through those challenges to be a more effective, more powerful and more successful leader.

For more information see our website
www.18challengesofleadership.com

The
Proactive Challenge

Learning to write the story

A. Understanding this Challenge

The first challenge in leadership development is to move yourself to a place where you are acting rather than reacting. When you are reacting you are acting without stopping to think, whereas when you are proactive you are seizing a moment to stop, think and have options and choices. There are three ways to think about proactivity.

1. Who Writes the Story?

When you tell people about your day at work you tell them the story. It's the story of how you felt when you got off the train, when you entered the office, the e-mails that greeted you, the meetings you attended, the surprise phone calls and interruptions, the challenges and deadlines, the conversation over coffee. The question surrounding proactivity is of who wrote your story today. Were you the author of what happened? While many things happened to you throughout the day, did you determine the pathway through it all or were you floated along on every-one else's agenda or script? How did you respond to what surprised you, your priorities, your task list? Did other people or 'circumstances' write it for you? To be proactive is that you write the story or that you take the initiative. To be proactive is to be the author of your story today at work or home or wherever, rather than being part of someone else's story. If you write your story you don't have to become a victim of circumstances or situations you find yourself in.

2. Find the Gap

All day, every day, life is throwing 'stimuli' at you and all day, every day, you are responding to what is coming along. The difference between being proactive and reactive is that proactive people find the gap between the stimulus and the response. It is in that gap that you can make a choice about how you choose to respond. Reactive people do not find the gap (see Figure 1.1).

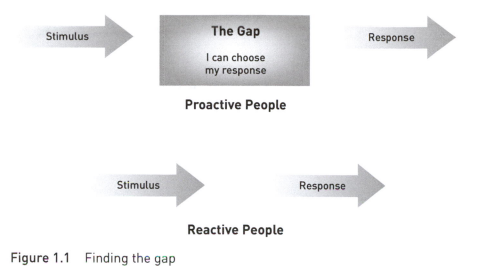

Figure 1.1   Finding the gap

3. Increasing Your Impact on Gravity

Gravity is a force that is constantly acting downwards and 'holds' things to the ground. Life is like the force of gravity that is constantly putting a downward pressure on you to react rather than act. There are always time pressures, unforeseen circumstances, other people's agendas, other people's demands and needs, urgent decisions needed, pressures of deadlines. All of these issues act like gravity, pushing you towards reacting. To be effective in this leadership challenge you need to develop the ability to constantly and every day work against gravity by increasing your impact on gravity rather than allowing it to increase its impact on you (see Figure 1.2). Whatever life is throwing at you, you need to develop your priorities, vision and strategies to influence your situation more than it is influencing you.

Gravity is all of those issues, events, relationships, attitudes inside and outside of you which, like gravity, constantly push you towards reacting rather than acting, being a victim rather than an author of your own life and actions.

Increasing your impact is about what actions you can take in each specific area of 'gravity' to increase your influence on the person, situation, event, and so on.

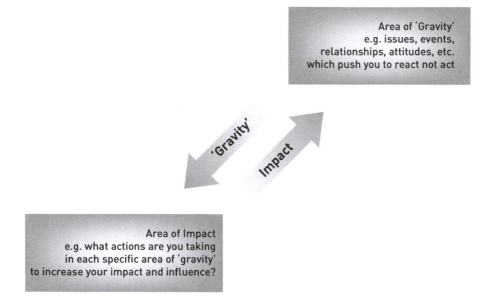

Figure 1.2   Increasing your impact on gravity

You can read more about this in Stephen Covey's books *The Seven Habits of Highly Effective People* (1989) and *First Things First* (1994) where he talks about it in terms of circles of concern and circles of influence.

How Does it feel to be Proactive or Reactive?

As emotions have such a big part to play in mood and motivations each day it's important to note the difference you feel when you are being proactive or reactive. To identify these feelings can act like the warning lights on the dashboard of your car. When a particular emotion associated with reactivity is 'flashing' at you then you can be alerted to making a different, more proactive, choice.

How does it feel when you are being reactive rather than proactive?

- You are too busy.
- You are stressed.
- You don't have enough time to do everything.

- You feel impotent in your organisation.
- You feel there is no point.
- You are always rushing around.
- Your behaviour feels habitual.
- You feel like it's always this way.
- You feel a victim of your circumstances or other people's agendas.
- You feel like you have no choice or limited choices.

How does it feel when you are being proactive rather than reactive?

- You feel like you are a step ahead of yourself.
- You feel like you are not reacting.
- You are anticipating.
- You are initiating.
- You are planning.
- You are taking charge or control of your situation.
- You are making a difference.
- You are increasing your influence.
- You have seen it in your mind's eye.
- You are keeping the main thing as the main thing.
- You are putting first things first.
- You are writing the story.
- You are influencing your concerns.

How Do You Talk When You Are Proactive or Reactive?

Stephen Covey in his best-selling book *The Seven Habits of Highly Effective People* (1989) identified the first habit of all effective leaders as being continually proactive rather than reactive. Proactivity is about always seeking to influence a situation rather than it influencing you. The language of the proactive person is different from that of the reactive person.

Proactive	Reactive
Can, will	You, they
I'll have a go	Can't, won't
Try, risk	I don't know how
I'll find out what's possible	It's not possible

Language shapes how you think and how you then act. Reactive thinking produces reactive people. If you say to yourself 'I can't do this', you probably won't and if you do the outcome will be less meaningful and the exercise itself will not be particularly enjoyable for you.

Proactivity and Stress Management

Every day you face many diverse pressures. Some of these you may enjoy and be energised by, others may drain your energy. As the draining pressures persist they can erode your feeling of control. Your greatest resource is yourself: your sense of who you are, what you know and what you are good at, and your ability to write your own story. Psychologists call this simply 'the self' (not to be confused with being selfish). The more you feel others are in control or writing the story, the more your sense of your self is diminished. This is why you may feel a lot of what is called *stress*. Your sense of self gets smaller so your feeling of control and resourcefulness diminishes. The proactive person deals with stress by constantly acting *on* their environment. This increases their sense of their self and increases their resourcefulness. All of their skills, experience, wisdom, ideas, etc. are available to them to use. (See Figures 1.3, 1.4 and 1.5.)

The worse-case scenario in not developing proactivity as an antidote to stress is that you eventually lose yourself totally. Once you have lost sense of yourself then it feels like everyone else or the organisation has taken

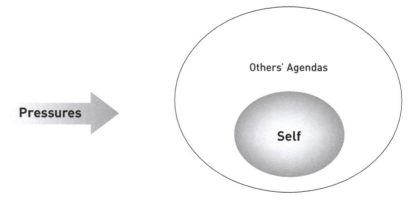

Figure 1.3 This is how life is

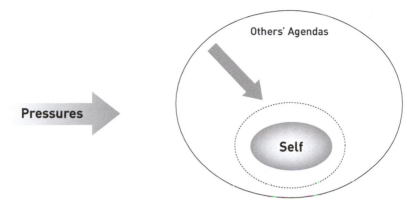

Figure 1.4 This is how life is for the reactive person: the sense of self gets smaller, stress levels increase

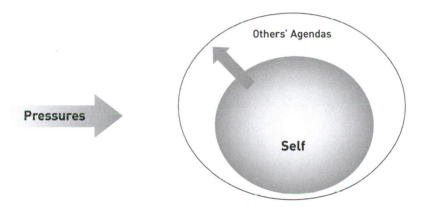

Figure 1.5 This is how life is for the proactive person: the sense of self increases, stress levels feel more under control

over and you have got lost. It is at this point that emotional or physical breakdown occurs or people simply 'check out' in terms of their perform-ance or leave the organisation to rediscover their self.

Other Factors That Influence Your Proactivity or Reactivity

Proactivity is like a muscle – if it isn't regularly exercised it gets flabby and when you try to use it again it's harder work than when you used it regularly. If you don't exercise your muscles regularly they get weak and ineffective; exercising the proactivity muscle is just the same. Leadership involves the daily training and development of proactivity. There are, however, two constraints that act against the development of proactivity: they are called 'time' and 'the market'!

Time pressure pushes even the best of senior managers into reactive mode where they end up managing the situation now rather than leading it towards tomorrow. I was told recently that the reason I was being asked to coach a senior manager was that the Chief Executive knew it was the right thing to be doing but he simply didn't have the time to be doing it. Time not only prevents people from managing and developing their staff, but it also forces people to get preoccupied with the problem and its solutions rather than core principles and creative possibilities.

This leads us to the second factor, 'the market'. 'The market' simply means any factor in your line of work, be it in the private or public sector, that is constantly changing the goal posts. Tom Peters's (1987) prophecy of the leader of the future being the person who would have to 'thrive on chaos' or Charles Handy's 'Age of Unreason' (1995) has come of age. Another word for 'chaos' is 'crisis'. Things change so rapidly these days that you can liken the manager's job to windsurfing, where they spend much of their energy just staying up on the board trying to keep their balance! Being proactive is about putting up the sails in anticipation of where the wind is coming from. Being proactive is about creating a dynamic movement with intent. If you can keep your balance, put the sail up, catch that wind, meet the wave – then you have managed to spot and use the 'gap'.

B. Personal Reflection

Now it's your turn to take a moment to reflect on how proactive you think you are. Why is it important to take time to do this? Einstein said that a problem could not be solved on the level at which it was created. So in order to start doing something differently you will first need to see something differently, some new perspective, new insight, a new way of seeing what is going on. Then you will immediately be aware of new options for action.

Definitions

Think through how you would describe what proactive and reactive mean to you and then reflect on how you feel when you are being proactive and how you feel when you are being reactive.

Example

One of our clients came up with this metaphor to illustrate what proactive–reactive looked like for them. They said that they have an image of themselves constantly being surrounded by deep turbulent rapids a few miles upstream from a waterfall. There are big logs coming downstream, moving fast and aggressively dragged towards the noisy waterfall. They could only see the logs coming towards them at the last minute. To stay alive and keeping going – to survive – they had to keep jumping.

Self-assessment of the Proactive Challenge

Read through all of the questions below and reflect on your work recently. Next, rate yourself in the box below on a scale of 1 to 10, where 1 = you are very ineffective in responding to this challenge (i.e. you are very reactive) and 10 = you are very effective at responding to this challenge (i.e. you are very proactive).

- Do you feel you are in control of your time or do other people largely control it?
- Do you spend your days on what is urgent more than on what is important?
- Do you act on your concerns or react to other people's agendas?
- Do you lead your day or manage your in-tray?

- Is your language 'I, Can, Will, What's possible?' or 'You, They, Can't, Won't, Don't know'?
- Do you seek to influence a situation more than be influenced by it?
- Are you more likely to say 'how can I change or influence this situation?' or 'that's just how it is and always has been'?
- Do you always feel you lack the time to do the important things in your work/life?
- Are you more preoccupied with the problem and its difficulties than the possibilities, principles and opportunities?
- Every time the goal posts shift do you redefine the goal and refocus or just hope the pressure goes away?
- Are you doing what you want to be doing or what you ought to be doing?

So where are you on the scale?

Challenge 1 – The Proactive Challenge

| 1 | 2 | 3 | 4 | 5 | 6 | 7 | 8 | 9 | 10 |

C. Developing Greater Proactivity

How a Proactive Person Behaves

The first step in developing greater proactivity is to be very clear about how highly proactive people behave. What would it look like if you were more proactive? Some of the behaviours that you would be exhibiting if you were high-scoring on this challenge would be:

- You are in control of your time rather than having other people determine it for you.
- You write the script for where you are seeking to go, what you are seeking to achieve, and the overall direction for your day.

- You make tough choices to invest time in your important goals not just the urgent issues dictated by others.
- You act on your concerns.
- You lead your day and your in-tray.
- Your language is 'I, Can, Will, 'What's possible?' rather than 'You, They, Can't, Won't, 'Don't know'.
- You seek to influence a situation more than be influenced by it.
- You are more likely to say 'how can I change or influence this situation?' than 'that's just how it is and always has been'.
- You make the time to invest in the important things in your work and wider life.
- You are more preoccupied with the possibilities, principles and opportunities.
- Every time the goal posts shift you start by redefining the goal and then refocus.
- You are motivated more by 'I want' than 'I ought'.

Can you think of others?

Face Your Concerns

Each day your head may be full of different pressures, challenges, deadlines, feelings and conversations. Let us call these issues 'concerns'. While your head is full of so many concerns there is little space to think, let alone plan and envision where you want to get to with each of these concerns. This is where your concerns act like gravity and push you into a reactive mode. To move from reactive to proactive you need to create a space in your head. The way to do this is to practice the discipline of doing a 'brain dump' by writing down in notes or free association everything (work-related or personal life issues) that is affecting, concerning and impacting you in your life.

Example

Writing the new procedures; new role in marketing; pricing the new product; leading a bigger team; my bonus was cut; less time with the children; spouse's health; where to go on holiday; boss interfering; not sure if I'm doing a good job at the moment.

Act on Your Concerns

When you have got what is in your head out on paper you are in a position to look at each concern. While it is locked inside your head you can't really see it or act on it. Much of it you can't even retain consciously in your head as people can only hold between three and seven blocks of information consciously at any one time. When you see the concern on paper you can now look at how you can act on that concern rather than have it acting on you. For instance, take *'I don't know if I'm doing a good job right now'* from the example above. What could you do to act on that concern? You could ask your boss for some feedback; you could ask for some feedback in Monday's team meeting; you could take 5 minutes to clarify in your own mind what a good job looks like and then assess yourself against this benchmark.

As soon as you create actions you are moving from a reactive mindset to a proactive one.

Now put this to work by influencing your concerns. For every concern or issue that you listed earlier write at least one action that you can take to influence this issue.

If you still feel stuck on this it may be helpful to unlock some thinking a little further by looking at each of your concerns and asking yourself what causes you to be reactive in this situation or area or issue. Is it an emotional reaction (does it cause you anxiety, fear, etc.?) or is it situational (large audiences, product not ready on time, etc.) or is it relational (e.g. you always have a problem with older male managers who reflect your father)?

Another area to consider is whether you are being too hard on yourself. You are saying that you are reactive in a certain area but how do you know that you are being proactive or reactive? Re-read the first section of this challenge and then reflect on the concerns you have outlined and consider what is the evidence that you are being proactive or reactive.

A final thought here is that if it feels like you have too many concerns, that you can see them all on paper and it all feels too much, then start by choosing one concern to create actions for. Either choose a concern that is central to many of the other concerns or choose a concern that you would most like to see some movement on.

Developing Motivation for Proactivity

It may be helpful to add some basic thoughts on motivation at this point. Often you may know the thing you want to do or be but you just don't do anything about it. Why is that? Here are three possible answers.

Answer 1. You haven't developed a strong enough picture of life as a proactive person

Reactive scripts are often what you know and are familiar with. You may react all of the time. It's a kind of default position for many people. To motivate yourself to choose proactivity you need to have a compelling and clear picture of what life would be like – how you would be behaving, how you would be feeling, what you would see yourself doing, etc.

In order to say 'no' to familiar, reactive patterns of behaviour you need a bigger 'yes' to move forward each day. Anchoring a strong picture of what you are seeking to be provides this bigger 'yes'.

See How a Proactive Person Behaves, above.

Answer 2. You haven't understood the payoff for your behaviour

Behaviour has a payoff. This seems a little perverse sometimes if the behaviour in question is causing you difficulty or pain or stress. However, you may know that you are sometimes prepared to live with stress rather than confront a difficult person at work and risk conflict. In thinking through this challenge ask yourself what are some of the disadvantages of your reactive behaviour patterns in the context of this issue and then ask yourself what are the advantages of your reactive behaviour patterns in the context of this issue.

Example

You are continually late to work on Mondays and miss the first part of the weekly project meeting.

Disadvantages: You are seen to be uncommitted to the project.

Advantages: Because you miss the first part of the meeting you avoid the discomfort of reporting the bad news.

Answer 3. You are running from something, not to something

While all behaviour is motivated by a goal (consciously or not) not all behaviour is motivated by what people are seeking to do. Some behaviour is motivated by what people are trying to avoid. Take Marianne Williamson's excellent piece of writing quoted by Nelson Mandela in his inaugural speech, 'your playing small doesn't serve the world'.

Our deepest fear is not that we are inadequate.

Our deepest fear is that we are powerful beyond measure.

It is our light, not our darkness, that most frightens us.

You can run away from being proactive because you fear the responsibility it might bring or like King Saul in the Bible you can run from leadership because you feel low self-confidence or self-esteem. We were working with a senior manager recently and his biggest struggle with proactivity was about how he'd spent the whole of his working life as number two to someone else. He was running from facing up to the emotional challenge of leadership which meant he had a vested interest in remaining reactive.

Reducing the Blockages

Revisit the explanations of the Inner and Outer Games in the Introduction.

The key issue here is that your performance in the 'outer' world is greatly affected by what is going on in your 'inner' world. For example, in your external behaviour, as you sit silently in a meeting it may look like you are not committed or involved, but in your inner world, inside yourself, you are struggling to put the words together for fear of sounding naive. So fear of looking naive is an inner challenge that has an external effect on how proactive you are in meetings. The same could be said for low self-confidence. So, as the next step, focus your attention on how this challenge is experienced in your outer game (work, family, team) and how it registers (feels like, looks like) in your inner game (inside of your self). The point of this reflection is to answer the following question.

What gets in the way in your inner world that affects how proactive you are in your outer world?

There are three ways to think about this.

1. What are the internal emotions and attitudes that affect your external behaviours when it comes to proactivity? For example, lack of confidence and fears of failure, exposure, ridicule, looking stupid.
2. Are there any patterns of behaviour in yourself that consistently seem to defeat your proactivity?

Example

Mike's first step was actually sitting down and verbally acknowledging to a friend at work that he had a genuine problem in following through on actions, which he felt went back a long way in his life but impacted his entire work within his current job. He realised he had cleverly hidden this from those around him, but admitting it was the first step to real change.

3. Are there any consistent themes around why you aren't as proactive as you need or want to be? In this case proactivity begins by addressing the blockages first and then going on to create more specific action plans.

Example

While you can see that you have three challenges that demand your immediate attention, your inability to deal with conflict is common to all of them.

Example

While you think you are pretty proactive in day-to-day issues, your challenge is to anticipate the impact of your choices: to be proactive about where your actions today will impact on tomorrow or next month.

Immediate and Important

Life is full of things that demand *immediate* attention from phones ringing, impatient bosses or shareholders, to 'urgent' e-mails. It is usually these things that people react to on a daily basis. There are also things that are *important*. *Important* can be defined as those things that must be done to achieve your vision and strategy, either personally or work-related. (See the Vision Challenge and the Strategy Challenge.) This means that some things that claim to be urgent are not necessarily important. They do not further the vision or strategy or business aims or strategic goals or personal mission. Conversely there are things that are absolutely important but are not urgent. Some things are both immediate and important. (Of course there are some things that are neither urgent nor important, but they still manage to fill the day!)

The greatest danger of being reactive is that the immediate pushes out the important, the good becomes the enemy of the best. Managing the in-tray suffocates leading the department. We often ask managers who are very reactive and caught up in the thick of management detail the following question.

> Whose job is it to lead this team/department, to set vision, to keep the compass focused on the right horizon?

They, of course, reply that they are responsible. The next question is obvious!

> If you are so busy reacting to the immediate agenda, who is leading the department? If you aren't, who is?

And, of course, again, the answer is no one.

Looking at Figure 1.6, write in the top right quadrant all of the activities you need to be doing as a proactive person: clarifying vision, planning, setting goals, coaching your staff, etc. In a different colour pen look at what you have spent your time doing in the past day, week or month, and place your activity into one of the four quadrants.

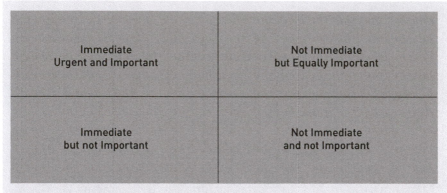

Immediate Urgent and Important	Not Immediate but Equally Important
Immediate but not Important	Not Immediate and not Important

Figure 1.6   Immediate and Important

What do you do with this insight? You plan the important non-immediate things into your diary as non-negotiable items. If you need to move one it should only be because something equally important but immediate (urgent) has come along and then only when you have found another space in your diary for it. If you let proactive choices drop out of your diary they will drop out of your behaviour. As we pointed out in the introduction to this chapter this is a muscle you have to keep on exercising and a gravity pull you need to keep on breaking.

> Ailsa Brimley did not believe in emergencies . . . the greater the emergency, the greater her calm. John Landsbury had remarked upon it: 'you have sales resistance to the dramatic, Brim; the rare gift of contempt for what is urgent. I know of a dozen people who would pay you five thousand a year for telling them every day that what is important is seldom urgent. Urgent equals transient and transient equals unimportant. (John Le Carré, *A Murder of Quality*)

I Don't Know Where to Start

Sometimes people just need a few practical and simple suggestions about what they can do to make a start on being more proactive.

Here are a few such suggestions.

- What three things could you do today that demonstrate proactivity?
- What three things could you do tomorrow that would demonstrate proactivity?
- Note the type of language you are using today.
- Create a process for anticipating what lies ahead.
- Write a short script for what you want your role to look like six months from now as a proactive person.
- Who else could you ask for more options?
- Who might have other ideas, solutions and insights about how to increase your proactivity?

The Final Question . . . What are you going to do now?
(See Appendix 1 for further development)

CHALLENGE

2

The
Influence Challenge

Making a clear impact

A. Understanding this Challenge

Influence Is at the Heart of Leadership

Every time you meet someone or they meet you, you make an impact – consciously or not. If leadership is about setting vision and a strategy on one side, then the heart of leadership is how you impact on people – whether it be one person or a thousand – to achieve the vision. If you cannot influence them you cannot lead them. If you accept that you influence knowingly or unknowingly every time you meet someone then the questions you need to be asking yourself are, 'What impact am I making on people?' 'Is the impact that I make the same as the impact I intended to make?' 'Are my intended actions the same as how others perceive my actions?'

Leadership is about influence. Everyone in the field of leadership agrees on this point, although they will disagree on much else. Just look at a few of the definitions of leadership, all quoted from Hughes et al. (1996):

'The capacity of a person to influence people.' (Roach and Behling, 1984)

'Leadership is the ability to create a story that affects the thoughts, feelings, and actions of other individuals.' (Gardner, 1996)

'The creative and directive force of morale.' (Munson, 1921)

'The process by which an agent induces a subordinate to behave in a desired manner.' (Bennis, 1959)

'The presence of a particular influence relationship between two or more persons.' (Hollander and Julian, 1969)

'An interpersonal relation in which others comply because they want to, not because they have to.' (Merton, 1969; Hogan, Curphy and Hogan, 1994)

'Team leaders cannot fly solo and must share the leadership task with the whole leadership team.'(Gardner, 1990)

'Leadership and followership are linked concepts.' (Heller and Van Til, 1983)

'The process of influencing an organised group towards accomplishing its goals.' (Roach and Behling, 1984)

A Familiar Story

There is an all-too-familiar scenario that we come across. You may recognise it. You train for a career in a specialist area. You do well in that area. You then get put in charge of a team. The team achieves its targets. You are offered a position in management, then senior management. The common thread is that you are indispensable to the company for your specialised knowledge or skill but your effect on others is somewhere between bearable and painful. The worst of it is that you are not aware of this because no one has ever given any honest feedback.

Creating and building trust amongst stakeholders is an essential ingredient. We are always a little surprised when coaching people at quite senior levels to discover that they have never had any training or development around influencing styles, personality preferences and the effects that they have on those they seek to lead. Too frequently I am told, 'X is a great technical director but is just not very good at the people stuff.'

Influential Leadership Styles

There is a danger that people become a little too 'monochrome' in their leadership style when it comes to influencing others. They may have a preferred style that they always use and it is effective in certain situations but very limited in others. Developing a range of influential leadership styles is important for those who seek to influence the performance, learning and development of others. Blanchard, Zigarmi and Zigarmi, in their book *Leadership and the One Minute Manager* (1987), describe four different styles of leadership that are useful in different situations. (If you are pushed for time this is one of an excellent series of books to read.) Their key point is that people need an approach to leadership that varies with the people and the situation. Their definitions of some of the leadership styles differ from use of language in the UK so we have adapted their model slightly for this culture. The four styles are outlined in the four quadrants in Figure 2.1.

Ask yourself the following questions. In what way did they influence you? What exactly were they doing? Be specific about the behaviours that influenced you.

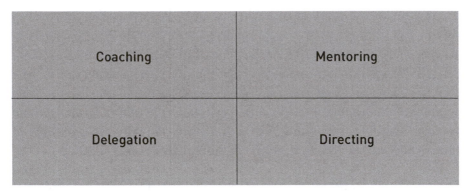

Coaching	Mentoring
Delegation	Directing

Figure 2.1 Leadership styles

Directing

This is where the leader tells people what to do. There is little discussion or negotiation. It can be done positively, with intelligence and with clear reasons or it can be done aggressively, unintelligently and in a 'pushy' way. In command and control situations (e.g. the armed forces or some hierarchical organisations) this may be the accepted way of passing instructions about performance targets down the chain of command. When someone is starting a new job or role it is entirely appropriate to spell out exactly what is required but if it remains the only style that is used it creates dependence on the part of staff and sometimes resentment.

Mentoring

The idea of the mentor is taken from the wise old sage sitting under the village tree who is visited by the younger person who seeks some help to know how to do something. The mentor is someone who shares their past experiences and helps others to then experiment with the *mentor's experience* in the *learner's situation.*

Coaching

This is a much more facilitative style where the responsibility is largely with the learner. The coach facilitates a conversation where the learner can come up with their own solutions by helping them set goals and achieve them. It has the specific aim of increasing the learner's performance while also advancing their learning and development.

Delegation

In this style of leadership responsibility and decision making are devolved to others over a period of time. As the leader becomes confident that others are clear about the goals, targets, values, mission and vision, she or he can begin to allow them to make their own decisions and put their own personal imprint on to how they do their job.

Who Do You Need to Influence?

Influence is not a 'woolly' subject. It is very specific. It involves other people who surround you in your role. Some of these people you may be aware of and some you can easily fail to be aware of. You need to consider who it is that you want to influence. Is it your team? If so, who exactly is in your team? Is it your board? If so, who exactly is on the board? Is it a specific group within the organisation? Is it the whole organisation? If so, who are the key influencers within the organisation? You need to become specific about who it is you want to influence.

Stakeholder Mapping

A stakeholder is anyone who has an interest or a stake in what you are doing or want to do in the future. Who has a stake or interest in the particular issue, project or outcome that you are looking at? There are two dimensions of stakeholder mapping. One is the visible stakeholders: these are the obvious, known people who have a vested interest in the issue. The other is the invisible stakeholders: these are not immediately obvious but they will be impacted by your decisions. For example, you want to influence your boss to make a particular decision to give you some resources (your boss is a visible stakeholder). What you don't see is how much pressure their boss is putting on them to reduce the head count in the department (your boss's boss is an invisible stakeholder). Stakeholders may be individuals or they may be whole groups (e.g. another department or another team).

One way you can draw out the stakeholders is as a mind map or spider diagram. In Figure 2.2 the solid lines represent the visible individuals and/or groups and the dotted lines represent invisible stakeholder individuals and/or groups. The purpose of a stakeholder map is simply to get a clear, visual picture of who it is you need to think about when influencing.

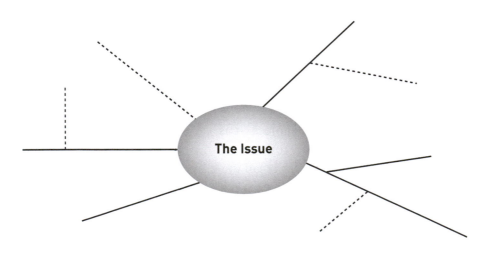

Figure 2.2   Stakeholder map

Proximity Mapping

Additional insight can be gained by constructing a proximity map. This is a way of looking at the relationship between people or issues to see how important they are in terms of influence. In a proximity map the circles may represent a person or they may represent an issue. The size of the issue or the size of influence a person has is represented by the size of the circle. A large issue or a seemingly very influential person is drawn as a large circle. When you have got all of the circles on the page the next step is to arrange the circles so that issues or people that have a close relationship to each other are placed close to each other on the map and people or issues that are far apart are drawn at a distance from each other. Let's say that in Figure 2.3 you are person 4, your boss is represented as person 3, but the person you need to influence is person 1. What this map tells you is that you feel your boss is a lot more influential than either you or your target person. It also tells you that your boss currently obscures the relationship you want with person 1 and that person 2 is a potential barrier. On the positive side it also tells you that person 2 may be a key person to influence in order to reach person 1 and that person 5 and you together may be able to have a more effective influence on your boss.

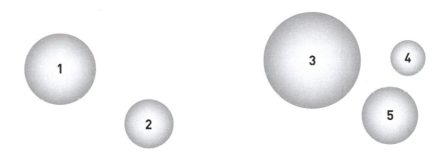

Figure 2.3 Proximity mapping

A good place to try this out is within your own team. If someone has a large influence on the team represent this with a large circle, if small then use a small circle. Arrange the circles in terms of proximity so that if one person is close to two others but distant from a third and fourth then represent the distance in relation by distance between the circles.

Leaders' Behaviour and Influence

In every interaction between people there is a dynamic movement of energy. No interaction is neutral. This interaction or energy is experienced as either *Push* energy, where an individual is operating according to their own agenda and he or she wants to Push you to agreeing with them, or it is experienced as *Pull* energy, where an individual is operating according to your agenda and he or she wants to understand you before they get you to understand them (read the fourth habit of *The Seven Habits of Highly Effective People* – Covey, 1989 – to expand your understanding of this behaviour). This idea of Push–Pull influence is one of the most widely used models about influencing people. Pictorially, it might look something like Figure 2.4. For examples, see Table 2.1.

Figure 2.4   The Push–Pull model: directive and non-directive styles

Table 2.1   Push and Pull behaviours

Push Behaviours	Pull Behaviours
Suggestions	Listening
Giving advice	Summarising
Feedback	Recapping
Telling	Reflecting
Asserting	Paraphrasing
Persisting	Exploring
Giving rational arguments	Looking for common ground
Instructing	Creating shared vision
Stating your point of view	Asking questions on the client's agenda
Stating what you want	

There are no right or wrong influencing behaviours but there are behaviours that are more or less appropriate depending on the situation or the relationship. If you persist in using Push behaviours you are likely to create a resistance in the other person or team. This may be because they feel 'pushed' or bullied or driven. Resistance may come from self-defence or protection. This would happen if the other person feels you are bigger or stronger than they are and that they may get hurt or lose out if they don't Push (resist) you back. Resistance may also come from ignorance. Your colleague may feel you are pushing them somewhere but they don't know where it is. They may feel this is a conscious manipulation on your part so they will resist manipulation or they may be uncertain and so resist out of fear.

If the only influencing behaviours you use are Push behaviours and you sense that they are not working then it is typical behaviour to borrow some energy to Push harder. Usually this extra energy comes from insecurities and so comes out as defensive comments, irritated remarks, or barbed comments. The Huthwaite Research Group call these 'Irritators' and they include statements that imply blame, or criticism, or which are formulaic and double-edged. For example:

- 'The problem arose when you failed to . . .'
- 'That unfortunate omission on your part meant that . . .'
- 'With respect, I hear what you are saying.'

While all effective influence is a combination of Push and Pull behaviours the most effective influence uses up to four times more Pull than Push. In the words of Covey (1989) effective influencers 'seek first to understand before seeking to be understood'.

Feedback – the Breakfast of Champions

Feedback is the most common way of finding out what you are currently doing in your behaviours that influence those around you. Feedback is helpful because it acts like the sonar echo from a ship. You send out a signal (your behaviour or attitude, verbal or non-verbal) that you intend to have a particular effect. Feedback is the 'beep' that returns to tell you the effect your behaviour has actually had on someone else (see Figure 2.5).

You may have had feedback through formal questionnaires like the Myers Briggs Type Indicator (self-feedback), OPQ or the Influencing Styles Questionnaire.

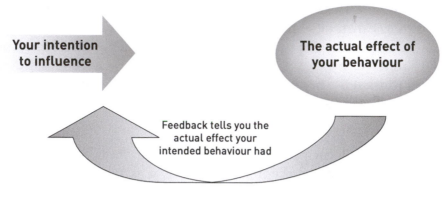

Figure 2.5   Feedback

You can get informal feedback by asking colleagues or your teams which of your behaviours or words are effective influencers, which of your actions or words are less effective and what you could do differently to improve your influence.

We say you have 360° feedback when you get feedback from a representative cross-section of all your relationships at work. Usually this involves four groups.

1. Yourself.
2. Your boss.
3. Your peers.
4. Those whom you line-manage.

The self–upward–peer–downward model of influencing relationships can be used by you to get some relevant data about your influencing behaviours (see Figure 2.6). We have created a questionnaire based around the Push–Pull model at the end of this challenge for you to complete by yourself or as a way of getting feedback from those around you.

Influencing involves creating trust between yourself and others. At the heart of trust is whether you are trustworthy. Trustworthiness comes from your integrity: that you have integrated your values into who you are and what you do and how you do it. Trustworthiness produces trust and respect.

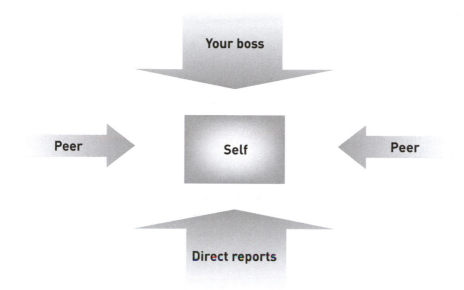

Figure 2.6 The self–upward–peer–downward model

Personality and Influence

For a more extensive exploration visit the Personality Challenge.

Energy

a. Some people are energised by their inner world of ideas, thoughts and concepts. They think first and speak second. They are reflective and 'deep'. They seek to understand something before they live it. Sometimes they can be seen as withdrawn, cool or detached.

b. Some people are energised by their outer world. They get energy from being with people and things. They are activists who have a breadth of interests. They prefer to live life and then understand it. They are outgoing and enjoy the interaction. They are good at action and networking but can be seen as intrusive, dominating or superficial at times.

Processing

c. Some people process all that is happening by a focus on the here and now, the present. They deal with facts, data, detail and usefulness. They are firmly rooted in reality. They can be seen as overly negative or pessimistic when new ideas or innovations are being discussed.

d. Some people process all that is happening by looking first for meaning and association between ideas. They search first for possibilities and follow their hunches and speculations. They create theoretical models of how life or projects might fit together and are happy to be focused on what might be, the future and imagination. They are seen by some as impractical, illogical and difficult to follow – a bit too 'pie-in-the-sky'.

Decisions

e. Some people arrive at conclusions and decisions through objective and logical thinking. They analyse a situation, looking at causes and effects, and are keen to make the right decisions based on impersonal criteria and their logic. They are able to be tough and to weigh up the costs of their decisions. Every decision has a reasoned basis. People may sometimes see them as cold and detached, critical or insensitive.

f. Some people arrive at decisions through a subjective process of appreciating the effects of the decision on people and their values. They are sympathetic to issues relating to people or values and approach decisions humanely and personally. They are in touch with their feelings and those of others and can persuade and reconcile where there are differences. Some people view them as over-emotional or too emotionally involved or illogical to make good decisions.

Life Management

g. Some people handle their lives by being very structured and organised. They plan and are decisive about that plan once it is formed. They set goals, are systematic in their execution and are in control of their life. Some people find them too rigid or inflexible.

h. Some people handle their lives by being very flexible and spontaneous. When they plan it is tentative and provisional in case new ideas or inputs arise to modify their approach. They like to let life happen to them and are not thrown by surprises. They are adaptable to new events or issues that may suddenly come along. Some people view them as disorganised, irresponsible and unprepared.

Think through How to Influence Different Personalities

To influence someone who is like person (a) you would let them have time to think and process their thoughts before looking for their response. You would invite them to contribute and not just assume that they will do it automatically.

To influence someone who is like person (b) you would enter into discussion with them as early as possible on any new ideas. You would create opportunities for discussion and brainstorming before you had gone too far in formulating your ideas or plans.

To influence someone who is like person (c) you would need to be careful with your facts, work out the details of a situation before speaking to them, think through and reduce the risks of what you are discussing. You would then present the information in a systematic way using concrete and practical examples that show the usefulness of your ideas.

To influence someone who is like person (d) you would present the big picture of where your ideas were heading and how they all fitted together before drilling down to the detail. You would create opportunities for new ideas and future possibilities to be generated. You would help them to see where the challenges lie and be confident and enthusiastic about your proposals.

To influence someone who is like person (e) you would use logic and show your analysis of the problem or situation. You would demonstrate the costs and benefits of your proposals while putting a high value on competence and clear conclusions.

To influence someone who is like person (f) you would be sensitive and friendly. You would pay as much attention to the people as to the task. You would focus on the values and people issues while listening and showing appreciation for their inputs and involvement.

To influence someone who is like person (g) you would be clear about structures and plans. You would put clear project plans in place with goals and targets and deadlines. You would be on time with your reports and updates. You would demonstrate to them that you were organised.

To influence someone who is like person (h) you would maintain a degree of flexibility and tentativeness about your proposals where possible. You would need to separate the crucial deadlines from the preferential deadlines. You would need to demonstrate where new ideas, insights or spontaneity could have their day.

B. Personal Reflection

Now it's your turn to take a moment to reflect on how effective you think you are at influencing.

Definitions

Think through how you would describe what effective influence means in the context of your work.

You can do this in two stages. First by thinking through what your definition of effective influence is and second by thinking through what constitutes effective influence and what makes up ineffective influence.

Reflect for a moment:

■ What is important about influencing in your own job right now?
■ How do you make yourself heard?

- How do you create trust?
- What affects how people see you, judge you, feel about you, respond to your requests?
- What is important in seeking to move your team to achieve the organisation's goals?

Self-assessment of the Influence Challenge

Read through all of the questions below and reflect on your work recently. Next, rate yourself in the box below on a scale of 1 to 10, where 1 = you are very ineffective in responding to this challenge (i.e. you have a low awareness of your style and its impact on others as well as a narrow range of effective influencing behaviours) and 10 = you are very effective at responding to this challenge (i.e. you do have a wide range of effective influencing behaviours).

- Do you display mainly Push (directive) behaviours (such as telling, explaining, persisting, suggesting, giving advice, asserting, giving rational arguments, offering guidance, stating what you want, stating your point of view, stating what you feel) or mainly Pull (non-directive) behaviours (such as listening, summarising, recapping, exploring, reflecting, paraphrasing, seeking to understand someone before getting them to understand you) or a full and balanced range of both?
- Do you have feedback evidence from your superiors, peers and subordinates to support your answer to the above?
- Do you create a story-line at work that affects the thoughts, feelings and actions of your staff or colleagues?
- Do you regularly ask for and give feedback?
- Do others describe your behaviour as helpful and influential or unhelpful, distant and critical?
- Do you expect and demand people to change or do you first seek to understand them before being understood by them?
- Do you build collaborative relationships?
- Do you seek to add as much value to your people as to the tasks they perform?
- Do you build relationships with key people in various functions?

- Do you usually win support with others easily?
- Do you let people know if they are performing well?
- Do you let people know if and when results are not up to expectations?
- Do you negotiate persuasively?

So where are you on the scale?

Challenge 2 – The Influence Challenge

1   2   3   4   5   6   7   8   9   10

C. Developing Greater Influence

Think about Your Own Influencing Behaviours

From your work throughout the previous sections what have you learned about your influencing style?

What have you learned about your influencing style when you are at your best? For example, when Trevor asked Shenaz this question she said:

- I use my intellect.
- Use my knowledge.
- I use my memory so they feel heard.
- I use humour.
- I use warmth.
- Sometimes I'm cool or severe.
- I use my voice.
- I'm very engaged.
- I'm a very attentive listener.
- I make people work hard at thinking.

What have you learned about your influencing behaviour when you are under stress? For example, when Shenaz asked Trevor this question he said:

- I get disengaged.
- I am sometimes quiet.
- I am sometimes irritated or have an edge to my voice.
- I get into a subtle form of blame.

Your Behaviours

From your own assessment or from feedback you have sought (using the feedback sheet at the end of this chapter), which of these behaviours are most in evidence in your management or influencing of people and which ones are less apparent?

Styles of Leadership

Look at the explanation around styles of leadership in the first section (Understanding this Challenge). Think about the people you lead. Who do you direct and in what aspects of their job? Who do you mentor and in what aspects of their job? Who do you coach and in what aspects of their job? Who do you delegate to and what do you delegate?

Learning from Who Influences You

Think of three people who have had the most positive influence in your life (colleagues, family, friends, media figures, historical figures, etc.).

In what way did they influence you? What exactly were they doing? Be specific about the behaviours that influenced you.

Indirect Influence

Having looked in detail at who has influenced you positively and consciously now take a moment to consider who has influenced you negatively or less consciously in your working context.

What was missing in the way they behaved towards you? What were they doing specifically? What were they not doing to influence positively?

Example

A colleague is regarded by everyone as a friendly, upbeat person but talks critically about people behind their backs. How might this influence you? Would you trust that person less and less?

What would you need to do to turn this into a positive influencing strategy? Maybe you will decide to talk about people only when you have evidence rather than perception or supposition.

Eight Keys To Creating an Influencing Strategy

Key 1. Be clear about your intent

Why are you influencing? For example, is it to manipulate or perhaps to win? Many people are now familiar with the expression win–win. What win–win actually means is coming up with solutions that both parties believe meet their needs. There are six different outcomes that are possible so you need to be clear which outcome you are honestly going for.

Outcome 1: Win–Lose. This is where you get what you want but the other party doesn't get what they want. This is a style of influencing that a lot of people seem to be educated in but it has a very short-term perspective. Once you have put the other party at the losing end of a win–lose situation they are unlikely to trust you or want to do further business with you. How do you think people feel if they are on the losing end of win–lose influencing?

Outcome 2: Lose–Win. This is where you don't get what you want or need and they do! How do you think people feel if they are on the winning end of lose–win influencing?

There is a form of lose–win that makes sense sometimes. It is called a 'loss leader'; this is where you choose to lose in the short term to establish a relationship or market share.

Outcome 3: Lose–Lose. This is where neither you nor the other party gets what is wanted or needed. Sometimes what is seen as a 'compromise' is a lose–lose because neither party gets what is needed from the situation. Initially, you can feel good that you came up with a solution and then, on reflection, feel bad that you have failed to get your minimum needs met. How else might people feel in a lose–lose influencing situation?

Outcome 4: Lose–Lose Crash and Burn. This is the lowest form of lose–lose. It is where the relationship between two parties breaks down so badly because of ineffective influencing that it will be impossible to get them back round the table to talk any further. How might you feel in such a situation?

Outcome 5: Win–Win. As we have outlined, this is where both parties get their underlying needs met through effective influencing. How might you feel in such a situation?

Outcome 6: Win–Win or Wait. In relationships where there is a very high level of trust and co-operation and two parties are keen to benefit each other as much as they can, it is possible to reach a win–win or nearly reach a win–win but instead the parties feel that by waiting for new information, new inputs, or by tolerating a time delay you reach a much better outcome for each other. Have you had any examples of this kind of influencing situation?

Key 2. Preparation

Preparation is crucial in influencing. If you don't prepare you end up acting instinctively or 'shooting from the hip'. When you prepare you need to think through the following.

- What you are trying to achieve.
- What your normal style of influencing is.
- What it needs to be in this situation.
- What the other person might need from this situation.
- What is their preferred style of influencing.

One of the most effective strategies in preparation is to step into someone else's shoes. Choose the person you seek to influence. Go and sit in a different chair. In this new place think through what you know about this person. What are their concerns right now? What do they want? What do they need? What are their personality preferences? How do they prefer to communicate? How do they prefer to be communicated with? When you have done this preparation you will be in a much stronger position to work out your influencing strategy with them.

Key 3. Where it takes place

The location and environment are crucial in influencing.

- Where will you feel most comfortable?
- Where will they feel most comfortable?
- Is the timing right?
- Have you allowed enough time?
- Do the environment and location match the occasion?
- What messages do they send to the other person?

Key 4. Be clear about what you and they want

Research shows that a high percentage of people enter influencing situations without being clear in their own minds about what they actually want out of the discussion or situation. Being clear about what you want and helping the other party to be clear about what they want is crucial.

Key 5. Be clear about what you and they need

Generally, what you *want* is just a solution to an underlying *need* that you have. Needs are deeper than wants. They are more fundamental. Needs are things like cash flow and self-esteem.

One way of getting to an underlying need is to take what you want and keep asking the question 'Why?' until you reach the real issue. This is the need. 'Why do you want that price?' 'Why do you want to complete by that date?' 'Why do you want them to phone first?'

Do the same for the other person you are influencing. What is it that they need? Help them to clarify this.

Key 6. Get creative about finding solutions that meet yours and their needs

This is the basis of win–win influencing. Use brainstorming to create as many ways as possible of meeting your needs, then use brainstorming to create as many ways as possible of meeting their needs. Look at the solutions that go some way to meeting both your and their needs.

A solution may not just be one thing: it may be a cluster of solutions that together meet the needs of both parties.

Key 7. Clarify that you are both satisfied with the outcome

Check that you both are happy with the outcome or solutions. Check that you both mean the same thing by the words or statements you are using. It is lack of robust clarification that can lead to many misunderstandings in influencing.

Key 8. Don't let it get personal

Effective influencing keeps the issue on the table and keeps the focus of attention on the issue. The alternative is to let the focus shift to the individuals involved. This is a dangerous route and can lead to the breaking down of the relationship we talked about in Outcome 4: Lose–Lose Crash and Burn. The classic saying is 'tough on the issue and not the person'.

Influencing the Organisation

This is a monumental topic and links into all aspects of change management and organisational leadership. However, there are two keys to consider.

Find and keep on telling the story of the organisation

People communicate each day with each other through stories, not through directives or three-point statements. A story is the thing that engages hearts and minds. Finding the story of the organisation up to this point and then creating the story for the future – which is just another way of saying 'create a compelling vision' (see the Vision Challenge) – is essential to influence the future of the organisation. Nothing less than this will engage hearts and minds. Once you have found the story you need to keep on telling it at every opportunity.

Communicate, Communicate, Communicate

In leading change you need to spend as much time on creating a communication plan as you do on the strategy. In fact the communication plan is a key part of the strategy.

Your Case Study

Take a specific issue where you want to improve your influence. For example:

- A relationship.
- A situation where you need to be more visible.
- A new role as team leader.
- A new project to manage.
- A new market to penetrate.

Step 1: Who? Identify the stakeholders (see first section, Understanding this Challenge).

Step 2: Identify any level of priority or importance in this list of stakeholders.

Step 3: Do a proximity map (see Understanding this Challenge).

Step 4: Who and what are the biggest challenges for you?

Step 5: Who and what are the most powerful influences?

Scenarios to think through

Think through these different scenarios as a way to understanding how you could be more effective at influencing others.

- How do you put yourself on the map in a meeting when your normal style is to be very quiet?
- How do you channel your energy in a meeting when you normally talk too much, like the sound of your own voice and overshadow other quieter people?
- How do you seek common ground when you strongly disagree with someone's point of view?
- How do you let someone know that you have truly understood their thoughts and emotions on a subject?
- How do you build consensus when you naturally want to control or manipulate?
- How do you keep exploring an issue with someone when your mind is already made up?

What is working and what isn't?

Choose the key stakeholders that you need to influence and review those behaviours you use that are working and those ones that aren't.

The Final Question . . . What are you going to do now?
(See Appendix 1 for further development)

Further reading

Further reading on different aspects of influence may be helpful:

General Influencing: Mills (2000), *Artful Persuasion*, Amacom.

Influence and negotiation: Fisher and Ury (1997), *Getting to Yes*, Arrow Business Book.

Influence and personality: Pearman and Albritton (1997), *I'm Not Crazy I'm Just Not You*, Davies-Black, also see the Personality Challenge.

Influence and teams: Wellins et al. (1991), *Empowered Teams*, Josey Bass Wiley.

Influence and change management: John Kotter (1996), *Leading Change*, Harvard Business School Press.

Influence and strategy: Thurbin (2001), *Playing the Strategy Game*, FT/ Prentice Hall.

Influence and culture: Rosinski (2003), *Coaching across Cultures – New Tools for Leveraging National, Corporate and Professional Differences*, Nicholas Brealey Publishing.

The
Reality Challenge
Understand where you are

A. Understanding this Challenge

Our rallying call for leadership is to 'lift up your head' but this must surely include the qualifying statement 'with your feet firmly anchored on to the ground'. Some leaders are idealists – they float above the ground and they rely on being surrounded by realists, if they are lucky! Some people shift between having their feet on the ground and their eyes on the horizon. We are suggesting these should be *both-and* rather than *either-or*. One leader we spoke to recently said that when new projects come along she gets so excited and involved that she loses a grasp of her own limitations and her existing commitments. The result of her feet 'leaving the ground' is that she over-commits and then finds herself frequently disappointing key stakeholders when she fails to deliver on time or has to back out of commitments at the last minute.

Leaders understand their current reality. This almost sounds a little 'new-agey'. It means that leaders understand their market, their sector, their subject and their clients. They understand how things are now. They understand the present. They may be great vision-setters but in equal measure they are realists. In sporting language, they 'read the game'. One of the skills taught on an Advanced Driving Course is the level of aware-ness of all that is happening around, ahead, behind and to either side while still being safely in control of the vehicle on the road. The same is true with leadership. While keeping the organisation or the team or the project on the road the leader is looking at what is happening today in all dimensions and directions in order to understand the current realities of the situation they are facing. They keep themselves informed and like to be kept informed.

Faced with the same situation an *idealist* team leader may assume that everyone is on board and equally committed, a *visionary* may focus on the future picture of what the team could achieve, the *pragmatist* may be thinking 'let's get this done' and the *realist* will be asking 'what do we already know?' The truth is most people probably have elements of each of these styles in them, but they may be more vulnerable in certain areas than others. The realist will be looking at:

- What is actually going on in the team.
- What they know about their strengths, weaknesses and development needs.
- What are the strengths, weaknesses, opportunities and threats to the current situation.
- What is currently known about their strategy.
- Who are the stakeholders – both visible and invisible.
- What are the realities around finance and resources.
- What are the politics of the situation.
- How much have people really bought in to a decision.
- How much of their focus is on the future and how much is on the here and now.
- What is going on in the marketplace.
- What factors will support or hinder their decisions and actions.
- How much does language or culture affect what they are seeking to do.

In a later chapter, the Personality Challenge, it becomes clear that some of the more 'sensing types' are excellent at using their five senses to look at what is the current reality. But just as vision needs both intuition and a firm grounding in reality so reality needs inputs, facts, data, information and some creativity and imagination to see the inter-relationships between these seemingly diverse pieces of information, in order to understand the real underlying situation and its possible impacts.

Example

The following is an example of a client who is strong on the Reality Challenge.

Alan, who is an advertising executive, was sitting at the table listening to his colleagues discussing a future advertising campaign. As they were discussing what the advertising might look like in the future, what it could be, what it should be, what it might be, what it would be aimed at, Alan was focused on what it is about now, how it would bring in revenue now and how it would impact on current sales of the product. He describes his internal challenge arising from feeling that his colleagues are 'airy-fairy', vague and unrealistic.

B. Personal Reflection

Think of some examples of great realists! Who do you know in your business that is an example of a leader who is a great realist? If you were to create a definition for the Reality Challenge faced by leaders, what would it be?

Self-assessment of the Reality Challenge

Read through all of the questions below and reflect on your work recently. Next, rate yourself on a scale of 1 to 10, where 10 = highly effective in this challenge (i.e. very realistic across all the dimensions of this challenge) and 1 = very ineffective in this challenge (i.e. not very realistic).

- Would you describe yourself as a realist or an idealist, a pragmatist or a visionary?
- Would your team or colleagues say that you have a firm grip on reality or that you have a great grasp on concepts, visions and ideals but lack a grasp on current realities?
- Are you well informed by your team and colleagues of what is going on around the business/organisation and outside of the business/organisation?
- Do you seek to be informed?
- Do you network with anyone within or outside of your organisation who can help you to keep a firm grasp on what is happening in your market sector, the economy or your team?
- Do you regularly conduct SWOT analysis, force field analysis, or similar, of your current situation?
- Would people who know you in your organisation say you 'read the game poorly' or that you 'read the game well'?
- Are you good at seeing the inter-relationship between the facts, data, information, etc. that you collect?
- Are you more focused on the present, the facts, the reality, what you can see, hear and touch, or are you more focused on the future, the possibilities, intuitions and ideas?

- Do you provide colleagues/direct reports/manager with access to up-to-date information?

So where are you on the scale?

Challenge 3 – The Reality Challenge

| 1 | 2 | 3 | 4 | 5 | 6 | 7 | 8 | 9 | 10 |

C. Developing strength in facing the Reality Challenge

Step 1. Learn to think as a Realist

The key to responding to this challenge is to develop a way of thinking through situations that ensures you are focusing on what is really going on. A realist has a thinking process that acts like a filter. Everything that passes through this mental filter is challenged in terms of reality. So, in terms of leaders being realists, what are the dimensions that are being considered? What are the areas that need to be thought through? See Figure 3.1 for an illustration.

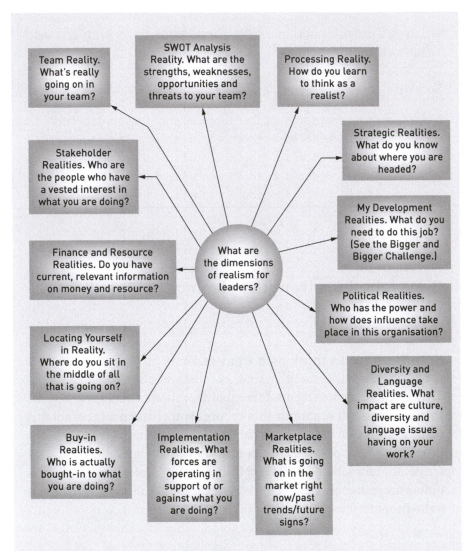

Figure 3.1 Dimensions of realism

Step 2. A Reality Audit

An audit is a way of checking what you already have. So, what do you already have in the way of understanding the current realities of your situation? Take time to do the reality audit in the next section by thinking through each of the areas below and also:

- Note the areas where you need to take action.
- Note the areas you find most difficult to look at (are there areas of reality that produce a blind spot for you?).
- Note the kinds of questions you have to think through so that you develop a way of thinking that will naturally look at reality.

Team Reality Check

- Do you know the development needs of each individual member of your team?
- Are you aware of the management style each of your team members currently needs from you?
- Have you agreed this with them or are you guessing?
- What is happening in the lives of your team members right now (personal or professional) that has an influence on their performance?
- Do you have all of the right type of people to form a complete response to this project or mission (provided by such instruments as Meredith Belbin's Team Roles or the Team Climate Survey)?
- What stage of team development are you in right now (forming, storming, norming or performing)?
- Are there important interpersonal issues that you are ignoring right now?

Is there anything you need to note? Are there any actions you need to take?

SWOT Analysis Reality

A SWOT analysis is a way of scanning the landscape of your current situation. It is called SWOT because each of the letters stands for an area you need to scan. They are S = strengths, W = weaknesses, O = opportunities, T = threats. To conduct a SWOT analysis is to ask honest questions in these four areas. Apply the questions both to your team and to the whole organisation. (See Figure 3.2.)

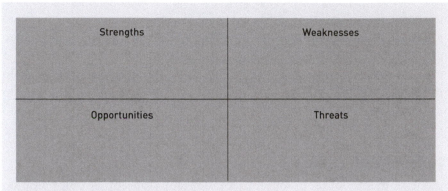

Strengths	Weaknesses
Opportunities	Threats

Figure 3.2   SWOT analysis table

Processing the Details of Reality

This aspect of the Reality Challenge is about learning to get the detail. The kinds of questions to learn to ask yourself are:

- What are the facts?
- What can you see or observe?
- What information is available?
- How can you use this?
- What are the details or specifics?
- Is the information accurate, current and relevant?
- What does your past experience tell you?

Strategic Realities

Strategic realities are the realities surrounding what lies ahead and can be identified by asking questions like:

- What are your high-level goals?
- What is your strategy?
- Is your vision credible, realistic and attractive to all of the key stakeholders?
- Are your plans robust enough to get your team 'from a to b'?
- Are there appropriate measures in place?

- Have you got a business plan?
- What resources are available/needed?
- Is your vision grounded in reality and is it shared?
- How do you know that your answer to the previous question is true? What is your evidence?

Stakeholder Realities

A stakeholder is anyone who has an interest or a need in the mission, project or decision that you are involved in. There are visible stakeholders (those it is easy to be aware of) and invisible stakeholders (equally important but often forgotten or whom it is easy to be unaware of).

1. Draw a 'map' of all of the visible and invisible stakeholders. You can do this in one of two ways. First, you can take a blank sheet of paper and list all of the people who have an involvement, a need and an interest in your project. Second, you can take a sheet of paper and put the same names down but spread them across the paper, drawing lines to connect relevant groups of people together. To ensure a robust response ask some people to challenge your map for thoroughness. Get them to ask you who might have an interest or a need but isn't obvious.
2. Now note the needs of each of these stakeholders or stakeholder groups.
3. Who are the people who are absolutely essential to the success of your current role? If the strength of your relationship with them was likened to a bank account, how healthy is each relationship?
4. Clarify your perception of each of these relationships? For example, consider who will help you in a crisis. Your response to this question may be just a perception or it may be true. If it is true then what is the evidence for your view?

Development Realities

You are a part of the reality you are looking at. When looking out of a glass window at a beautiful view, you assume the window. It is a dangerous thing to forget to see yourself in the picture. Consider the following.

■ Where do you fit within this organisation right now?
■ What are your personal development needs?
■ What are your current strengths and what do they need to be twelve months from now?

At this point it may be helpful to note that we examine development realities specifically in the 'Bigger and Bigger Challenge' Challenge to help you deal with any mismatch between the skills you currently need and the ones you currently have.

Finance and Resources Reality

Up-to-date financial information is essential for effective decision-making and strategic planning. Knowing who is on the team and what skills they bring is also a crucial part of the picture. High levels of redundancies bring a high level of human capital reduction; for example, when Bill got made redundant the company not only lost Bill, it lost 25 years of knowledge of the business. Managing knowledge as a resource is increasingly recognised as being of strategic importance. Therefore, some questions that it may be helpful to ask are:

■ Is there up-to-date and relevant financial information?
■ Are projections based on fact or wishful thinking?
■ Has an audit of the team's skill, knowledge, competences and experience been carried out?

Political Realities

Robbins and Finley (*Why Change Doesn't Work*, 1997) talk about the different roles leaders need to play in managing change. One of the roles they call 'The change maker as game player'. Interdepartmental wars, jealousies, competitions, relationship positioning, career back-stabbing, conflicts, power games – they all go on. Internal politics is a huge area in some organisations. While paranoia isn't necessarily the route, neither is naivety. So how could a realist think through the political arena of their context? Some questions you might consider are:

- Where is power located in the team/organisation?
- Is it in positions, titles, role relationships, processes – or all of these? Whose interests are in conflict with whose?
- How does politics get played out in the organisation?
- How do resources get shared, especially in times of change?
- Where are the informal and formal communication channels in the organisation?

Buy–in Reality

So often, when talking with leaders about their vision for their organisation, team or project, we find they are convinced that others share their vision. When challenged about this they tell us that they have told the team at a recent meeting what the vision is or they wrote it down in a recent document. This is not a shared vision and it provides no indication of whether people agree, understand or have any enthusiasm for the vision. Therefore, you will need to consider the following.

- Have you checked with each team member what their actual level of buy-in to your vision is?
- Ask team members to note their level of buy-in on a scale of 1 to 10, where 1 is low and 10 is high.

■ Get team members to note down all of the questions or issues that they need answering to move their buy-in figure significantly higher, up to at least 7 or 8.

Implementation Realities

When you make decisions or come up with great visions and strategies you need to be a realist about the chances of success. It may be an exciting plan, it may be an innovative plan, but you need to know that it will be a 'robust enough' plan to get off the ground. A Force Field Analysis looks at the forces operating on your decisions or actions that will support them in making a successful start. Much like a hot-air balloon, there is the gas that gets the balloon off the ground and there is gravity holding it back down to earth. To do a Force Field Analysis you can follow through these steps:

1. Make a list of all of the forces that will support your decision or action in getting off the ground.
2. Make a list of all of the forces that will hinder your action or decision in getting off the ground.
3. Brainstorm ways of strengthening the impact of the supporting factors that you have listed.
4. Brainstorm ways of reducing the impact of those hindering forces you have listed.
5. Consider, on balance, whether this decision is likely to succeed.

After you have taken the steps listed above you may decide to take one of the following actions:

■ Go
■ Stop
■ Redesign the plan.

Marketplace Realities

Understanding the context you are in is essential. The context is not just your office or your organisation but also the market you are in. What is happening in your sector right now? What were the previous trends? How does the current pattern fit with past patterns? I (Trevor) was coaching a senior manager recently who was just about to fly into a very reactive mode after receiving some figures until we stopped and compared them with figures for the same months over the past five years and saw that the pattern was normal for his market for this time of year. Some of the questions you might want to consider in trying to understand marketplace realities are:

- Who are your competitors?
- What is going on in your market right now?
- What other areas does your market impact on?
- What are the opportunities?
- Where are you vulnerable to shifts in your other markets?

Diversity and Language Realities

We deal with this in more detail in the Confusion–Complexity–Chaos Challenge. Organisational culture, language differences and international cultures will all affect how people hear what you are trying to say or do and the way you are doing it. Such realities can affect the rate at which you are able to effect change and affect the outcome of change. For example, imagine reorganising your call centre to one that is internationally staffed. Language difficulties in a call centre will always have an effect on the speed of getting your messages across to the team.

- Do you know that all members of your team mean the same thing by the same words?
- How do the different cultures or language groups define key areas like leadership or negotiation?

- How do different cultures' personalities reflect the way they do business with you?

Step 3. Developing Robust Thinking

Some people have very robust thinking processes whereby they challenge their own ideas and the ideas of others. Others have quite weak thinking; for example, one man we spoke to in the voluntary sector had a vision for an organisation of two to three thousand people in an area where the total population hardly exceeded this!

Robust thinking involves asking yourself all of the kinds of questions outlined in Step 2.

What do you need to put in place that will ensure robust thinking? Look through all of the answers and insights you gave in Step 2 and decide what you need in place. Maybe you will need to ask a person who does think robustly to mentor you.

Is there a process you could design, such as a set of questions you could answer yourself, to ensure that you challenge your thinking?

Warnings

- Don't ask for feedback for a reality check if you don't want to hear the answer!
- Proceed carefully, gently and respectfully when giving your perception of reality to others. Gain their agreement for receiving your thoughts where at all possible.

Step 4. 360° Assessment as Reality Testing on Yourself

The subject of 360° assessment and feedback is discussed in the Influence Challenge, so you may wish to visit that chapter. A 360°

assessment tool is designed to help you assess yourself realistically. It can be used to solicit the views of a wide range of people:

- Your views.
- The views of those you report to.
- The views of those you aspire to report to in the future.
- Your peers.
- Those who report to you.
- Those who know you well.
- Those who have only recently met you (they have an excellent and fresh view of how you present yourself in new situations).

This book is designed as a reality check on your leadership and helps you to check:

- What you know.
- What you don't know.
- What you need to know.

It acts as a 360° assessment tool for yourself and for your team.

Step 5. How to Bring People from Their Perception of Reality to a Grounded Reality

The problem you face, with regards to reality, may not reside solely with yourself. Your challenge may be bringing one of your direct line reports or even your team to a point where they are effective at this leadership challenge. You can use the 'blunder and force' approach by telling people they are wrong or stupid; however, we suggest a process that pays attention to how to influence people effectively using the Push–Pull model outlined in the Influence Challenge. People hold their views reasonably tightly and in order to create a new or different view you need to help them loosen their grip on their current perspectives and help them then to create new ones.

How you actually go about loosening another person's grip on their current perspectives is a process that is not necessarily immediate. The behaviours you will need to adhere to in helping create a new perspective are outlined in Table 3.1.

Table 3.1   Creating a new perspective

Hear what they are saying.	Generally people need to be heard and understood before they are ready to take on change, a challenge or an adaptation to their views, especially if these perspectives are held rigidly.
Validate what they are saying.	Giving credence to what they have already understood is important. One way of doing this is not just to listen but to recap, paraphrase, summarise and explore what you hear them saying.
Don't collude with what they are saying.	Listening and understanding doesn't mean you have to agree with a perspective that you don't share. Collusion is an unspoken agreement – conscious or not – to not tell the truth to each other, and this will not help to build a picture of reality.
Respect what they are saying.	However, maintaining respect is crucial. If someone's perspective may be easily challenged you should assume that there are good reasons why they hold the view they do. Dismissive or patronising responses just build up resistance to change.
Gently question it to understand and clearly what they are saying.	Once a perspective has been heard and validated then you can begin to challenge their views by gentle questioning. This will have a twofold effect: it will help them to understand why they have the perspective

	that they do and will also raise new awareness and insights.
Creatively challenge it.	Increase the level of challenge by using a few of the tools we outline below.
Find the core issues or principles.	Help them to find what the core issues or principles are on which reality needs to be based.
Build a grounded picture around the core issues or principles.	Once the principles are established help them to flesh out the details of reality.
Leave them with a success formula for action – a plan that will work.	Leave them with a way forward: a new way of both using the reality they have uncovered and ensuring that they can get a more accurate perspective next time.

Some Useful Tools for Creatively Challenging People

Advantage or disadvantage

People are often characterised as 'glass-half-full people' or 'glass-half-empty people'. They see all the positives of their position and few of the disadvantages of their position or vice versa. One tool is to get them to look at their position from four different viewpoints. First, what are the advantages of their position? Second, what are the disadvantages of their position? They can increase the challenge by, thirdly, looking at the disadvantages of the advantages they have identified and, fourthly, by looking at the advantages of their disadvantages. This method of challenge ensures that you and they walk right round an issue to establish reality.

Try out this tool using a real issue you face at work, perhaps taking time to write your observations in a box similar to Figure 3.3.

What are the advantages of your position?	What are the disadvantages of your position?
What are the disadvantages of your advantages?	What are the advantages of your disadvantages?

Figure 3.3 Checking the advantages and disadvantages

Self-limiting Beliefs

A key area of reality is governed by the beliefs people hold about themselves or a situation they face.

- 'I could never do that.'
- 'I always fail to do this.'
- 'I'm useless at that.'

Aaron Beck (1991) introduced the idea of challenging these self-limiting beliefs by asking questions. The questions are designed to establish the reality of the situation.

Take a fear of mine. I do a lot of public speaking. I am often limited by two fears. One is that people will get so bored that they start ripping up the seats or something. The other is that I will run out of material.

These beliefs may be true or they may not be based on reality. So I could ask myself a set of questions like:

- Has this ever happened before?
- How many times and in what situations?
- How many talks have I given and how often has this happened?
- Where is the evidence for what I am saying?

Other questions for different situations might be:

- Can you clarify how you draw that inference or conclusion from what happened?
- Is this actually your responsibility or someone else's?
- How do you know that is what people were thinking or feeling?
- Is there an in-between position other than the two polarised ones you have given?
- What is the evidence that they are as good/bad/incompetent/brilliant as you say?

Checking out buy-in, motivation or clarity on an issue

One method that coaches often use to bring people from vague generalities to a more concrete reality is borrowed from the world of Brief Solution Focused Therapy. It is called *Scaling*. People are presented with a scale of 1 to 10 and asked to rate themselves on the scale where 1 is low and 10 is high.

Examples may be:

- On a scale of 1 to 10, where 10 is very clear, how clear are you about your goals this year?
- You say that you feel a little miffed with your boss right now; on a scale of 1 to 10 where 1 is mildly irritated and 10 is ballistic, where are you?

The benefit of this tool is that it ensures that people focus on the reality of their situation. It is also helpful in creating a future reality. For example, *'you've scored yourself a 6 in terms of clarity on your goals this year. If you were to transform that into an 8 or 9, exactly what would you have that you don't have right now?'*

Techniques for 'drilling down' into underlying realities

Often people only give the headlines of what they want to say. They are asked a question and then answer it in the shortest form they can, but often there is a lot more detail or a lot more substance below the surface answer. How do you get the 'full' reality behind a person's sentences? There are two useful techniques for drilling down into underlying realities. One is to ask the question 'Why?', up to five times; the other is to ask someone what they really want.

Example

You want to get the partners in your law firm to be more effective in leading their staff.

Why?

Because ....

So why is that important?

Because ....

What do you want?

A few years ago the Spice Girls seemed to corner the market on what people really, really wanted. We think their question is a good way of finding out underlying realities.

- What do you want to pursue that particular market for?
- What do you really want from pursuing that market?
- What do you really, really want from pursuing that market?
- What do you really, really, really want from pursuing that market?

The idea is to persevere with the question until you feel you have hit the underlying reality. This might be achieved by asking the question once or a few times.

Both of these drilling-down techniques need to be done as genuine explorations and not inane repetition or done in a way that suggests you didn't believe the first answer you got!

Planning to be a Realist

Choose

Choose one of the dimensions of reality that has been touched on and create a strategy to explore that particular dimension thoroughly.

For example, you might choose team reality. How will you go about getting a robust picture of what is really going on with your team right now? We have worked with senior managers who think their teams are in great shape but their staff tell us quietly when we are on the way out of the building that some members of the team are thinking of leaving because they can't stand their boss's attitude.

Note

Make notes on the reality of the situation you have chosen. Take this opportunity to write down everything you know and don't know about your chosen area. It is often as you write down what you do know that you will see clearly what you don't know or where you are making assumptions with no evidence to back them up.

Plan

How do you plan to retain a firm grasp on reality?

For example, if you chose the area of team reality and you have now discovered things you didn't know before, what do you need to put in place to ensure that you keep a grasp on reality from now onwards?

Or, for example, you may have chosen the area of financial and resource reality. In the past you may have shied away from getting to grips with the figures yourself because they intimidate you, so perhaps you may create a plan that involves learning to read figures and then setting aside time each month to study the new figures with the aim of feeling you have a first-hand, rather than a second-hand, understanding of them.

Planning a Step Change

So, if you were 5% more realistic in the way you work, consider:

- What would you start doing?
- What would you stop doing?
- What would you keep on doing that you are already doing?
- What other areas might you explore?

The Final Question . . . What are you going to do now?
(See Appendix 1 for further development)

The
Vision Challenge
Creating an engaging picture
of the future

A. Understanding this Challenge

Not much happens without a dream. And for something great to happen, there must be a big dream. Behind every great achievement is a dreamer of great dreams. Much more than a dreamer is required to bring it to reality; but the dream must be there first. (Robert K. Greenleaf, *The Servant Leader*, 2003)

Definitions

The *Collins Concise Dictionary* (1988) defines vision as the ability or an instance of great perception, especially of future developments and fore-sight characterised by idealistic or radical ideas, especially impractical ones.

How do we define the Vision Challenge? We would say something like: 'Leaders create and articulate a compelling picture of the future that is shared by others.' There are three key elements to vision in this definition. The *first* is about creating something. A statement of mission or purpose defines what a person or organisation is about, what the core business is. It is often stated in present-continuous tense, i.e. it's always true. Take for example this statement from Gillette.

The Gillette Company is a globally focused consumer products marketer that seeks competitive advantage in quality, value-added personal care and personal use products. We are committed to building shareholder value through sustained profitable growth. (Available on *www.gillette.com*)

A vision, however, looks at what that mission or purpose will actually look like in five years (or whatever horizon is set) from now. What will people see going on? Vision is about defining the future. A lot has been said in recent years about the different functions of different parts of the brain, where (amongst many other things) the left brain controls the details and the right brain the big-picture thinking. Vision is a visual, right-brain activity. Some of the elements of vision are that it is attractive, credible and a future state. Visions are not just limited to organisations; they can be for a person or a team.

The *second* element in our definition is that it needs to be verbalised. Often vision can be held intuitively inside a person and they can assume everyone else sees what they see when they look towards the future. This is seldom the case. The leader needs to find words to express the picture of the future. As Executive Coaches we will ask a leader to tell us about their vision and as they talk we ask them lots of questions for clarification. This does two things. It helps us to know how clear their vision really is. If they can't get us to see clearly what they see then we assume that they will have a problem getting others to see the vision clearly also. Secondly, by writing down copious notes to catch as many words as we can, they have the basis of a whole document full of words that describe the vision.

The *third* element of the definition is that for vision to motivate change it needs to be shared. This does not just mean that the leader shares with the team or organisation, it means that the team or the organisation actually sees what the leader sees. Often a leader will share their vision with a team and assume that the team has bought into the vision and is on board. This is frequently a mistaken assumption. Sharing a vision with a team of people is *vision casting*, but getting the team to share that vision is *vision creation*. It is this process that is essential if the people within an organisation are to put their energy into pursuing the vision. Therefore, the leader needs clear vision but this vision needs to be shared if it is to motivate others.

Vision And Change Management

Where an organisation is involved in any kind of strategic change a verbalised, shared vision is essential. Research into why change succeeds or fails reveals that the presence or lack of a clear and shared vision is always at the top of the list. The successful implementation of any strategic change involves the clarity of a vision that captures the organisation's purpose, values, leadership requirements, key deliverables, key processes for delivering them and the sense of empowered decision-making by everyone involved in the change. Vision drives all of the components of strategic change by engaging and organising the imagination in a big picture of what the change will look like when it is complete, who will be involved, how they will be involved, and how resources will be used.

Intentional change involves two creations. First, there is the *mental* creation. This is what goes on inside people's heads to get the picture clear for themselves. Second, there is the creation in *reality*. This is the actual doing of it. Vision is the mental creation. Successful athletes mentally recreate repeatedly the whole of their event through to victory. This mental creation clarifies and focuses all of the available energy and resources to reach an agreed goal. For example, the athlete will imagine what it will look like to win. He or she will focus on gaining a picture of winning that is so clear that it enables him or her to ensure that every known or potential obstacle is worked through before the real event begins.

Vision and Leadership

Vision creation is a leadership function rather than a management function. It seeks to create what currently does not exist rather than simply manage what does. This was Handy's point about leaders when he said, 'A plan or strategy which is a projection of the present or a replica of what everyone else is doing is not a vision. A vision has to reframe the known scene, to re-conceptualize the obvious, connect the previously unconnected dream' (*The Age of Unreason*, 1995). Where serious attention is given to the creation and maintenance of vision, the managerial processes are allowed to remain flexible to fulfil that vision. Where vision is lacking or becomes outdated the managerial processes are in danger of becoming inflexible and contribute less. The following are taken from Handy's book:

'Without a vision the people perish.' (Proverbs 29 v.18)

'Leadership is the ability to create a story that affects the thoughts, feelings and actions of other individuals.' (Gardner, *Leading Minds*, 1997)

'All the significant breakthroughs were breaks with old ways of thinking.' (Thomas Kuhn)

'The significant problems we face cannot be solved at the same level of thinking we were at when we created them.' (Albert Einstein)

'If we live out of our memory, we're tied to the past and to that which is finite. When we live out of our imagination, we're tied to that which is infinite.' (Stephen R. Covey)

Choosing the Arena for Your Vision

As with many of the challenges, you may feel you are more effective in certain dimensions of the challenge and less effective in others. To make a good assessment of yourself it may help you to focus on the Vision Challenge across *four areas* and *two dimensions*, as in Figure 4.1.

Personal	Relational or Interpersonal
(For my life)	(For my relationships)
Managerial	**Organisational**
(For my team, department or project)	(For my company, hospital, PCT, Borough Council, charity, organisation)

Figure 4.1   The four areas of vision

The first area is Personal Vision, which is linked to the Internal Compass Challenge and looks at whether you have a vision for your own life including your relationships and your career. Related to this is the second area of Relational or Interpersonal Vision, which involves getting clear about specific key relationships in your life. If you are in a long-term relationship then what do you want that relationship to look like 30 years from now? How would you want your relationship described and what will you be doing? The third area of Managerial Vision involves questions like What will your project look like when it is complete? What will you be doing? How will you be working with others? Finally, there is the whole Organisational Vision area. Take our earlier example of Gillette's mission. You only need to look at the Mach 3 razor alongside a 1940s version with replaceable blades to know that Gillette did not stand still. However, did people think in the 1940s that Gillette would own four leading brands in the marketplace and reorganise the way they do business around Europe? Along the way people have to keep translating the core mission into a picture of the future that is verbalised, clear and shared so that the whole workforce can move towards it.

Vision Shapes Action to Create a Future

Example – Personal Vision

A retiring CEO has spent his whole life in the City but has not invested time on creating a bigger picture of his life. He now feels very depressed, as if his life has ended.

Example – Relational Vision

When Jane took time to look at her relationships she had a vision for being a real friend and support to her nephews, providing support and enrichment beyond that of their parents. When she had clarified her vision of her relationship with her nephews she realised that she hadn't spoken to them for months. She picked up the phone that evening.

Example – Managerial Vision

When Alan realised that he and his team had little vision and did something about it, it transformed the way he spent his time. He no longer spent his day fire-fighting but rather spent his time ensuring the right resources were in place for his team to achieve the vision. He also discovered that he had time to meet each team member personally on a monthly basis.

Example – Organisational Vision

When Sheila's board finally took vision seriously they not only created a picture of the future that they were aiming for, they also created four alternative scenarios that might occur if the market changed so that they now felt they were acting rather than reacting for the future.

As you will learn from the Personality Challenge some people are more values- or relationally focused and others are more task-focused. This translates into two key dimensions when considering the Vision Challenge. One dimension (probably the more familiar) is a *doing* focus. This is a vision about the tasks or activities the person, team or organisation is seeking to develop. Just as important, however, is the *being* dimension. This is much more focused on how people will be: how they will experience their values in the future. How will they be feeling? What will be important to them? Some people really struggle to create a picture of what they want to do in the future but have a much greater sense of how they want to be.

The six key questions to consider from this are:

1. Do you have a vision for your own life? (Links to the Work–Life Balance and Internal Compass Challenges.)
2. Do you have a vision for key interpersonal relationships – both personal and work? (Links to the Influence Challenge.)
3. Do you have a vision for your team, department or project and for your management of your team, department or project?
4. Do you have a vision for the organisation that you lead and/or do you share the vision of the organisation to which you belong? (Links to the Proactive Challenge.)
5. Do you want to focus on a vision that looks more at what people will be doing?
6. Do you want to focus on a vision that looks more at how people are being?

B. Personal Reflection

Take time to consider your understanding of vision. Where do you see its importance?

■ For you personally?
■ For your work?

In which of these four areas do you see your greatest challenge right now?

- Personal (for your life).
- Relational or interpersonal (for your relationships).
- Managerial (for your team, department or project).
- Organisational (for your company, hospital, Primary Care Trust, Borough Council, charity, organisation).

Self-assessment of the Vision Challenge

Read through all of the questions below and reflect on your work recently. Next, rate yourself in the box on a scale of 1 to 10, where 1 = very ineffective in responding to this challenge (i.e. not very good at creating and communicating vision) and 10 = very effective at responding to this challenge (i.e. very good at creating and communicating vision).

- Do you have a vision for your own life that is clear, compelling and attractive to you?
- Do you have a vision for your organisation/business/team/project that is clear, compelling and attractive to others?
- Do you feel at ease with 'blue-sky' thinking or does the need for getting on with the job now, short-circuit the vision creation process?
- Do you feel comfortable with the language of creativity, possibility, intuition, hunches, concepts, principles and values?
- Do you have a clear process that you use to create a shared vision?
- In your vision for your business/organisation/team/project can you 'see' how the goals, values, leadership activities, key deliverables, key processes, decision making, etc. all fit together?
- Can you see, hear and feel what your business/organisation/team/project will look like when it is fulfilling its future vision?
- Do you do both the first, mental, creation and the second, reality, creation when you are planning for the future?
- Is your vision unexpressed and located within yourself or is your vision shared, owned and developed by your team or others?

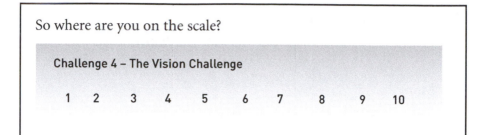

So where are you on the scale?

Challenge 4 – The Vision Challenge

| 1 | 2 | 3 | 4 | 5 | 6 | 7 | 8 | 9 | 10 |

C. Developing the Ability to Create and Share Vision

Informal surveys by Gary Hamel and C. K. Prahalad suggest that senior managers devote less than 3% of their time and energy to building a collective vision of the future. (Paul Schoemaker, *Profiting from Uncertainty*, 2002)

The Need for Shared Vision

In this section we will give you four different processes that you can use to create vision. First, however, there is a need to underline a key point we made earlier in the chapter. This can be achieved by looking at two hypothetical stories.

Story 1

Three people went to start up a new restaurant together. They were excited, passionate and focused. Everything was fine until the building started to be erected and decorated. 'Hold on', says one person, 'it should be painted green and red.' 'No, no,' says another, 'I wanted pagoda shapes and lanterns.' 'No, no,' says the third person, 'it needs to be arches all over the place.' Over the following weeks more and more conflict broke out between the three of them. Finally, it emerged that one had in mind a Chinese restaurant, another had in mind an Italian restaurant and the third had in mind a French restaurant. The problem? No shared vision.

Story 2

One man set out to build the most amazing Thai restaurant, the like of which had never been seen in his area. His charisma, energy and excitement drew in a team of staff and they made a great success of this new restaurant. As the years passed by the original staff moved on and new ones appeared who were inheritors of the success of the founders but had little interest in working as hard as they had done. The founding boss was resentful that the new staff were unreliable and he couldn't delegate to them. They always wanted to do things in new ways and were lazy. The founding boss was tired and wanted a rest but there was no one he could trust his restaurant to. The problem? No shared vision.

Where vision involves others – which apart from personal vision, it does – then the important fact to note is that it is not just vision but *shared vision* that motivates others. Although a leader may be clear and motivated it does not necessarily mean his or her team will share that leader's vision to any extent or be motivated to put their energy into it.

There are two ways to create shared vision.

Route 1

You have a clear vision that you cast to others. They gather around you and your vision and you then engage in a process with them where 'your' vision becomes 'our' vision.

Route 2

A group of people gather together and create a shared vision from a blank sheet of paper or from a given objective.

So, who needs to share your vision or whom do you need to create vision with?

Four Processes for Creating Vision

Before we take you through four different processes you can use to create vision and shared vision it may be helpful to give you an example of someone's vision.

Example

Louis Arnitz and his travel company FAO had a vision long before the Internet was an accepted part of daily commerce that people should be able to book their own travel. This is the picture they described in their 1999 annual report.

'Imagine: Our traveler of the future has to travel to London on a business assignment. He opens the calendar on his computer desktop and clicks on next Wednesday. He uses his mouse to drag the date over the travel icon and drops it there. The travel software is automatically launched and opens a map of Europe. He clicks on London and the software, connected to more than 700 airlines through the Internet, returns a list of available flights, flagged by company preference. Another click secures a seat on the 8 a.m. service. One more click on Thursday, and the intelligent booking software automatically displays return flights for his selection.

'As soon as the traveler has made these choices, the application displays a city map of London, pinpointing the corporation's headquarters and several other important points of interest. More so, the software also displays hotels on the city map that fit two criteria: they are approved by corporate travel policy and have rooms available. Upon contact with the cursor, the little hotel icons open a window that displays the name, rate, facilities and amenities of the selected property. Upon a single click a room is booked. The application returns a complete travel itinerary and at the same time performs a number of transactions in the

background. These transactions secure the traveler's preferred seat and meal, take care of payment procedures and enlist in frequent travelers programs. The traveler is not bothered by these transactions – they are all controlled by his detailed profile, which is governed by the corporate profile his online system uses. The traveler drops the itinerary onto the calendar for future reference and e-mails several copies to other staff members, his contacts in London and to his family. Upon request the online system will start a special agent software that will pull together a 'Smart Itinerary' for his trip. This itinerary will contain recent currency exchange rates, weather forecasts, a map of the hotel's vicinity and up to date information on cultural and sports events. It will be automatically e-mailed to him in good time for his trip.' (Paul Schoemaker, *Profiting from Uncertainty*, 2002)

From this example it is evident that vision is not merely a few intuitive brushstrokes – it is a picture of the future in action. It enables people to see what you or others will be doing. When you have a clear vision you can look at it and see the crucial areas you must focus on. (Strategic goals – see the Strategy Challenge.)

We would now like to walk you through the four different processes that you can use to create vision with your stakeholders.

Process 1 – Engaging a Team

1. Split your (leadership) team into small groups of three or four people maximum.
2. Each group is given pens, a large sheet of flip-chart paper, a large pile of varied magazines, scissors and glue.
3. Each group has to create a picture, with no words, of what the team/product/organisation will look like in five years from now (approximately 20 minutes or while there is still energy and engagement in the activity).
4. Bring the groups back together.
5. Each group explains their picture in as much detail as possible.

The other groups can ask questions for clarification but not make comments or judgements.

6. When all of the groups have finished ask the whole group what they have noticed or observed about what has been shared. What are the themes, main strands or main ideas that all groups shared and which ones were specific to only one or two groups?

7. Distil the four or five main brushstrokes of the vision (they may become the key goals).

8. Start asking very detailed questions about each goal to create a detailed picture of what will be taking place if this goal is actually realised.

Variation 1

Taking a large sheet of flip-chart paper, draw a large circle on it. Stick pictures inside the circle that will illustrate how this team or organisation will look from the inside and stick pictures on the outside of the circle to illustrate how this team or organisation will look from the outside, e.g. to customers, other departments, competitors.

Variation 2

If you don't have lots of magazines handy then use flip-chart pens of different colours to draw images and pictures.

'My team would think we're going soft if we use pictures!'

The purpose of using this method is that vision is obviously visual and you and your team need to use as much of the 'right brain' as possible to do this. Images and pictures engage hearts and minds on a different level than words.

Try it! You'll be surprised at the fun you can have once you've got past the scepticism.

Process 2 – From Mission to Vision

Step 1

Start by writing out, in one sentence, your mission statement or the statement of purpose for your team.

There are many definitions of vision, mission, purpose, etc. This book bases its use of these words on the following definitions.

Mission or purpose = something that will always be true. Your core reason for being.

Vision = a picture of the future if you were achieving your mission. It is more time-bound, and, once achieved, you will create new vision. Purpose or mission will remain unchanged.

Example

The purpose of The Executive Coach is to influence the leadership conversation around the world or, more informally, to lift up people's heads.

Step 2

Create a list of questions that you could ask of your statement in order to put 'flesh on the bones' or to bring the statement alive with a picture of what it would look like if you were achieving your mission.

The questions below are just some of those you may want to ask to flesh out your statement, but take time to think of others.

- Why is this important to you?
- What would you be doing if this were achieved?
- What excites you or gets you out of bed in the morning in this mission?
- Describe what is going on when you are achieving this mission.
- Who else is involved?

- What are they doing?
- What will it look like if things are going well/badly?
- What would I see going on?
- What would I hear you talking about?
- What would you be feeling?
- What would others be seeing/hearing/feeling?
- Who would be doing what?
- How will resources be being gathered/managed?
- Tell me some stories that you would like to be circulating around the organisation in five years from now if you were achieving all of this.

Step 3

After you have asked questions of your mission statement jot down in note form all of the details from your answers.

Step 4

Think through your values. What is important to you, the team, the project and the organisation in order to achieve this mission? List the values and the observable behaviours you would see if these values were being lived.

Step 5

Stories engage people's hearts and minds much more than stock-piling words. Take time to write down and share three stories about your team or organisation that link the past, present and future.

Step 6

Metaphors or pictures act like a coat hanger to hang the detail of the vision together in a way that people can envisage.

- 'I see the future looking like . . .'

■ 'Imagine a future where . . .'
■ 'I see this team looking like . . .'

What image or metaphors could provide an engaging way of bringing together the vision in both the big picture and detail so that people have a clear sense of what the future can look like and see themselves as being a part of it?

Step 7

Now bring all of the notes from steps 1–6 together and create a picture or vision of the future.

Recap: What is the Vision Challenge?

The Vision Challenge is not about coming up with a plan or a strategy – so what is it? Charles Handy's definition says, 'A leader shapes and shares a vision which gives point to the work of others.' Handy's checklist has five key points, the answers in each case being taken from Handy (1995).

1. Is it different? 'A plan or strategy which is a projection of the present or a replica of what everyone else is [already] doing is not a vision.'
2. Does it make sense to others? 'Stretch their imagination but still within the bounds of possibility.'
3. Is it understandable? 'It has to be able to stick in the mind.'
4. Do I live the vision? 'It must be seen in you, your words are not enough.'
5. Are others signing up to follow? The vision is the work of others. 'A leader with no followers is a voice in the wilderness.'

Process 3 – 'Tell me . . .'

This process is based on asking a certain question repeatedly with different focus.

The formula of the question is 'tell me'. The reason we use this type of question is that it is an open question that allows people to think through an issue from a different perspective, hopefully in ways that they haven't thought about before. You can ask the question to yourself or if you are working as a team then one of the team can act as a facilitator and ask the team the question.

Asking the same question a number of times allows you to move beyond the surface answers.

- Tell me what you are doing.
- Tell me why you are doing it.

Choose a point down the road; 1, 3, 5, 10 years from now. Taking your chosen time-frame:

- Tell me what you want to be doing/what you want to be in x years from now.
- Tell me what it will look like if you are excelling in what you doing.
- Tell me, who do you exist for?
- Tell me, how did your organisation begin?
- Tell me, what are the principles from this story that need to be central to the future?
- Tell me, given all of your answers to these questions, what will this team/organisation look like x years from now?

Describe

This process is very similar to the 'tell me' process. The difference is more about trying to get creative descriptions from the team. Take this first question.

Describe what it is that you/your team/your organisation does.

'Describe' gets an answer that is more than simply stating what you do; it seeks actual descriptive detail and processes.

- Describe the four or five things you must do to achieve this.
- Describe, each one in turn, what you are doing when you are doing these four or five things.
- Describe what it would look like if you were excelling at each one.
- Describe what it would look like if you were under-performing in each one.
- If you had 60 seconds to engage me in the vision for the future as a part of your team/organisation, describe what you would say.

Process 4 – See–Hear–Feel

Choose a point in the future that will stretch your thinking sufficiently. If the horizon is too short you are likely to repeat what you already have; if the horizon is too far then it may be demotivating. Use the idea of *See–Hear–Feel* to describe what will be happening in this organisation, team or project in the future.

- What will I see happening?
- What will our customers see happening?
- What will our team see happening?
- What will I hear going on? Stories people are telling? Overhear in corridor conversations?
- What will I be feeling?
- What will the team be feeling?
- What will our customers be feeling?

Now write a 30-second version of your vision.

Vision and getting people out of the stands

> 'The fundamental ability of an inspirational leader is to change the energy in those around them.' (Olivier, 2001)

Daniel Goleman (2001) has produced research on the role that a leader's mood plays in motivating people within his or her organisation and it is no surprise that a leader's mood affects the performance of those around them. It is important to understand what moves people from observer to engaged employer, out of the grandstands on to the pitch as a player. Just saying 'I ought' or 'you ought' won't do it. So what does?

The missing link is vision. A leader who has a clear vision creates within them an energy or passion; it is this that inspires others (see Figure 4.2).

Vision ➤ **Passion** ➤ **Inspiring others** ➤

Figure 4.2 Linking vision to motivating people

So, here are three questions to ask yourself.

1. Do you have a clear vision of the future?
2. Does your vision excite you?
3. Does your vision excite others?

Vision and the Impact of Personality

It is important to recognise the impact of different personalities on this challenge. Different people will respond to the Vision Challenge in different ways. This is not only important for you and where you start on this challenge, but also for how you might lead the different personalities within your team or organisation through this particular leadership challenge.

Table 4.1 outlines the different personality types and how they might respond to the Vision Challenge.

Table 4.1 How different personality types respond to creating vision

Personality Type	What Challenges Do They Face in the Vision Challenge?
I get my energy from being with other people, from interacting with them, knocking ideas around together, stimulating and challenging each other in order to find out what I think myself.	They can fill the space up so that others don't engage in the conversation and subsequently don't feel involved in the vision creation process. They lack reflection sometimes and so there may be great breadth but insufficient depth to the vision.
I get my energy from thinking and reflecting internally before I share my ideas with others. I need space to work out what I feel before I share it with others.	They can appear detached and uninvolved in the vision-creation process. The team may ignore them, assume them to be on board with the vision or become irritated by their seeming lack of interest and involvement.
I love the 'big picture' stuff. I enjoy creating ideas and systems and visions of the future. I can just 'see it' without anyone telling me what is involved or delving into information, facts and details.	They can see the vision so clearly in their own mind's eye that they find it difficult to explain it to others, make it concrete for others or help others see how they arrived at that particular idea. They are in danger of assuming that everyone sees as clearly as they do and because it is all self-explanatory they don't explain themselves.
I love the detail. I need the details, facts and inform-ation. They are like the building blocks from which I create or build towards a picture of the future. I focus on what 'is' in order to build towards 'what is not yet'.	They can be so rooted in the current situation, the problems and the realities that they are held back from going forwards. Their thirst for reality can discourage visionaries by seeming to shoot down every good or new idea on the basis of its potential problems.

Table 4.1   continued

Personality Type	What Challenges Do They Face in the Vision Challenge?
I am very analytical in my approach to vision creation. My thinking is systematic and thorough, seeking to understand the implications and ramifications of all that we might do in the future.	They can come across as cold and a little harsh. Other people's good ideas are not acknowledged or praised. Sometimes doing the right thing is at the expense of others' feelings.
I am most interested in who is involved rather than what we are doing. How the vision impacts on people is my primary concern along with a concern to maintain and deepen the organisation's or my own values. A good idea is a bad idea if it cuts across the values of others and pays little regard to their feelings.	They can appear a little irrational or 'touchy feely' sometimes. Doing the right thing commercially seems to give them great pain at times. Their explanations can come across as a little confused or unclear.

Communicating Vision

Vision Casting v. Vision Creation

We have already said that it isn't vision that motivates, it is shared vision that does. *Vision casting* is where we have a vision and we want to get you to be involved; *vision creation* is where we sit down and create the vision together. In reality the communication process is an interplay of the two.

Some wrong assumptions:

- We have communicated clearly with others about vision just because we are clear in our own minds.
- Because we have told people once at a meeting or presentation what our vision is they will have caught it.
- Because we are clear and enthusiastic people will catch the vision by accident.
- People will remember your brilliant PowerPoint presentation from yesterday – given that the mind can only consciously hold three to seven blocks of information this is unlikely.

Using one or more of the four processes outlined earlier with your team will be useful in ensuring a shared vision is created.

A more typical process that can be used in organisations is as follows:

- You cast the vision to the group using a clear and engaging presentation.
- You then ask people to write down a figure privately on a sheet of paper in front of them. It is important to tell them that they do not have to share this number with anyone. The number needs to be between 1 and 10, where 10 is 'I totally buy in to the vision I've just heard' and 1 is 'I don't buy into this vision at all'.
- Once everyone has written down a figure ask him or her to write down all of the questions that they would need answering in order to push their figure up towards the higher end of the spectrum.
- Gather in all of the questions and begin discussion groups around them or answer the questions from the front of the group. (There needs to be small-group interaction in this process that revolves around meaningful debate.)

What is the message?

In order to communicate vision you need to distil the message into different lengths of presentation. A key version of any presentation is the 30-second version. The reason for this is that often we only have very short gaps of time to communicate important messages.

■ What is the 30-second message of your vision?
■ What is the 2-minute version of your vision?

Who do we need to communicate it to?

Time needs to be spent on working out exactly who you need to communicate with. To answer this question you need to write down all of the stakeholders. Remember stakeholders include anyone who has an interest or need in what you are seeking to do.

See the Influence Challenge to learn how to create stakeholder maps.

A good exercise is for you or your team to put yourself in your board or team's shoes for 20 minutes and ask yourself what this vision will look like from their position and then ask yourself, what do I need to adjust in my communication strategy?

What is the Best Way of Communicating Vision?

Here is a checklist for you to think through what are the most appropriate ways to communicate in your situation.

Vision through ideas

Ideas, theories and concepts can be communicated through:

■ Words
■ Graphics
■ Metaphors
■ Examples.

Vision through written communications

Written communication may involve using:

- PowerPoint slides
- Books
- Articles
- Letters
- News sheets
- E-mails
- Intranets
- CD-ROMs.

Vision through experience and seeing

Effective ways of communicating might include:

- Showing them other places where it is happening.
- Talking to people who have experienced completion of a vision.
- Seeing a structural model of a completed vision.
- Hands-on experience of having a go themselves through workshops or simulations.

When Is the Best Time to Communicate What?

Finally, you will need to create a 'master plan' that covers whom you communicate what to, and when?

It is no good communicating with your divisional team until your boss has bought in and signed off the vision you are proposing.

Do you have a stranglehold on the vision?

The Final Question . . . What are you going to do now?
(See Appendix 1 for further development)

The
Strategy Challenge
Defining a path to the future

A. Understanding this Challenge

Any Route Will Do?

> Alice stands at a crossroads utterly perplexed which way to go.
> 'Which way should I go?', she asked. 'Where are you going to?',
> someone asks her. 'I don't know', she replies. 'Then any route will
> do.' (Lewis Carroll, *Alice in Wonderland*)

Strategy is about the route to where you are going. Suppose you have done a great job on the Vision Challenge. You have a big picture and that picture is now being shared by and motivating a key group of stakeholders. The *'where are you going?'* question is reasonably well answered. The Strategy Challenge is about how to answer the first question Alice asked, 'which way should I go?' Unless there are clear routes to achieve a vision then the vision will either be left as a dream or only partially achieved by accident rather than design. To be a good leader you need to have clarity and focus, a clear picture of the end you are pursuing and clear plans on how to get there that respond to the ever-changing environment.

Is There a Key to Successful Strategy?

The current climate on thinking about strategy is divided. Do people plan to get from *a* to *b* or does the pathway from *a* to *b* emerge as they put one foot in front of the other? Either way, the challenge for leaders is to be strategic and to think strategically. Research shows that there is no single strategy that will make an organisation successful. To keep the issue at its simplest, the challenge for the leader in thinking strategically is how to bridge the gap between reality and vision. Some of the skills leaders need in order to think strategically are listed below (don't worry if some of these are not familiar to you).

- Stakeholder analysis.
- Scenario planning.
- Understanding the organisation's culture and its politics.
- Analysing the forces for and against decisions working out.

- Identifying the key objectives.
- Understanding what leadership tasks need to be fulfilled.
- Clarifying the values and behaviours needed to deliver the vision.
- Identifying the roles people need to take.
- Identifying the deliverables.
- Understanding where the decision making is to be located.

On top of all this there is the need to understand:

- What your market share is.
- How to increase it.
- Product cycles.
- Marketing strategies.
- Resource allocation.
- Budgeting.
- Investment.

(Of course the list needs to include cunning, political awareness, flexibility and large doses of luck!)

Five Stages to the Strategy Challenge

Freedman and Tregoe in their book *The Art and Discipline of Strategic Leadership* (2003) outline a simple and practical five-stage process to responding to the Strategy Challenge. This model has been adapted for you in Figure 5.1. The process is what is called 'iterative' in that each stage gives new information that you can go back and review and so keeps building up a stronger and stronger strategy. In the diagram the upward arrows represent this process.

Find out what is going on

The first stage will link into the Reality Challenge. It's all about gathering and analysing all of the data available to you that may be directly or indirectly relevant to the journey you are about to embark on. What are the kinds of analysis that you can do?

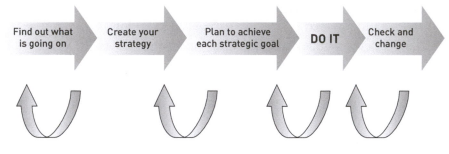

Figure 5.1 Five-stage model

- **Stakeholder analysis.** Who has a need or an interest – both obvious and formal relationships as well as informal or invisible stakeholders?
- **Trend analysis.** What are the five major trends or forces that will have the greatest impact on your business over the next three years?
- **Financial analysis.** What is your financial map for the past three years, this year, next year, the next five years? What shape is the economy in generally, within your sector or business?
- **Risk analysis.** What are the risks and consequences of doing this and not doing this?
- **SWOT analysis.** What are the strengths, weaknesses, opportunities and threats to the organisation, team or project?
- **Competitor analysis.** What are your competitors doing? What are they doing differently from you? What would they do in your situation?
- **Needs analysis.** What are your needs, the needs of your team, customer needs, stakeholder needs?

One way to then take this analysis into the future is by *scenario planning*. This is where you sit down and create different scenarios of what the future might look like if certain factors from your analysis were to continue. Examples of scenario planning often start with the question 'what if . . .?'

Example

Five years to travel six weeks!

The year 2000 saw the first successful unsupported walk to the Geographical North Pole. Alan Chambers spent five years planning for his six-week journey.

Strategic planning is the result of thorough analysis.

Create your strategy

Having got a clear vision and an analysis of the domain the next step is to turn it into a concrete strategy. The first step to doing this is to distil *strategic goals*. Strategic goals are the key areas (we usually recommend an optimum of up to five because beyond this it is hard to retain focus) that you must focus on if you are to achieve the vision. A strategy needs to make sense of three key areas. Does the strategy show clearly the route to achieving the *task*, the *communication* and the *change*? (The areas of communication and change are dealt with later in this chapter.) The task is the 'hard-edged' dimension of financial targets, products, markets, etc. The communication strategy is the route to ensuring that people are fully included in all of the flow of information and understanding around achieving the task. The change dimension takes account of how you will manage the changes implicit in achieving the task.

The final strategy takes into account all three areas and integrates them into the grand plan.

Plan to achieve each strategic goal

Each of the strategic goals needs a detailed project plan with milestones and accountabilities. The success of achieving vision will be equal to your success at achieving all of the numerous projects that constitute the strategic goals. The success of achieving each of the individual projects will depend on the clarity of the project plans, the milestones that tell you if you are on track and the responsibility and accountability of each project owner or leader.

Do it

Strategy is about taking the first, mental creation, which you read about in the Vision Challenge and turning into the second creation, i.e. reality.

Check and change

The need is for continual review of projects against agreed plans and reviewing these against the strategic goals. The strategist wants to know three things:

1. What is the right track?
2. Is the project still on track?
3. Is this still the right track?

As a strategist you want to know as soon as possible where there is slippage or distraction from the strategy so you can either get back on track or change the strategy where new information dictates that it is necessary.

B. Personal Reflection

What is your definition of strategy?

Consider the following questions.

■ Where will you need strategic thinking?
  – Leading the whole organisation
  – Leading your team
  – Leading your department
  – Leading a project
■ What are your priorities?
  – Are you clear on the strategy?
  – Have you ensured that others are clear?
  – Are you clear about how to manage any change in order to achieve the strategy?
■ What do you already do well in the areas of the Strategy Challenge?
■ Where are your gaps?

Self-assessment of the Strategy Challenge

Read through all of the questions below and reflect on your work recently. Next, rate yourself in the box below on a scale of 1 to 10, where 1 = very ineffective in responding to this challenge (i.e. not very strategic) and 10 = very effective at responding to this challenge (i.e. very strategic across all of the dimensions of this challenge).

- Do you build a clear path between current reality and future vision?
- Do you have clear and verbalised strategic goals that focus your time and your team's time, energy and resources?
- Do you confidently use tools and processes like stakeholder analysis, scenario planning, force field analysis and balanced scorecard?
- Are you clear about market share, market opportunity, product cycles, marketing strategies, resource allocation, budgeting and investment?
- Do you have a clear logic for achieving vision?
- Do you have immediate, intermediate and longer-term concrete steps and timetables for implementing your strategies?
- Do your plans have clear 'task', 'financial' and 'people' dimensions?
- Do you have a strategy for managing change and transition?
- Do you have a communication strategy for seeing through change?

So where are you on the scale?

Challenge 5 – The Strategy Challenge

1	2	3	4	5	6	7	8	9	10

C. Developing Yourself as a Strategist

Developing a Strategic Mindset?

A good place to start is to outline the scope of strategic thinking. If you were a person who was thinking strategically what would your mind be focused on? The first thing to say is that it would be based on a foundation of proactivity not reactivity (see the Proactive Challenge). The benefit of Figure 5.2 (which is based on an original schema from Wellins, Byham and Wilson, *Empowered Teams*, 1991) is to illustrate that to have a strategic mindset is to bear all of these components in mind. The big picture means more than holding a vision in your mind; it means holding the overall picture in your mind. This is another way of underlining our definition of leadership that it's about 'lifting up your head'.

Over the next pages we will give a short explanation of each of the components of strategic thinking and ask some questions to help you think through each component.

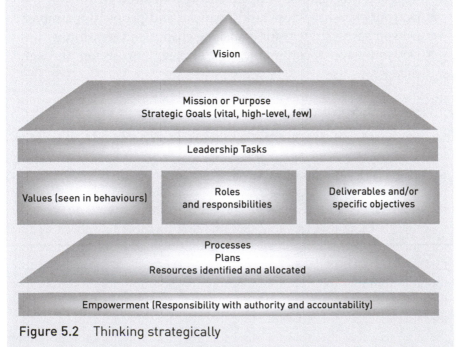

Figure 5.2   Thinking strategically

Vision

Vision can be defined as 'an articulate and compelling picture of the future' (for a full explanation see the Vision Challenge).

An important point to note here is that a lot of organisations have come up with what they call a 'vision statement'. Often this is more like a mission or purpose statement. Vision is about creating the detailed picture of what will be going on, who will be doing what, what you will see, etc. To reduce it to a sentence often loses the important creative, engaging dimensions.

Mission or Purpose

A mission or purpose statement captures the reason for being. Generally a mission will always be true, whereas the vision will be achieved and then recreated for a future point.

A mission statement needs to:

- Be focused on the present.
- Identify clearly what you do.
- Specify where your organisation/team/project adds value.
- Capture your core business.
- Be a clear focus for all employees' attention.

One route to creating a purpose or mission focus is to answer the following questions. (Take time to write down your answers but limit each answer to one sentence.)

- What does your team/business exist for?
- What is your team/business goal?
- What does your team/business do?
- How do you add value for your customers, employees and shareholders? What do you do to add value?

Example

An admin team at a housing association defined their purpose as:

To be effective in providing support, focus and excellence to all of our customers.

The strengths of this statement are its brevity, its aspirations and its focus. The weakness of this statement is that it could be applied to almost any organisation.

So write out your mission or purpose in a sentence that is brief, focused, engaging for your team, not too wordy and easy to remember.

Strategic Goals

Look carefully through your mission or purpose and then look in detail at your vision. What are the vital few, high-level areas that you *must* focus on in order to achieve the vision? These need to be high-level, strategic goals, not detailed projects or actions. The detail should fit with each of the strategic goals. Some people are calling them BHAGs (big hairy audacious goals!).

What are your strategic goals? Try to keep them to no more than five.

Example

An engineering company that makes specialised tools for the automotive industry had four goals:

- *To always be competitive on price with all of their competitors.*
- *To reduce order-to-delivery time to 24 hours in the UK.*
- *To manufacture their own tools (they were currently reliant on other companies).*
- *To create 35% of annual turnover from outside of the UK.*

Leadership Tasks

The leader has certain leadership tasks to perform, like maintaining a ruthless grip on the vision and ensuring alignment between the team/project and the overall business objectives – but certainly not all of them. What are the leadership tasks that need to be performed in order for the team to realise its vision?

Choose from the list below and then add your own.

- Setting vision and strategy.
- Ensuring organisational alignment.
- Building the team.
- Decision making.
- Coaching.
- Managing performance.
- Resource gathering and allocation.
- Influencing stakeholders.
- Monitoring key processes.
- Budget setting.

You can then decide which tasks you need to do and which ones others can do.

Values

Values look at how you need to achieve your vision. What is the culture you need in your organisation or team? What matters to you? What is important? Values should translate into behaviour. They are not just 'nice to have', they need to answer the question, 'How do you need to be or behave in order to deliver your vision and mission?'

Here are some questions that will help in creating values.

- What does it need to be like in your office/organisation to achieve best performance?

- If you value and respect people how will that show itself in your behaviour?
- If you value your customers how will that show itself in your behaviour?
- If you value excellence how will that show itself in your behaviour?
- If you value work–life balance how will that show itself in your behaviour?

List three core values that your situation needs and then think through how each value would translate into specific behaviours.

An American Management Association (AMA) 2002 survey on corporate values revealed the following stated values in organisations (*www.amanet.org/research/pdfs/2002_corp_value.pdf*).

Customer satisfaction	Ethics/Integrity	Accountability
Respect for others	Open communication	Profitability
Teamwork	Innovation/Change	Continuous learning
Positive work Environment	Diversity	Community service
Trust	Social responsibility	Security/Safety
Empowerment	Employee job satisfaction	Have fun

Roles and Responsibilities

Roles and responsibilities are about who does what and who is responsible for what. Remember that responsibility needs authority! One of the biggest complaints within flexible or matrix management structures is that people no longer know who does what, or whom they are responsible to, or how what they do overlaps with others' jobs. Such a lack of role clarity reduces performance.

Think through your own team in light of the vision and strategic goals and ask yourself what roles people have and exactly what they are responsible for. When you have done this check with them that they have exactly the same understanding. Leaders bring clarity, and assumptions are not the same as clarity!

Team roles

Meredith Belbin (1995) is famous for spelling out the nine different roles that are needed by teams. They provide a helpful reminder when thinking about leadership as well.

1. **Plant** – these are creative, imaginative, unorthodox people who are good at solving difficult problems.
2. **Resource investigator** – usually extrovert, enthusiastic and communicative. They explore opportunities and form great networks.
3. **Coordinator** – mature and confident, they make good chairpersons. They promote decision making and delegate well.
4. **Shaper** – they challenge, are dynamic and thrive on pressure. They have the drive and courage to overcome obstacles.
5. **Monitor-evaluator** – sober-minded and discerning. They see all the options and make wise judgements.
6. **Team worker** – cooperative, perceptive and diplomatic. They listen well, build relationships, avert friction and calm turbulent waters.
7. **Implementer** – disciplined, reliable and efficient. They turn ideas into actions and get things done.
8. **Completer** – they deliver on time, search out the errors and fix them with their painstaking conscientiousness.
9. **Specialist** – single-minded and self-starting. They provide knowledge and skill in specialist areas.

Deliverables

Often a strategic goal will require a dozen or more specific things to happen in order to achieve it. The first step is to identify what you need to deliver and then create a goal that will focus on achieving it. Having created a goal for each deliverable then how will you measure that you have achieved it? What are you aiming at as a target? Exactly what initiatives will you put in place to achieve the goal? Who will take responsibility for the initiative (be the owner) and when do you need it done by (deadlines)? How will you monitor how it is going at any point in time? Table 5.1 provides an example of how you may want to record your answers to these questions for purposes of clarity.

Table 5.1 Clarify the deliverables in your strategy

Goals	Measures	Target	Initiatives	Who	When	Status
(What?)	(How will you know you've achieved it?)	(How much?)	(What actions will you pursue?)	(Who is owning this initiative?)	(Deadlines)	(How is it going?)

Processes

Processes look at how people get things done. A key process in many businesses is how to move from issuing a contract all the way through to billing for the completed work. Processes might be 'hard' systems like IT or 'soft' like Customer Relationship Management processes. Other examples of processes are how people run their meetings, how they make decisions, how they manage their projects, how they manage risk and what their safety procedures are.

What processes are crucial to the effective, smooth achievement of your vision?

Planning

We talked about this in section A. Planning is ensuring that you have clear project plans to achieve each of your strategic goals. There may well be plans within plans. This means that there may be a plan to achieve a strategic goal that has a number of projects attached to it with different owners. These projects then have their own plans. The success of planning is laying out a pathway of achievable milestones between now and realisation of the vision. It is also thinking through every eventuality and planning for it.

Resource Identification and Allocation

It is one thing to have grand plans and visions, but what resources do you have available? What resources do you need? What do you need to get the job done? What could you do to get the resources you need?

An Empowered Team or Person

The final line of the model in Figure 5.2 is called 'empowerment'. Literally this means 'putting the power into someone'.

The aim of leadership is about achieving through others in such a way that they own their achievements. Empowerment is, therefore, about ensuring that each person is clear about vision, mission, strategic goals and their role within them so that they can be trusted to make their own local decisions with their own teams. It would be disastrous to simply devolve power to people who don't share the vision and the values (see the 'Managing the tension between holding on and letting go' Challenge); similarly you simply cannot do it all yourself. You need to be confident that the people you empower have the same compass inside of them that you do, so that when it comes to decisions, while you cannot vet everyone, you can be confident that people will make decisions based on agreed criteria (the vision, mission, strategic goals, values, etc.).

Think through the questions below for your team members or key stakeholders and answer them as 'definitely yes', 'maybe/not sure' or 'no'. Once again you may want to write your answers in a table like Table 5.2 to help you achieve greater clarity.

Table 5.2 Identifying how to influence stakeholders

	Are they very clear about the vision and the overall strategy and core values?	Are they clear what their goals, measures and deadlines are?	Are they clear what their next steps are?	Have we made explicit agreements about how they will be managed and supported?
Person A e.g. Jim	e.g. Not sure	e.g. Yes	e.g. No	e.g. No
Person B				
Person C				
Person D				

As a result of this analysis what conversations do you need to have with whom and about what?

Communication Strategy and Change Management

Change management fails where there is, amongst other things, lack of strategic planning. Managing change has two dimensions. Change needs a *project strategy* that will look at many of the elements you have covered so far in this challenge, but it also needs a *communication strategy*. The overall strategy needs to be a combination of overlaying the communication strategy on to the project strategy. Only when this is done is the strategy likely to be effective in the Influence Challenge.

Formulating a communication strategy involves answering the following questions.

- Who do you need to communicate with?
  - Who are the known stakeholders?
  - Who might be secondary stakeholders?

- What do you need to communicate?
  - The big picture?
  - Why are you making this change?
  - What is the driver?
  - What is the rationale and what will the result of the change be?
  - What is and what is not changing?
  - Who will benefit and how?
  - What does the situation look like from their point of view? What do they know/feel?
  - What do they need to see?
  - What do they need to hear?
  - What do they need to know?
  - What do you want them to feel?
- How do you need to communicate?
  - Written – e-mails, memos, letters, newsletters
  - Audio
  - Projection
  - PowerPoint presentations
  - Briefings
  - Ask them into your office
  - 'Chance' encounters at the water cooler!
  - Coffee meetings
  - Focus groups.
- When should you communicate?
  - This will emerge through the overlaying of the communication strategy on to the project strategy. What is important is to continually clarify whether what you think you've communicated is what has been heard.

Conclusion

Which of the following tools do you need to investigate to equip you for this challenge?

- The Balanced Scorecard for strategy implementation.
- Stakeholder analysis.

- Scenario planning.
- Risk assessment.
- Clarifying key goals.
- Setting clear deliverables.
- Market share.
- Product life cycle.
- Resource allocation.
- SWOT analysis.
- Force Field Analysis.
- Needs analysis.
- Gantt charting.

Which area of the Strategy Challenge do you need to develop most in?

- A strategy to get the task done.
- A communication strategy.
- A change strategy.

If you were to develop a strategic mindset in all aspects and situations of your life what three things would you habitually do? For example, you might ask yourself three questions.

- Where is it that you are heading?
- Have you spent as much time 'planning' as you intend to spend 'doing?'
- Have you a set of robust milestones in place?

'Doing' Strategy or Being Strategic?

It is one step to learn how to think through a specific project, team strategy or organisational strategy. The next step is to be someone who thinks strategically as a habit. They don't just 'do' strategy – they are being strategic in their approach to all situations in or outside of work.

The Final Question . . . What are you going to do now?
(See Appendix 1 for further development)

The
Wisdom Challenge

Applying your learning from
experience

A. Understanding this Challenge

Wisdom: the ability or the result of an ability to think and act utilising knowledge, experience, understanding, common sense and insight. (*Collins Concise Dictionary*, 1988)

Last week you may have got five days' worth of experience but it doesn't mean that you have five days' worth of wisdom. Our definition of wisdom is: the ability to turn your experience and knowledge into a resource that can be used in new situations.

Experience is not the same as wisdom. It is only a part of it and only the beginning of the process of creating wisdom. Wisdom is a reflexive process (it's an ongoing habit, not just a once-off activity) that involves reviewing past experiences (immediate or longer-term), gathering the learning from that experience and applying this learning into tomorrow's action. In the world of psychology we talk about 'the compulsion to repeat' in the context of people who despite all that happens to them just keep on doing the same things, repeating the same unproductive patterns of behaviour. Lack of wisdom is manifested in repeating patterns of behaviour, repeating approaches to problems, repeating 'shooting from the hip'. People place too high a value on experience, assuming that experience is the same as wisdom. It results in that well-known saying, 'If you keep on doing what you've always done, you will keep on getting what you've always got!'

Many people say 'oh, I learn from my experience'. Probe a little deeper and it is evident that what they really mean is that they have a lot of experience that has not really been processed to any depth and an overly high reliance on their intuition or habits. What they may have is two years' experience repeated many times over a twenty-year career span. Note the difference between the person who says 'in my last job we did so and so, so why don't we try that' and the person who says 'in my last situation we were faced with a number of different challenges, the principles we discovered at the heart of what we did were these . . . why don't we see if and how these principles might apply in this different situation'. While most people obviously carry a level of 'unconscious' wisdom from all of their experiences in life, effective leadership is about consciously uncovering the depth of your wisdom and applying this learning to new situations.

Example

Lucy was an IT manager who remarked at a team event that I (Shenaz) was leading that, 'We never seem to learn. We go from one project to another at such speed that we just don't learn from our last project. We don't think anything through and do the same old unproductive processes again and again.'

Wisdom is a proactive process that starts with experience, has a lot of reflection and analysis, and ends up with new actions. There is, therefore, an inner game and an outer game to play in the Wisdom Challenge. The outer game of the Wisdom Challenge is seen in experiences and new actions or behaviours. The inner game is seen in internal reflections, analysis and overcoming self-limiting beliefs or perspectives.

Ideas and terminology constantly change and so the 'old economy' became the 'information' economy', and then the 'knowledge economy' and now the word on the street is of a shift to the 'wisdom economy'. Actually there is nothing new about wisdom, as the story of Solomon will testify. Patrick Thurbin, in his book on leadership and strategic thinking, *Playing the Strategy Game* (2001), says, 'One more thing that top strategists share is an ability to convert experiences and knowledge into a personalised skill base that sustains all of their effort' (p. xiv).

In other words, leaders need to continually build a reserve of wisdom. So, what do you have in your reserve of wisdom? Do you know what you know? Ask yourself some of the following questions.

- What do you know about building high performing teams?
- What do you know about building strong families?
- What do you know about building good friendships?
- What do you know about your area of work/business activity?
- What do you know about building life–work balance?

A CEO's Story about Wisdom and Strategy

When a managing director of an engineering company in the south of England made the decision to reduce order-to-delivery times down from 6 weeks to 24 hours and create a minimum of 33% of business in new markets abroad, he was using wisdom. He was drawing from past and current experience of getting caught in a recession and being at the mercy of other people's cost-cutting in the automotive industry. He was also drawing on an accumulation of twenty years of knowledge about his industry and creatively applying that experience and that knowledge to the current predicament. To achieve this he had to take the time to analyse the lessons learned from each experience and apply that learning into the new situation (wisdom) rather than just spending twenty years moving from one experience straight to the next without understanding the consequences or the repercussions of those experiences.

A Middle Manager's Story about Wisdom and Influence Styles

Mary is a middle manager who objected to being sent on a course about dealing with aggression in the workplace. With hindsight she realised that she had not been aware of her influencing style when she was involved in new projects. Her tendency was to be very sharp in her manner by the way she asked questions, and she would usually end up bombarding the team with directives on how to do things differently. Team members would react and she would repeatedly find herself in conflict situations. She would get quite aggressive and would then raise her voice, cry or walk out. During the course, through a process of continual reflection, role-play and feedback on her past experiences, she realised that this was a pattern. She now had new insight into her behaviour that provided the opportunity for new choices. Twelve months later she was in a new job with a new team and was using her newly discovered wisdom by first listening and pausing to find out what was going on and then choosing the best response, rather than jumping in with both feet.

B. Personal Reflection

How would you define wisdom?

Where do you need help? Now you have some understanding of the challenge what would be the benefit to you at work in increasing your levels of wisdom?

In what specific areas do you think you would need to improve your levels of wisdom? (Specific work situations? Work relationships? Your health or well-being?)

Do you see yourself as someone who learns easily from your mistakes or past experiences, or do you find yourself saying 'I never seem to learn?'

Example

When we had finished the CD assessment for the 18 Challenges (see www.18challengesofleadership.com) and had launched it in the City of London we hurried straight into producing the book. 'Hold on,' we said to ourselves, 'we're missing the Wisdom Challenge here.' So we paused and asked ourselves what were some of the internal blockages that led us to avoid stopping and reflecting and learning. Some of the things we listed were:

■ *No need to stop – we've been successful; let's crack on.*
■ *No time to look at what we've done – we've got a January deadline for the first-stage completion of the book.*
■ *We know it all anyway – I don't think there's much to be gained by spending time talking about what we did, how we did it, lessons learned. It would be an expensive and indulgent luxury that we don't have time for.*

Then we asked what some of the external blockages and constraints were. The main one was that making time together is difficult given our difference in geography (London and Dublin) and our other work and family commitments.

Self-assessment of the Wisdom Challenge

Read through all of the questions below and reflect on your work recently. Next, rate yourself in the box below on a scale of 1 to 10, where 1 = very ineffective in responding to this challenge (i.e. never pause to translate experience into wisdom) and 10 = very effective at responding to this challenge (i.e. very effective at creating space to convert experience into lessons that can be applied quickly in new situations).

- Do you conduct a personal review of each of your major interventions at work that involved dealing with people, with tasks, with finance and with business processes?
- Do you conduct team reviews of your major interventions at work that involve the team's dealings with employees, customers, objectives, finance and business or organisational processes?
- Do you carry out an audit of what you have learned from your experiences in terms of increased skills, knowledge and new behaviours?
- Do you act more effectively today as a direct result of what you learned from your actions yesterday?
- Do you regularly receive challenging feedback from your peers, bosses and subordinates?
- Is there evidence that you change approaches, behaviours, how you treat people as a direct result of feedback?
- Do you move rapidly from one experience to the next or plan in time to reflect, debrief and learn from your experiences?
- Do you celebrate your successes?

So where are you on the scale?

Challenge 6 – The Wisdom Challenge
1   2   3   4   5   6   7   8   9   10

C. Developing Wisdom

A Model – The Wisdom Cycle

Figure 6.1 is a model to provide a mental map of how you can go about developing wisdom from everyday experience.

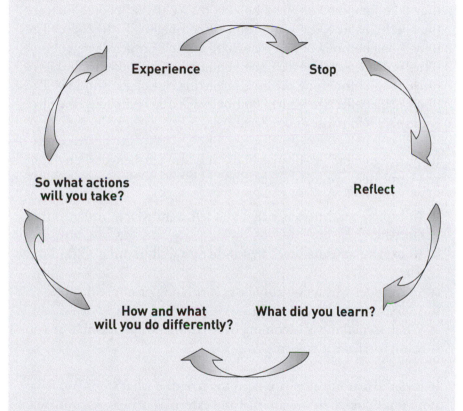

Figure 6.1 The wisdom cycle

Step 1. Experience

Experience is where you start in this cycle. Every day your life is filled with challenges that you react to. This is the diet of your daily experience.

Step 2. Stop

Given that life doesn't wait for you or present you with space to reflect, you need to create it for yourself (see the Proactive Challenge). Taking time to ponder and reflect can be refreshing, a way of gaining fresh resources, balancing and useful. It makes business sense. People often think that it will diminish their performance if they take time out to reflect but the reality is that people increase their effectiveness by significant percentages if they do. The underlying humour of Ken Blanchard's One Minute Manager book series is that every time the eager young manager comes to the boss's office to ask something the boss is looking out of the window! The point is that effective leaders do not live at 100% capacity, they live with space – to pause and reflect.

If you are going to be effective in the Wisdom Challenge when might you stop? Here are some suggestions.

■ To explore an experience that you felt went well in order to find out why.
■ To explore an experience that didn't go well in order to find out why.
■ To consider why an outcome was surprising or unpredictable.
■ To make sense of something.
■ When something is becoming over-familiar or predictable or you think you have it 'sussed'.

In order to learn to stop you need to recognise what stops you from stopping. Often there are internal and external barriers. Ask yourself:

■ What are the internal barriers you face that stop you making time to reflect?
■ What are some of the external barriers that you face that prevent you from stopping to reflect?

Step 3. Reflect

The key to reflection is externalising your experience in some way. The mind only consciously holds a very small number of units of information at any one time. In order to reflect you need to download all that you currently know, and this will free the creative depths of your mind to access what you don't yet know consciously. How can you externalise in order to reflect?

Write it down

People do this in different ways. Some people find it best to write everything down by free-associating over a sheet of paper, simply dumping everything they can think of on paper. Others do the same but in a more structured way like mind-mapping (see Tony Buzan's *www.mind-map.com* for the definitive view on the subject). Mind-mapping may begin by writing the issue or core experience in the centre of the page. You then draw main branches off this centre point. Each branch represents a major strand of the issue. As secondary ideas or insights occur then you draw them off the relevant main artery. You end up with something that looks as if a spider has crawled out of an inkpot and walked all over your paper but it actually maps out your reflections in a very orderly way.

Say it

Speaking out loud to a friend or using a coach or mentor is an excellent way of verbalising in order to reflect on experience. A lot of the benefit people derive from their time with coaches arises out of just having someone create a space to listen to them, but more than that, to hear themselves and what they think.

Other ways you might want to consider as the first step in reflection

■ Meditation.
■ Regular team reviews.

- Regular project reviews.
- Regularly soliciting feedback.
- Identifying where you do your most effective reflection.
- Visiting other managers in similar organisations to yours.
- Visiting other managers from totally different sectors.
- Being part of an Action Learning Set.
- Peer reviews.
- Continual professional development.

One simple reflective model that can be used on a daily basis is based on the following questions.

- What went well?
- What went less well?
- What would you do differently?
- What will you keep doing?
- What will you stop doing?

Think carefully about how you prefer to reflect on your experience.

You know more than you think you do. You have more wisdom than you think you have. In the next four exercises we will seek to draw out some of the latent or less-than-conscious wisdom that you have.

- Exercise 1 involves reviewing key events from your work experience.
- Exercise 2 involves mapping your career history around key experiences.
- Exercise 3 is focused on key people who have influenced you.
- Exercise 4 is focused on your wisdom regarding each of your team.

Exercise 1. Reviewing key events from your work experience

Stop Name three big, important, but different projects, work events or life events. (Try one where you felt you excelled, one where you felt at your worst or least effective and one where you felt average.)

Now choose one of these three to start working on.

Reflect Spend some time reflecting on your chosen event using these questions.

- Why did you/your team do it?
- What were the steps you/your team took?
- How did you/your team manage the project/event?
- What did you feel?
- What were your anxieties?
- What were your intentions?
- What were your fears?
- What were your hopes?
- What were the obstacles and how did you overcome them?

Think it through It is important that you make no self-judgement in this exercise.

- So why did you choose to do it in this way?
- What were you actually doing?
- What would others have seen you doing?
- What kind of person were you on that occasion?
- How did it sound?
- If another person could have put their finger on your pulse what would they have felt?
- If another person were able to record your thoughts what would they have recorded?
- If you believe you were at your best/worst/average during this event – how would you describe yourself or your team at this time?

So, what have you learned?

- About yourself?
- About the ways you work when you are:
  - Most effective?
  - Least effective?
  - Average?

- About managing projects, conflicts, change, people, and so on?
- About yourself as a leader?

Example

When we reviewed ourselves and the task of creating and producing the 18 Challenges assessment on CD-ROM, we realised that a key learning point for us was around the differences in our personalities and how that affects the way we work.

Exercise 2. Mapping your career history around key experiences

A different dimension of wisdom is in thinking through the journey you have taken to get to where you are in your career. First, make a chronological list of where you studied and worked from an early age until now. Mapping your education and work history can be done by asking yourself the following questions.

- What did you learn from each experience?
- Is there any theme or anything you notice as you look at the list?
- What were the key moments in your school history when you learnt something that has had a continuing influence on your working life?
- What were the key moments in higher education when you learnt something that has had a continued impact on your working life?
- What were the key moments in your first job when you learnt something that has had a clear influence on your working life?

Exercise 3. Focusing on key people who have influenced you

You may have learned a lot from other people as you grew up, particularly those who you saw as key influencers.

Take three of your key role models over the span of your adult/working life so far. What do you most admire about them?

Imagine yourself sitting down with them over a cup of coffee and asking them what wisdom they would have about your role if they were doing your job.

Exercise 4. Focusing on your wisdom regarding each of your team

You probably work with your team day in and day out. It is likely that you do not pause to reflect on what you are picking up from these daily contacts. Construct a table that contains the name of each person, that lists what you have picked up about them from your time spent with them, and then check what this wisdom is based on. Is it fact or perception?

Your table may look something like Table 6.1. If you don't have a team you can do this exercise on any part of the organisation, the project, your work schedule, etc.

Table 6.1 What do you know about your team?

Team member	What is your wisdom about them?	On what evidence are you basing your wisdom?
e.g. Jane	Astute; good communicator; excellent at building rapport quickly and maintaining long-term relationships.	Strong, well-developed networks and client groups; people like meeting her; well organised in her admin and management of these relationships.

Step 4. What Did You Learn?

Following on from the process of reflection within the wisdom cycle, the next step is to consider the question, What did you learn from this experience?

Step 5. How and What Will You Do Differently?

The point of the reflective process is to understand what is working well and needs to be kept or developed and also to identify what isn't working well and needs to be done differently.

Step 6. So What Actions Will You Take?

The final stage of the model is committing to doing something differently. It is here that you need to translate the mental process of learning into the action stage of trying something new or different. It can be difficult to break out of old patterns of behaviour and old ways of doing things. Gently experimenting with your behaviour is a key way to doing things differently.

The Final Question . . . What are you going to do now?
(See Appendix 1 for further development)

7

The
Insight Challenge
Seeing beyond the obvious

A. Understanding this Challenge

What Is Insight?

Insight is the ability to see clearly and deeply and to understand a situation and its outcomes. It is easy to see one-ninth of the iceberg. Insight is seeing the other eight-ninths. Another way of putting it is, how do you see what is in front of you in a different way? A more subjective definition is, you know you have insight when you say 'ah-ha'.

Leaders face the challenge of not only seeing what is going on around them, but also seeing into what is going on around them. There are four dimensions to insight that leaders need to develop.

Seeing into is another term for perception. The leader is not just taking things at face value, she or he is asking herself or himself and others, 'What does this mean?' 'What is at the heart of this?' 'What is the underlying principle here?'

Then there is *seeing beyond*. The novelist Paulo Coelho coined the phrase 'walk with your eyes on the horizon' (*The Valkyries*, 1996). The interpretation is that a leader should be focused on that point where the two rails of a railway track converge into one – the horizon. Research into why change management fails suggests that leaders do not take this longer view. Instead, they are distracted and react to short-term trends and cycles. Seeing beyond means looking beyond the immediate to ask the question, 'Where is all of this going?'

The third dimension of insight is to *see beneath*. When a CEO was recently doing an assessment of what was going on in his customers' minds he was not just looking at what their stated needs were, he was also trying to determine what lay beneath the surface or behind their stated needs. What might their underlying needs be? Were they conscious of them or not?

The fourth dimension of insight is to *see between*. When a leader that I (Trevor) worked with years ago in Austria began to form a strategy to take relief-aid to Sudan and Micronesia, he had to look beyond the individual actions that were being proposed. He also had to take into consideration the effects and the inter-relationships of those actions. But that wasn't the end – he also had to consider and accommodate the effects of the proposals upon another culture along with the social and political implications.

What Are the Dimensions of Insight?

Personal Insight

This book has already touched upon the area of Emotional Intelligence, and it is evident that self-awareness or personal insight is fundamental to excellent leadership.

A well-known tool often appears at leadership development courses. It is called the JoHari window. Legend has it that two chaps called Joe and Harry invented it on a table napkin one lunchtime! It looks at four dimensions of personal insight (see Table 7.1).

Table 7.1   The JoHari window

	You know	**You don't know**
I know	There are things that both you and I know about me. e.g. my name e.g. my job title These things are Public.	There are things I know about myself but you don't. These things are Private.
I don't know	There are things about myself that are clear to you but I can't see them. These things are Blind Spots and the greatest need here is for feedback.	There are things about me that are out of sight to both you and me but affect my behaviour and my impact on others. These things are Unconscious and it may be helpful to look at the Pathology Challenge.

Relational Insight

An important issue for managers is that every relationship has a text and a subtext – what is being said and what is going on beneath the surface.

Some examples of subtext are:

- *Transference* This is where someone in your team or organisation transfers on to you attitudes, feelings, fears and wishes from long ago. At some deeper level you become mum or dad or older/younger brother or sister for them. There are two dimensions to this. One is that people try to repeat how the relationship was in the past and the other is that they seek to replay how they wished it had been. So you, the manager, may be seen as the cold, indifferent dad they had or as the warm, loving dad they had wished for, or a mix of both. The problem is that this is going on while you think you are having an adult-to-adult conversation about the IT project you are both working on.
- *Counter-transference* This is more about what another person's personality, behaviours and attitudes stir up in you. You may wonder why there are certain people you like and others that you take an instant dislike to. For example, if there is a depressed woman, you find yourself deeply wanting to make it better for her. The myth of management is that in this room there is one person who is needy and one manager who has it together. There is a hidden drama in the relationships at work where people's history of deepest needs, wishes, fears and impulses interact with the leader's own issues. Counter-transference is when you, the leader, have a hidden drama that is awakened by something in someone in your team or direct report which produces feelings and behaviours towards them that don't belong to them.
- *Projective identification* This is a hidden form of influence. It is where one person in the conversation or relationship may be full of anger but will not admit it to himself or herself, and the other person walks away from the conversation feeling angry. Somehow the denied emotions of person A get projected into person B; and person B, not realising what is going on, acts out these emotions for person A. They may walk away thinking 'I felt fine a minute ago, before I had that conversation, and now I feel awful!'

Deep stuff? Yes, certainly. But as you seek to build on your leadership skills it is essential that you gain more insight into relational dynamics.

Character Insight

This is an art in good leadership. How do you know who are the right people when interviewing? How do you know, if someone performs well at interview, that they will perform well in reality? Will the characteristics that shone at interview be borne out in the character the person shows when in the job? Will they be honest and reliable, act with integrity, be fair? Succession planning is crucial within organisations to equip them with leaders for the future. How do you know who are the people who will go further in your organisation's leadership values as well as plans?

Systems Insight

Systems theory reveals that where there are groups of individuals or groups of teams or departments, they do not function on their own – they function as part of a system.

I (Trevor) was witness to an example of this at work in a team where one member seemed to be always angry and was being isolated by the rest of the team. It all came to a head during a meeting when the angry person challenged the rest of the team.

'Surely I'm not the only one who thinks this is unfair?', she said angrily. 'Well, no, I think it's unfair too,' someone replied, but with a passive tone. 'You don't sound very angry about it,' said the angry lady. 'Well, I am,' was the reply, with a bit more emotion. 'Me, too,' said someone else.

Over the next thirty minutes each member of the team began to admit how angry he or she was about some particular injustices. Quite remarkably as the team owned its anger the original angry lady got quieter and calmer. They had stopped denying their emotion and she no longer had to carry it for the team.

I (Shenaz) was working with a man who was head of a local government department. He felt crushed by some feedback that another department in the organisation refused to work with him. It took a few hours, but as we unpacked what was going on we discovered that within the wider system there was a lot of insecurity and anxiety around recent changes and people had taken the opportunity to focus their angst on to this one person whose behaviour, while being unhelpful, in no way warranted the depth and strength of negative feedback that was dumped on him.

Systems insight is about understanding what belongs where within the team, within the department, across the departments, across the supply chain and across the processes.

Organisational Insight

- *Politics* Who are the key players, where is the power located and how is it used? Where is the influence located?
- *Culture* How are things done in the organisation?
- *Values* What really matters in the organisation? What are the true values as opposed to the ones that are pasted on the office wall? When one company did an audit of the reality around values it revealed that one of the lived values was 'workaholism'! The one on the wall said 'work–life balance'. Insight around the organisation's values is important because there may come a point when your personal values are at such dissonance with the corporate values that you need to move on.

Wider-context Insight

Every part of an organisation sits within the wider context of that organisation and every organisation sits within a context itself.

To have insight into the wider context is to have insight into:

- The market.
- The environment.
- Macro-politics and economies.
- The local community – its priorities, values and spirituality.

What Are the Conditions for Gaining Insight?

Insight needs space to grow

To develop insight requires time to stand still. Time to stop. Imagine that you are like a filing cabinet. You need to pause for long enough to open the drawer, dust off some files (what you already know), see something in those files that you haven't seen before, or note something that could be in those files that isn't there yet, take out that file and look at all of the other files, and then put the old file back in a new place.

Insight needs an open and questioning mind

You need to ask and be asked challenging questions to uncover what lies in, beneath, between or beyond the obvious. We asked someone recently, 'What makes you so confident that you are a good strategist?' 'I just know', they replied. 'What do you know?', we persisted. She then paused and began to give examples of what a good strategist would do in their job. She clearly had a level of intuitive insight but had never verbalised it. To have a questioning mind means not accepting the status quo or the obvious as obvious. To ask searching questions in order to create insight in others requires a high degree of trust to provide them with the safety to explore the depths of their own experience.

Insight needs an openness to be surprised

If one plus one equals two then there is nothing left to understand; but what if it doesn't? If you are closed down or convinced that something is just as you think it is, then you shut down the possibility of discovery. The insistence that the earth was flat meant that there was no point in exploring too far. The possibility of a round earth opened up an adventure.

Theorists in information processing reckon that individuals can only retain three to seven blocks of information in their conscious minds. This means that there are thousands upon thousands of thoughts and experiences and perceptions that you have stored away in your internal filing cabinets.

B. Personal Reflection

What is your definition of insight? Why do you think that it is important for leaders to develop insight? Of the six different types of insight described above, are there one or two areas that you feel you need more development in?

Self-assessment of the Insight Challenge

Read through all of the questions below and reflect on your work recently. Next, rate yourself in the box below on a scale of 1 to 10, where 1 = very ineffective in responding to this challenge (i.e. not very insightful) and 10 = very effective at responding to this challenge (i.e. very insightful across all of the dimensions of this challenge).

- Do you see yourself as a person of insight?
- Do others see you as a person of insight?
- Do people often reflect back to you in conversations, 'that was a really good question you just asked'?
- Do you take situations and information at face value or do you find yourself asking, 'What does this mean?' 'What is the underlying principle here?' 'Is this just a symptom, and if so what is the root cause?'
- Do you keep your eye firmly on future goals while dealing with the present?
- Do you look for underlying trends, underlying needs, unconscious motivations in situations?
- Do you look for connections, relationships, effects and consequences in your own and others' decisions?

So where are you on the scale?

Challenge 7 – The Insight Challenge

| 1 | 2 | 3 | 4 | 5 | 6 | 7 | 8 | 9 | 10 |

C. Developing Yourself as an Insightful Leader

Preparing to Gain Insight

Personal constructs theorist George Kelly (see Bannister, 1971) has a model of what is necessary to gain insight. We call it the *Tight–Loose–Tight* model, illustrated in Figure 7.1).

Figure 7.1 Tight–loose–tight model

According to this model, people start by holding on to their perceptions, ideas or world views tightly. These are what they know and are familiar with. Sometimes these are so deeply rooted that people define who they are by these ideas or views. People who hold their views so tightly need to loosen their grip for a while. They need to engage in a period of 'not knowing' or not holding on so fiercely to what they know. Sometimes they need to read about new ideas or speak in-depth to people who hold very different views from their own. It is in this 'loose' place that new insights can come (as shown by the vertical arrow).

But they then need to 're-tighten', as Kelly puts it. They need to re-form some structure around their new insights to provide a foundation for new action.

We shall take a look at six different ways of gaining insight.

Gain insight through psychometric tools

There is a wealth of psychometric or other tools that are currently on the market for gaining personal and relational insight. Among the well-known psychological tools in use are the following.

Myers-Briggs Type Indicator™ This looks at personality preferences and is useful for personal insight, relational insight, influencing, leadership styles, change management and organisational character and style. (See the Personality Challenge.)

FIRO-B™ The *FIRO-B* (Fundamental Interpersonal Relations Orientation – Behaviour) instrument is one of the most widely used tools for helping people understand their own behaviour – and that of others – in interpersonal situations. The assessment lets you quickly gather insights about your interpersonal needs and how those needs affect your interactions. This information helps illuminate why some relationships click and others don't. The *FIRO-B* instrument is based on three basic interpersonal needs identified by renowned psychology pioneer Will Schutz.

- Inclusion – participation in forming relationships and associating with people.
- Control – decision-making, control and influence.
- Affection – closeness and loyalty between individuals.

It then looks at these needs along two dimensions:

- Expressed – the extent to which a person initiates a particular behaviour.
- Wanted – the extent to which a person wants others to initiate the behaviour.

OPQ (Occupational Personality Questionnaire) Licensed by SHL®, the OPQ looks at personality dimensions in terms of management competencies. The kinds of issues that it looks at are:

1. Specialist knowledge – do you understand the technical and professional aspects of your work and continue to develop your knowledge?
2. Leadership – how well do you motivate and empower others in order to reach the organisation's goals?

3. Creativity and innovation – do you create new and imaginative approaches to work-related issues? Do you identify fresh approaches and show a willingness to question traditional assumptions?
4. Flexibility – do you successfully adapt to changing demands and conditions?
5. Attitude – what are you capable of doing?
6. Style – how do you relate to your colleagues, your team and the organisation?
7. Motivation – what sort of energy do you bring to your job and tasks and what motivates or demotivates you?

There are many, many other excellent tools around. The 18 Challenges of Leadership is designed to increase your own and your team's levels of insight around leadership.

Gain insight through raising your awareness

Insight is increased by simply raising your awareness. Try the following exercise.

Look out of the window. What do you see? Keep asking yourself this question for three minutes. Your level of awareness will have risen greatly by doing nothing other than focusing your attention.

Now take it one step further. What did you assume, so that you failed to be aware of it? Answer? The window! Assumptions are like glass that you look through. They shape your awareness and you need to be aware of them as well.

Another dimension of awareness raising is to get inquisitive or get interested. A younger manager was struggling with being seduced away from necessary leadership tasks by details and mini-crises that he found really interesting. I (Trevor) suggested to him to 'get interested'. In his case in particular the challenge was to get interested in leadership more than in details. As we talked further he told me how he enjoyed people's personal stories of how they had solved various problems, so I came back to the suggestion 'get interested' but developed it further to 'get interested in the kinds of stories people would be sharing if you were doing the leadership tasks you know you should be doing'.

A further way of raising awareness is to look at an issue in front of you and ask yourself these questions:

- Where is all this going/leading? Where will it end up?
- What lies underneath this issue? Underlying needs? Unspoken agendas?
- What connects these issues? How do they link up? Do they share a common theme?
- What is at the heart of this issue? What is the core, the essence?

Gain insight through others

Insight is increased by simply talking to new people, especially those who have a different perspective from ours. Often people are so busy trying to convert, influence or change the minds of those around them that they fail to learn from them. The suggestion here is that you initiate conversations with a variety of people. Have you spoken to someone recently just with the intention of learning from them?

- Someone with political differences?
- Cultural differences?
- Personality differences?
- Gender differences?
- Known experts in the area?

Gain insight through different perspectives

'What would it look like if you were blind?' the children had to ask themselves. The teacher's intent was to get the children to walk around the house with their eyes shut for thirty minutes and then write about the experience. In training leaders as negotiators it is good practice to get them to prepare a negotiation from their own perspective first, then to get them to physically move and sit in a different chair. From this new perspective they can start to describe the person they would negotiate with as if they were that person. They can take their place for a while and prepare the negotiation from inside their world. It is always amazing how much insight can be gained by thinking through someone else's motives, needs and perspectives. The key here is to walk in someone else's shoes and think through the situation from their perspective.

A friend in a National Health Service Trust recently led his department through a strategy and planning meeting for the next year. As well as preparing the strategy and planning with his own staff, he asked some patients and local services and local authority stakeholders to contribute thoughts on what the plan would look like from their point of view.

Another organisation got all of its managers off-site for a strategy meeting. Once they felt they had created a robust strategy they then pretended to be their chief competitors and spent the next hour trying to create a strategy to do their own original business out of work. Once they had gained the insights from such a vantage point they went back to being themselves and built these new insights into the original plan.

Gaining situational insight

Situations confront you all of the time. How can you learn to think quickly about these situations in a way that will develop insight fast? One way to gain such insight in a particular situation is to ask four questions.

- What does this mean?
- Where is this going/leading/heading?
- What are the underlying needs and issues?
- What are the connections, relationships and consequences?

Gain insight through expanding your knowledge

A simple way of raising awareness is to expand your knowledge in a particular area by reading widely on the subject or area. We have provided an extensive reading list with comments on areas that relate to the 18 Challenges of Leadership.

The Key

The key to insight is to ask the right questions.

The buzz gained from developing leaders does not occur when they say to us 'that was good advice' but rather when they say 'that was a good question'.

- Why was it a great question? Because it created insight.
- Where do great questions come from? Powerful, attentive, engaged listening.
  - Powerful listening is where someone listens to understand, not to tell.
  - Powerful listening is without ego, agenda or distractions.
  - Powerful listening raises awareness.
  - Powerful listening focuses people's attention.

Such listening creates a space for people. It is in that space that insight is gained.

Developing Emotional Intelligence

Emotional Intelligence could quite justifiably be put with the previous section on personal insight but we want to focus on it specifically in this part of the challenge because of its clear link to leadership effectiveness.

What is Emotional Intelligence?

> Emotional Intelligence (EQ) is the distinguishing factor in leadership. Whilst highly effective leaders have a high IQ or level of skill, research shows that they have EQ at a ratio of 2:1 more than IQ or skill.

Emotional Intelligence (affectionately abbreviated to EQ) is all about the inner world of emotions and reactions, how aware people are of them and how much they are able to channel them into appropriate and constructive actions and responses. Why is it so important to leadership? Goleman's research (1998b) into the importance of the EQ factor in leadership showed that while IQ (the leader's intelligence as normally understood) and cognitive skill (big-picture thinking, long-term vision, etc.) were very important, 'Emotional Intelligence proved to be twice as important as the others for jobs at all levels'. Furthermore he went on to say:

> The higher the rank of a person considered to be a star performer, the more emotional intelligence capabilities showed up as the reason for his or her effectiveness. When I compared star performers with average ones in senior leadership positions, nearly 90% of the difference in their profiles was attributable to emotional intelligence factors rather than cognitive ability.

The higher you are in your leadership position within an organisation the more responsibility you have to understand your own EQ and the impact you have on those around you. EQ is about understanding your inner world of emotion – your impatience, your frustration, i.e. what is going on in your inner game – and then being clear about how it impacts on your outer game (the office, the team meeting, the family, friends, your PA). Where do you deal with or leak out your inner game? Does your PA suffer, or your partner, or your kids, or your own health? When you are feeling so empty because you have been working long hours does it translate into cutting comments, offloading frustration on to your managers or peers, or can you identify what is going on inside you and translate it into constructive and appropriate behaviour towards others. The higher you climb in an organisation the more stretched your outer game becomes through the challenges you face, but is the development of your inner world keeping up with the challenges of the outer world? Too often the increase in pressure externally leads to neglect of a person's inner world and often people fail to become intelligent in how they deal with themselves and others. Women and men often have different challenges because of cultural stereotypes, language and expectations in developing appropriate responses in the outer game.

Primal Leadership

Recent research by Goleman, Boyatzis and McKee (2001) showed that of all the factors that influence people's performance one of the greatest, but hidden, drivers is the leader's mood:

> If the leader's mood and accompanying behaviors are indeed such potent drivers of business success, then a leader's premier task – we would even say his primal task – is emotional leadership. A leader needs to make sure that not only is he regularly in an optimistic, authentic, high-energy mood, but also that, through his chosen actions, his followers feel and act that way too. Managing for [results] then begins with the leader managing his inner life so that the right emotional and behavioral chain reaction occurs.

Six Key Assessments

The key to developing Emotional Intelligence is first *self-awareness* (do you know yourself painfully and honestly well?), followed by *translation* (how do you turn self-awareness into something that is appropriate and responsible behaviour?). Goleman identifies five elements of the emotional world that are crucial to how people lead others and themselves. A sixth area is emerging from current research.

Area 1. Self-awareness

The first element is self-awareness (recognising and understanding your moods, emotions and drives and their effects on others).

Rate yourself On a scale of 1 to 10, where 10 = very self-aware and 1 = have not really thought about this before, rate your level of self-awareness.

| 1 | 2 | 3 | 4 | 5 | 6 | 7 | 8 | 9 | 10 |

Ask yourself, what are you aware of about yourself that has an impact on your work performance with people and tasks?

Ask yourself, which of your behaviours demonstrates that you are good at translating your self-awareness so that it results in appropriate and constructive behaviour?

Ask yourself, what areas of self-awareness do you need to invest in?

Ask yourself, in which contexts or situations do you need to have great emotional awareness and intelligence?

Sometimes you may be aware of a first reaction, a feeling that occurs before being aware of the main emotion. For example, impatience or getting sharp with people may be the first indication of your anger. Another example may be when you disconnect or withdraw. What 'first' emotions are you aware of in yourself?

Area 2. Self-regulation

The second element is self-regulation (controlling and channelling your most disruptive impulses and moods by thinking and suspending judgement before acting). You may be more familiar with the term 'self-control'.

Rate yourself On a scale of 1 to 10, where 10 = being able to spot and control your more damaging or disruptive impulses and make constructive choices about how to deal with the situation and 1 = have never thought about it, rate your level of self-regulation.

1	2	3	4	5	6	7	8	9	10

Ask yourself, what are your disruptive impulses or emotions in the work situation that have an impact on your work performance with people and tasks?

Ask yourself, how do they affect others or the tasks you perform?

Ask yourself, what do you do that demonstrates that you are good at controlling or channelling these impulses so that it results in appropriate and constructive behaviour?

Ask yourself, what areas of self-awareness do you need to invest in?

Ask yourself, in which contexts or situations do you need to have greater control or channelling of disruptive emotions or impulses?

Area 3. Motivation

The third element is motivation (working for reasons beyond money or status). You may have things that motivate you that could be seen as positive or negative, e.g. recognition could be positive, but if you tread on other people to achieve it then it could be seen as negative.

Rate yourself On a scale of 1 to 10, where 10 = very clear about your motivations at work beyond money or status and 1 = have never thought about it, rate your level of motivation.

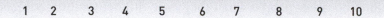

Ask yourself, what are your motivations at work beyond money or status?

Ask yourself, how do they affect others or the tasks you perform?

Ask yourself, what do you do that demonstrates that you are good at controlling or channelling these motivations rather than being controlled by them to the detriment of people or tasks?

Ask yourself, what areas of self-awareness do you need to invest in?

Ask yourself, in which contexts or situations do you need to have greater understanding or control over your motivations?

Area 4. Empathy

The fourth element is empathy (understanding the emotional make-up of other people and being skilled in handling them and their emotional reactions).

Rate yourself On a scale of 1 to 10, where 10 = possessing a good understanding of other people's emotional make-up and being skilled in handling them and their emotional reactions and 1 = have never thought about it, rate your level of empathy.

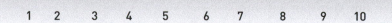

Ask yourself, what is your understanding of different types of emotional make-up in people?

Ask yourself, what do you do that demonstrates that you are skillful in handling other people when they have different emotional reactions or are in different emotional states?

Ask yourself, what areas of self-awareness do you need to invest in?

Ask yourself, in which contexts or situations do you need to have greater understanding of other people and their emotions or emotional states?

Area 5. Social skill

The fifth element is social skill (good at managing people, relationships, networks, finding common ground and building rapport).

Rate yourself On a scale of 1 to 10, where 10 = very good at managing people, relationships, networks, finding common ground and building rapport and 1 = have never thought about it, rate your level of social skill.

1	2	3	4	5	6	7	8	9	10

Look at the following areas and ask yourself specifically where they are important in your work.

- Managing people.
- Managing relationships.
- Managing networks.
- Finding common ground.
- Building rapport.

Ask yourself, what examples do you have of the impact on people and tasks when you do these things well?

Ask yourself, what examples do you have of the impact on people and tasks when you do not do these things well?

Ask yourself, what areas of self-awareness or development do you need to invest in?

To find out more, why don't you try the full test?

The *Emotional Competency Inventory* (ECI) is the only tool that Daniel Goleman himself recommends as being the genuine article for measuring EQ. You can find out more by visiting *http:// ei.haygroup.com/products_and_services/*.

Area 6. Emotional Intelligence in teams

A sixth area of Emotional Intelligence has been highlighted by recent research. This suggests that EQ is not simply an individual matter but is a team issue. Vanessa Urch Druskat and Steven B. Wolff published their research in the *Harvard Business Review* in March 2001 under the title 'Building the emotional intelligence of groups'. Their summary conclusion was: 'In an era of teamwork, it's essential to figure out what makes teams work. Our research shows that, just like individuals, the most effective teams are emotionally intelligent ones' (p. 90).

Assessing your team's EQ Using their research as a base line, here are some questions to ask yourself and your team.

■ Do you take time away from tasks to get to know each other?
■ Do you check at the start of meetings how each person is doing?
■ Do you seek to find out why a negative contribution has been made without its becoming a blame or attack session?
■ Does the team leader tell the team what they are thinking and feeling right now?
■ Do you check with each person whether they agree with a decision or do you assume silence is agreement?

- Do you have playful or humorous ways of pointing out unhelpful behaviours?
- Do you have ground rules that are explicit and applied?
- Are individual perspectives and differences respected?
- Are contributions all explicitly valued?
- Are difficult comments made constructively without being demeaning or attacking?
- Do you discuss the emotions around an issue as well as the issue itself?
- Do you allow members to call for a 'process check' where the relational dimension of the meeting is discussed?
- Do you reflect together on where the team is at while it pursues its tasks?
- Do you acknowledge the emotion in the group?
- Do you seek to give regular feedback to each other in the team meetings?
- Do you give feedback to yourselves as a team?
- Do you seek the feedback from your customers (internal and external) as to how they feel you are doing?

Putting Words on Emotions. Developing an Emotional Vocabulary

A crucial part of developing self-insight as well as insight in managing others is the ability to spot an emotion in yourself (or others) and give it an accurate name. For instance, when you ask a teenager these days how they feel they might say 'stressed'; however, when you clarify what is going on they talk about frustration or anger. They call it 'stress' because it is an emotion that is experienced in the body as stressful. One way of helping your development or your team's development in this area is to take a well-known emotion and find as many words as possible that can be used to describe the whole range of that particular emotion.

For example, take anger. What is the range of words you can use to describe the varying states or emotion of anger? They may include pique, 'ouch', frustration, annoyed, irritated, angry, malicious, ballistic, furious, rage. What other 'anger' words can you think of?

Now try and work out a range of words for the following.

■ Anxiety
■ Aggression
■ Depression
■ Guilt
■ Other emotions.

What Do Emotions Tell You?

Emotions are like the red lights on the dashboard of a car. When there is a problem with the oil pressure a light flashes; when there is a problem with the petrol level a light flashes (on more modern cars). The problem is not the light on the dashboard – it simply alerts you to something else that is going on. Emotions are like this. As you have seen in other places in this book, people are motivated at a deep level by their needs: those things they feel that they need in order to live. These may be basic needs for food and clothing, or deeper needs for meaning, or love or security or recognition.

Without going into deep psychological or counselling theory it is sometimes helpful to have a simple diagnostic understanding to recognise the emotion and what it is alerting you to. Table 7.2 gives three examples.

Table 7.2   Understanding your emotions

Emotion	What is going on?	Illustration
Anger	Your goal for getting your need met is being blocked or frustrated in some way	You ask someone to do a task and he simply refuses
Anxiety	Your goal for getting your need met is being threatened in some way	You are new to your job and you are concerned that you will not make your targets this month
Depressed or low	Your goal for getting your need met seems hopeless or unattainable	You are 45, you've applied for three positions and haven't got any of them

The Final Question . . . What are you going to do now?
(See Appendix 1 for further development)

The
Confidence Challenge
Developing self-belief

A. Understanding this Challenge

Examples

Jack is a recently appointed finance director in a public-sector organisation. His role often demands a directive style with his other finance managers. He genuinely feels comfortable in being supportive in a coaching style but he outwardly and inwardly lacks confidence when he needs to be directive. He fears that they will laugh at him or they will just not listen and will ignore his requests, which in turn will lead to conflict.

Mandy is project manager for an IT company. She frequently finds herself being asked to make presentations on her work. Some are informal to her team, some are more formal to the company's senior team and others are very formal to large groups of stakeholders. She often finds herself making excuses to get out of doing these presentations but when she cannot avoid it she has sleepless nights and feels nauseous for days beforehand.

Jim has been a team leader for seven years in his PR company. His performance record is outstanding but he resists all attempts to advance his career. He feels that he would never be able to deal with the pressures at senior management level.

The issue of confidence is one that everyone faces at different times. Right now your confidence may be high and rising, it may be okay but descending or it may be very low and well disguised from those around you.

True or False Confidence

Self-confidence doesn't mean 'bravado' or 'bullshitting or 'pulling the wool over people's eyes'. Some people's image of confidence is the archetypal used-car salesman blagging his way through life: a 'confidence' where nothing fazes him, upsets him or gets to him. Our definition of confidence separates true self-confidence from false self-confidence (see Figures 8.1 and 8.2). True self-confidence is when you honestly face and manage your internal resources to meet the external challenges or demands of your role. False self-confidence is when you create a façade of confidence that does not draw off your internal resources and therefore lacks integrity and is not sustainable in the long term. The challenge you face is not to get caught up in trying to manufacture an external confidence that doesn't have a resourceful foundation because at some stage you will not be able to keep up the façade. This does not mean that you need to parade your anxieties, fears and crises of confidence to everyone at work, but you do need to integrate what is honestly going on inside you with the demands of the external work situation if you are to create a sustainable, true self-confidence.

Imagine you have two rooms. One room is full of the confident resourceful you: all of the things you know you can do, have done, skills, gifts, abilities, positive experiences. In the other room is the more vulnerable you: less experienced, with known weaknesses or vulnerabilities. If you seek to maintain a confident front to others by hiding away this other room it results in a false self-confidence. If you admit to yourself and others both parts of your humanity, then you can confidently draw off the energy from your whole person rather than just a small part of it.

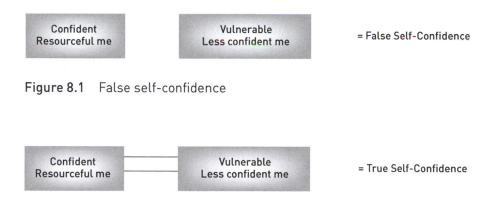

Figure 8.1   False self-confidence

Figure 8.2   True self-confidence

Sometimes in more macho cultures people feel the need to hide or split off the weaker bit to bolster the more confident bit of themselves. This has exactly the opposite effect to the one they desire.

- True self-confidence involves an admission and management of both parts of yourself.
- True self-confidence lies in acknowledged weakness as well as strength.
- True self-confidence involves owning the tougher emotions while accessing the resourceful emotions.

Confidence isn't something that is necessarily tied to age and experience. 'The older or more senior you get the more confident you become.' True or false? In our reckoning, the answer is 'false'. Sometimes the younger a person is the more naive they are and the more confident they feel. Age and the school of hard knocks may make people more reticent. The higher they go up the ladder the more aware they become of the potential sources of a fall.

The Effects

- When your confidence is low you find yourself avoiding situations where you feel that you may fail or underperform or be found out to be incompetent.
- When your confidence is low your performance level goes down. Energy goes more into coping than in rising to challenges.
- When your confidence is low your projection of your visions, your strategies, your leadership and yourself is affected.
- When your confidence is low your non-verbal communication is affected. Your voice is less certain and your shoulders can droop.
- When your confidence is low you set an uncertain tone or may vacillate in decision making.

'The Impostor'

Many leaders (we would say *most* leaders from our experience), regardless of their level in the organisation, while appearing outwardly very confident, fight an internal battle where they fear that their perceived incompetence may be found out. Psychologist C. G. Jung called this fear 'the impostor'. He said it was one of the fundamental archetypes of the human condition (i.e. foundational in all people) that they feel that someone will come along and discover that they cannot really do this job, that they don't really know what they say they know. New challenges, new teams, new markets, new skill sets and environmental pressures all act to erode confidence. On top of all of this certain managers and organisational cultures seem committed to undermining confidence!

Given that research shows that one of the biggest stresses line reports face is their manager, then it is likely that you, as a manager of others, are having a real effect on the confidence of those around you. I (Shenaz) was struck with a contrast to some organisations and managers I have worked with when I watched my son's Saturday-morning football coach at work a while ago. He spent the whole hour shouting words of affirmation and encouragement for everything he could spot to encourage in every child. He didn't lie. He didn't praise something that was clearly bad, but he did find something in everyone to encourage. He was committed to laying a foundation of confidence in the team.

As coaches we are most aware of this confidence issue by the issues our clients *avoid* in their conversation or activities rather than the ones they pursue. We have had a number of conversations that reflect the same misgivings.

> **Coach:** 'We've focused a lot on the short-term problem but what is your vision for the future?'
>
> **Client:** Pause. 'Actually I don't really know how to do vision. I'm really not confident in that area.'
>
> **Coach:** 'I can see the picture of what you are trying to achieve tactically but what is your long-term strategy here?'
>
> **Client:** 'Strategic thinking is an area I don't feel comfortable in.'

The issue of confidence may only be around a particular aspect of leadership such as strategy or vision. It could be because of a shortcoming or limitation in knowledge about finance, budgeting, marketing or sales. A crisis of confidence may also be about working with certain personality types or at certain levels of an organisation or with certain emotions.

Confidence and Self-esteem

Is there a difference between talking about 'confidence' and talking about 'self-esteem'? Our view is that confidence is more about feeling capable and being seen to be capable whereas self-esteem is more about your identity – who you see yourself to be, about feeling loved and valuable and having worth. The dangers in the area of mental and emotional health at work arise when confidence is over-identified with self-esteem. 'I'm not very good at this' quickly becomes 'I am not a very good person'. Therefore, self-esteem is more private; people don't quickly talk about their self-esteem and others don't usually make a quick judgement about someone's self-esteem, but people do make quick judgements about yours and others' levels of confidence.

B. Personal Reflection

Some questions to ask yourself:

- When was the last time you felt really confident?
- Describe what others observed when you were in that confident space.
- Describe what confidence looked like from the inside for you at that time.

So, what is your definition of confidence?

One way to identify your current level of confidence is to take a look at Figure 8.3 and see if you can pinpoint where you are right now.

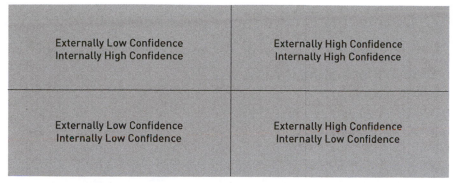

Figure 8.3   Pinpointing your level of confidence

Self-assessment of the Confidence Challenge

Read through all of the questions below and reflect on your work recently. Next, rate yourself in the box below on a scale of 1 to 10, where 1 = confidence is very low and you are not good at managing it and 10 = confidence is high and you are good at managing it.

- Do you feel confident in your current role?
- Do you feel confident that you have the right skills, experience, personality and qualities for your current role?
- Are there areas or situations within your job that you find yourself avoiding (e.g. visioning, strategic planning, close dealings with your staff, business planning)?
- Do you live with the constant unease of someone discovering that you are not up to the job?
- Do you regularly or seldom feel like you are 'in the flow' or 'in the zone' or have a relaxed and focused concentration in your job?
- Are you confident that you have the right people to support you and compensate for your weaknesses and vulnerabilities?
- Is your self-esteem and emotional reserve being depleted more than it is being built up in your current role (or vice versa)?

So where are you on the scale?

Challenge 8 – The Confidence Challenge

1   2   3   4   5   6   7   8   9   10

C. Developing Confidence For Leadership

Step 1. Pinpointing the Issue

The first step in building confidence is to notice how your confidence levels are doing. One way of pinpointing your confidence is to check four different areas of your life: your feelings, your situation, your roles and your relationships. Think through the following questions in each of these four areas.

Feelings Check

- Describe how you feel when you lack confidence.
- Describe how you feel when you have self-confidence.

Situational Check

- Which situations/tasks do you feel confident in?
- Which situations/tasks do you lack confidence in?

Roles Check

- Which roles do you feel confident in?
- Which roles do you feel less confident in?

People Check

- Who do you, as a manager, feel confident with? (Your team, some of your team, senior management, the board, etc.)
- Who do you, as a manager, feel less confident with?

Pinpointing needs to become specific. Consider the scenario of situation, person, role or task (be specific; what is the evidence?).

- What?
- When?
- Who?

- How?
- Where?

People are sometimes dismissive when others admit to low self-confidence. 'What, you?' 'You don't feel that, do you?' Such responses shut down the opportunity to develop that person's confidence. The key is always to listen and validate your own as well as other people's perspectives, however unbelievable they may seem to you. So, accepting what's honestly going on for you right now, pinpointing the situation and your internal as well as external reactions will help you to be even more specific.

Example

I am not confident at . . .	Internal reactions	External behaviours
Challenging bullying	Uptight	Avoid
	Choked	Overly aggressive
	Heart pounding	Tight, defensive tone

Step 2. Understanding your Issue

The key is to get factually clear about what your low confidence is about. This in itself can be very helpful in reducing the size of the issue. Often the size of the issue is perceived as equal to the size of the emotion we feel and not to the reality of the situation. So in order to gain rational, emotional, visual and internal understanding of your confidence issue ask yourself these four questions.

Gaining rational understanding: this is about what is going round inside of your head – the story you are telling yourself.

- What is your worst-case scenario?

Gaining emotional understanding: emotions, especially fears, may keep you avoiding being honest with what is actually going on. Fear makes you look away from rather than at the issue of concern.

■ What are your fears?

Gaining visual understanding: images have a powerful effect on your emotion and motivation. It is important to identify the images that are controlling your levels of confidence.

■ What do you see actually happening in this situation, relationship or incident?

Gaining internal understanding: you may often associate present situations and emotions with past situations or emotions. For example, one manager said he felt like a little boy of 10 when his boss was telling him off about something.

■ What images do you have when you feel low confidence?

Step 3. Deal with the Confidence Sappers

Just as being outside on a hot day saps energy, so confidence can be sapped by a number of different things. You need to identify what is sapping confidence and create a strategy to deal with it. In this section we identify four confidence sappers, illustrated in Figure 8.4.

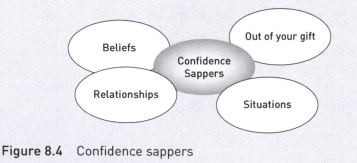

Figure 8.4   Confidence sappers

Confidence-sapping beliefs

When Wimbledon tennis champion Venus Williams said 'most times when we lose we defeat ourselves', she was talking about the battle that goes on in a person's mind. You probably hold conversations with yourself and replay irrational, self-defeating beliefs that serve to undermine your confidence. Just a few of the habitual statements you may use on yourself are:

- 'You idiot.'
- 'You're useless.'
- 'You knew you would do that again.'
- 'You're useless in these situations.'
- 'You always get these wrong.'
- 'You were told you should never attempt these situations.'

So what could a strategy be for dealing with these irrational, self-limiting beliefs?

Expose them Name the thoughts. One way of doing this is to map out the pattern of unhelpful thinking, as outlined in Figure 8.5. By mapping the shape or pattern of your unhelpful thinking you are able to actually see what you are thinking. It also allows you to do the next step, which is to challenge the elements of this thinking.

You hate doing presentations; they always go wrong

When you do presentations your mouth goes dry and you cannot remember anything that you had planned to say

You get up and start talking and you begin to stutter

You can see people are embarrassed

You get more anxious

Your words get jumbled

The presentation goes badly

That confirms what you always thought

Figure 8.5   Self-limiting thinking patterns

Challenge them   Think of some questions that would challenge the belief pattern of Figure 8.5.

- What evidence is there that the presentation went badly?
- Who said so and what specifically went badly?
- What does 'badly' mean?
- Does this always happen in every situation?

- Do all your words get jumbled each time?
- What evidence do you have that people were embarrassed?

Build some new supportive sentences to replace the unsupportive ones
What else could you say to yourself that would be more supportive? Imagine these old sentences to be like an old video or audio tape; what images or sentences would it be helpful to put in their place? The sentences need to be true of you and not just hype or wishful thinking. Examples of these might be:

- You can do most presentations well.
- When you are prepared you do well at presentations.
- When you have cue cards and clear OHPs then you are quite fluent in your presentations.
- No one has ever walked out of your presentations.
- No one has ever given you feedback that your presentations are bad.

Confidence-sapping relationships

Your working world is full of different relationships. When you are with certain people you feel confident and resourceful, yet when you are with other people you feel anxious and uncertain and confidence begins to waver. Here are some questions to help you think through your relationships.

- Which relationship is sapping your confidence?
- What do they do specifically that saps your confidence?
- What happens inside you when you find your confidence being sapped?
- How much is about what they do and how much is about what goes on inside you when they do it?
- What are the opportunities to give feedback to this person directly or through an 'open-door' policy to senior management?

- What can you do to re-wire your own internal responses to this person?
- Have you had some coaching on how to deal with this relationship?

Confidence-sapping cultures

Why is it that some companies create a culture where people thrive and others create a culture where people become defensive and operate in survival mode? Some organisational cultures seem to undermine people's confidence. How?

- By their aggressive stance and behaviours.
- By a set of values which are at variance with your own.
- Over-controlling management.
- Lack of trust demonstrated through lack of delegation.
- Over-paternalistic culture that doesn't take risks.

Think through the following three areas in relation to the organisation you currently work in. Contrast this with other organisations that you have experience of and ask yourself what is the difference.

- Describe the culture of your organisation that you feel undermines your confidence.
- Visit the Proactive Challenge and look at how to create a plan to influence your own situation within the culture.
- Is this the right organisation for you? Do your own values match those of the organisation?

Out of your gift?

People are good at some things and less good at others. Working in areas, skills or roles that are not in line with your core abilities or 'gifts' is always going to be draining and will eventually affect confidence. Three key questions to face in this area are:

- What are your top abilities or 'gifts'?

- Are these the ones being dominantly used in your current role?
- If not, what are you going to do about it?

Step 4. Building a Resourceful Picture of Self-Confidence

In many organisations it is not uncommon to hear people commenting when others have done something wrong. People internalise this behaviour and often spend their time catching themselves doing things wrong and ignoring the things that go well. Logging successes, positive experiences and strategies is absolutely key to developing healthy self-confidence. These bundles of images, emotions and thoughts act as a pool of resources that confident people draw from to counteract the weight of unhelpful emotions or beliefs that undermine their confidence.

Follow through the model in Figure 8.6 to see what happens.

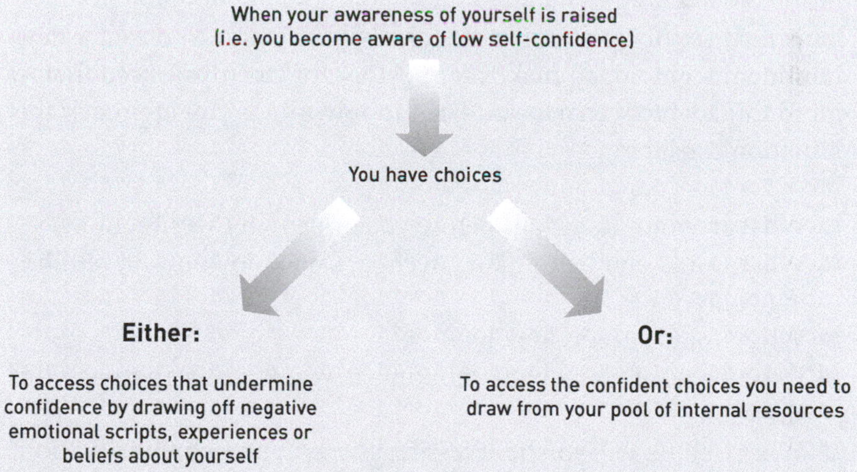

When your awareness of yourself is raised
(i.e. you become aware of low self-confidence)

You have choices

Either:

To access choices that undermine confidence by drawing off negative emotional scripts, experiences or beliefs about yourself

Or:

To access the confident choices you need to draw from your pool of internal resources

Figure 8.6   Choosing to build confidence

Why don't you begin to store up a pool of resourceful emotions, experiences and achievements? Here are some questions to help you do this.

- Write down four examples of people or situations that you have handled well.
- What are your top five achievements at work so far?
- What would your best friends say you are really good at?
- What did you do, say and look like when you were confident in these situations?
- If you were to build a strategy for the future from your successes of the past, what would the key steps be?

Step 5. Creating a Confident Scenario

Step 4 involved creating a bag full of experiences, emotional connections and beliefs that act like a resource to you to counteract the confidence sappers. The next step is to take the scenario you don't feel confident about and rework the video in your head to create a scenario where you see yourself doing the same action, having the same conversation, but with a high degree of confidence.

This next set of questions is designed to help you to create a new, confident scenario. To make the most use of them you need first of all to think what scenario you need to rework. As you approach this situation consider:

- What are your intentions before you approach this situation?
- What would you be thinking, feeling, saying to yourself, reminding yourself of?
- What would success look like?
- Describe what you will be thinking as you actually approach this situation.
- What feelings will you be accessing as you approach this situation?
- Describe what an observer would see if you were handling this situation with true self-confidence.
- What would your ideal internal image be as you confidently deal with this situation? For example, if it isn't being 10 years old again, then what is it?

Finally, create a few paragraphs that tell the story of what a confident 'you' would sound like, feel like and act like in this situation.

Key Beliefs

- No one needs to be a victim of their circumstances or biography.
- There are always alternatives available – so you have choices.
- You can be hugely imaginative and creative when your awareness of a situation is raised.
- Experimenting with how to make your work more enjoyable is both possible and fun.

The rewards of increasing confidence are enormous!

Step 6. Creating a New Structure for Yourself

This step particularly applies to people who are moving into senior management positions. A confidence sapper that we have noted for very senior managers is that previous roles were well defined, they knew what success looked like, they knew what was expected of them and they knew what their objectives were, whereas in very senior roles they are told 'here's your desk, get on with it'. This sudden vacuum of expectation or clarity causes some people to falter and lose confidence. They no longer know whether they are doing a good job; they don't even know how they would measure a good job for themselves.

The important shift for senior managers is to realise that they are now expected to be able to tell themselves what their job is and to tell themselves whether they are doing well. If this is new to you then put these four things in place.

1. Put in place a vision for what you are personally seeking to achieve.
2. Put in place approximately five key strategic goals or areas you must focus on to achieve the vision.

3. Put in place some measures to tell yourself if you are on track.
4. Create a feedback culture around your key stakeholders so they can tell you if they think you are on track.

DO NOT work in a vacuum of expectation or feedback because over time this can severely drain your confidence.

Step 7. Supporting Yourself through this Challenge

It is hard work dealing with the Confidence Challenge, especially when it taps into painful stories in your past or present. When we were working on this challenge we were very aware of how significant people in our past had a big impact in boosting our self-confidence or undermining it. We suggest that you get support from a colleague or coach. Tell them your specific situation and challenge and tell them what you are now going to do as a new approach. Keep in touch with them by arranging telephone or e-mail contact at short intervals while you are trying out new behaviours and growing your confidence. You need to be gentle with yourself and celebrate the little wins.

Step 8. Building Confidence in Others

Leadership is not just about managing your own confidence, it is about developing the confidence of others.

Research has shown that one of the greatest stressors in a person's life is their boss's behaviour. If you are a manager then you could quite possibly be the cause of someone else's erosion of confidence.

Self-assessment

Here is a short reflective exercise to think through how you are doing in creating confidence in others.

Rate yourself on a 1 to 10 scale, where 10 is very good at building others confidence and 1 is not good at all.

| 1 | 2 | 3 | 4 | 5 | 6 | 7 | 8 | 9 | 10 |

What is the evidence to justify your score?

- What feedback (anecdotal or formal) would back up the score that you have just given yourself?
- What are your behaviours that build others' confidence? (Think of exact behaviours or examples or incidents where you have sought to build the confidence of others.)
- What are your behaviours that undermine others' confidence? (Think hard about some of the ways that you may undermine the confidence of others by what you do or what you fail to do. For example, certain personalities seem to assume in their own minds that when someone has done a good job that it is obvious and doesn't need mentioning, while at the same time feeling they should just point out some little problem that needs correction. This can come across as quite unsupportive and critical.)
- Do you have a structure for giving positive feedback? What is it?
- How do feel about receiving and giving positive feedback?

Some people find it hard to receive compliments or positive feedback. When they do, they dismiss it or shrug it off. Sometimes it is harder for such people to give positive feedback because they do not want to put others through the embarrassment that they experience.

Building confidence through positive performance management

Good management builds confidence. It creates clear agreed goals, it supports and challenges people to achieve these goals and it provides a range of appropriate management styles from direction to coaching to help people achieve their goals. Here is a simple checklist for good management practice in creating confident people.

- Set agreed, measurable, specific performance goals for each of your direct reports or project members.
- Coach your staff rather than 'tell' them most of the time.
- Have regular one-to-ones with them to see how they are doing and to coach them in areas of lower performance or uncertainty.
- Discuss with your team what a 'no-blame' culture actually means.

A question for reflection

How does your level of confidence in your team affect their performance?

The Final Question . . . What are you going to do now?
(See Appendix 1 for further development)

NB: It is very important if you feel that your confidence is ebbing to not let this go on too long. In the worst cases this can affect performance and then emotional and physical health. Set yourself a date when you will commit yourself to take action if things have not improved. Who will you go and talk to on that date?

9

The

Internal Compass Challenge

Lead yourself
so you can lead others

A. Understanding this Challenge

Are You Leading Yourself?

Every day you are making choices. Some are conscious; many are unconscious. Some are big and involve lots of people, money and implications; some are seemingly small and affect maybe only one person or even just yourself. The question is, *on what basis do you make this myriad of choices?* Are they reactive to others or reactive to your pathology – feeling important, needing praise, money, adrenalin, peer admiration, grandiosity? Or are they proactive? To be proactive is to write the script. Victor Frankl, in his biographical work *In Search of Meaning* (1984), based on his experiences in a Nazi death camp, talks of the ultimate human dignity being personal choice around what people think and believe: that in between a stimulus (or something that happens to you) and your response (or how you react to the stimulus) is a space, a gap, a moment – in that moment you can decide the direction you take. An internal compass is a clear personal mission and vision, providing values and goals.

There is a point of disconnection for some people in organisational leadership. They talk about the vision of the organisation and how crucial it is, but they don't practise the same principle in their own lives. They talk about the values of the organisation and how crucial they are, but they don't get clarity about their own values. The core premise behind this challenge is that a leader's capacity to lead others ultimately rests on their ability to lead themselves. If you don't know where you are going, how can you lead others there? An internal compass is a core set of values and beliefs that acts as an essential navigational tool. When the sky is clear and the route is familiar you don't need a compass. When the sky is dark, foggy or (to change the metaphor) the waves are getting bigger, the landscape is unfamiliar, confusing, contradictory and unpredictable – when the environment is changing all around you, how do you navigate?

Principle-centred Leadership

I have always been a fan of what Stephen Covey named 'Principle-centered Leadership' (1992). The idea behind this phrase is that of the internal compass. It relates back to the issue of wisdom but goes further. In the real world and for many centuries a compass has given people direction irrespective of the geography in which they have found themselves. But people are also blessed with an internal compass, which is their own personal set of values. These are deeply embedded, forged over years by experience and wisdom: they govern the choices people make about the direction they take in any given situation. For instance, I believe in fairness, honesty and acting ethically, but my real values show themselves if I find myself 'bending the truth' for financial gain. It may be that there are underlying values around greed or entitlement. The Internal Compass Challenge is to decide on a personal governing set of values and then act in ways that are consistent with these. This is integrity – 'walking the talk'.

The Key to Gaining the Trust of Others

The reason why this is so crucial for leaders is that the basis of all interpersonal trust (the Influence Challenge) is trustworthiness. If people do not sense that what you say equates to how you act, then they will not be inclined to trust you. Business negotiations and deals need a foundation of trust, although on some occasions it is not forthcoming. However, successful long-term commercial or organisational relationships are based on a foundation of trust. You can have a lot of beliefs but your values will be the real determiner of what you do, particularly when you are under pressure.

You will not lead the organisation to discern its guiding values and behaviours and perform them unless you are truly a value-driven person (link to the Strategy Challenge). If values are just a 'nice to have' in your leadership portfolio, then you will probably lack the motivation and commitment necessary to lead others to embed them in your organisation. You may lead an away day on listing what the organisation's values should be, but without that motivation and commitment they will remain on flip charts at the bottom of a drawer or on the floor of the seminar room for the cleaners to consign to the bin. Outstanding leaders have the capability to discern, verbalise and embody a core set of values.

A Tough Challenge

This challenge is deep stuff! Why? Because, maybe for the first time in your life, you are drilling down to uncover what matters most, and when you reach the bedrock of your personal values and vision it creates an emotional buy-in that will enable you to make choices. The choice to 'leave the office at 5.30 p.m. today', the choice to 'not take on that piece of work', the choice to identify 'this is important and needs my commitment' – all rely on having done a deep piece of work on yourself first in order to have an internal compass that sets the direction for the tough choices each day. When you make these kinds of choices you grow in character and integrity. It confirms something in you; it does not diminish you. However, in the confusion and busyness of life you may often make choices that don't come from the internal compass, and they will often have the opposite effect on you.

Examples

A CEO we spoke to recently was close to retirement and fearful of how he would spend his time. I asked him whether he'd ever investigated his own internal compass beyond his job role. He said 'no'. He was 58 years old!

In contrast, a CEO at 39 years old invested in understanding his own internal compass and it revealed that he'd invested twenty-one years in something that he once believed in and now was able to admit that it didn't fit with what he wanted for the next twenty-one years. He began to rewrite the script immediately.

'I spent a lifetime climbing up the corporate ladder and I've just realised my ladder has been up against the wrong wall.'

At a training seminar for a group of high potentials in a global IT company we did an hour-and-a-half exercise just getting them to connect with their own internal compass. The effect was profound. Comments were made by individuals that they had never had the time to find out what matters most to them or that they had just discovered what their core values were and with that had come a realisation that they were not living them.

Summary of the Benefits of Being Clear about Your Internal Compass

- You always have a starting point when navigating in the dark.
- You have clarity about your direction even when you don't have a map.
- You have access to your best resource – yourself.
- Your whole life matches what you preach to your organisation or team about the primacy of vision, values and strategy.

If all leadership is about influencing others then personal integrity – the integration of who you are, your personal vision, personal values and personal strategy – is the foundation of interpersonal trust. Do you have integrity at the foundation of your character to inspire trust from others?

B. Personal Reflection

Do you have a sense of having an internal compass? What does this mean to you in your own language?

Self-assessment of the Internal Compass Challenge

Read through all of the questions below and reflect on your work recently. Rate yourself in the box below on a scale of 1 to 10, where 1 = do not have a clear sense of your own mission, vision, values and goals for your own life beyond who you are at work and 10 = do have a very clear sense of your own mission, vision, values and goals for your own life beyond who you are at work.

- Do you have a clear set of personal values?
- Have you got examples of where your values have manifested themselves in your behaviour in this past week?
- Do you have a personal mission statement that guides the choices you make in your work and in your relationships?

- Do you have a vision and mission for your life that is greater than your work?
- Do people actually say, 'You are a person with values and integrity'?
- Do you build high-trust relationships?
- Have you discovered, verbalised and embodied the core values of your team/role/organisation?
- Do you have a clear mission in life?
- Do you have a governing set of values?
- Are you clear about what matters most to yourself and does this act like a compass to your life?
- Are you clear about all the roles you have in your life? (As a parent, boss, aunt/uncle, leader, communicator, etc.) Are your mission and values demonstrated in each of these roles?

So where are you on the scale?

Challenge 9 – The Internal Compass Challenge									
1	2	3	4	5	6	7	8	9	10

C. Developing an Internal Compass

For this challenge you are definitely going to need to get yourself a notebook or pad of blank paper.

In the sections that follow you will be taken through a development process for each of the areas illustrated in Figure 9.1. In part this will be done through a series of questions. Don't get stuck on any question; if you do, just move on to the next one. The questions are there simply to stimulate your thinking and reflection.

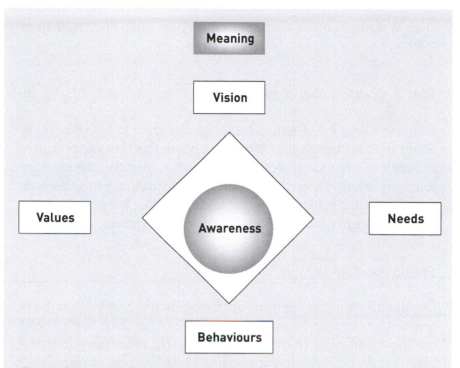

Figure 9.1 A model of the internal compass

Developing a Personal Vision

A personal vision is a picture that you can have in your mind that captures something of the future that you desire to have. It may be a vision of what you will be doing, or it may be a picture of how you will be or what will be important to you. In order to create personal vision try the process outlined below.

Step 1. Choose the time and place

Developing a personal vision can only be done by finding a clear space of time, uninterrupted and in a place that is 'yours', i.e. not at the office or a place where you will have competing demands for your attention. You are going to dig deep into your own self and so you need all the help you can get from the environment. Choose music if that helps; sometimes people do this work by finding a comfortable chair at the local coffee shop or when they are on holiday away from it all.

Step 2. Create a pool of your insights

Below is a long list of vision questions, designed to help you think about what is important to you. Using blank sheets of paper answer as many of the vision questions as you can. Just free-associate by jotting down all of your thoughts without trying to organise them or shape them for yourself or for an audience. The key is to tap your deepest thoughts and insights without censoring them.

Step 3. Read and shape

Once you have brain-dumped your thoughts and insights to as many questions as you can answer, re-read all of your answers to the vision questions and begin to shape an answer to the following question – 'what are the main thing(s) in your life?' Or 'what is the picture of your future?'

See also the Personality Challenge.

Those of you with a more extrovert personality may find it more helpful to do this process with someone else so that you can think out loud and discuss it with them.

Step 4. A vision that engages you

Get your *main thing* into a verbal, visual or tactile form that engages you, so that whenever you read or look at it you have a sense of connecting with something that is vital to who you are. Some people prefer a vision expressed in words (a paragraph, a poem, a series of bullet points), other prefer it in pictures (a painting or collage).

The Vision Questions

1. It's your 75th birthday party. Three people from your life stand up and talk for five minutes each about what you have meant to them. For example, you might choose your wife, your son and your closest friend. Choose your three people.

   What would you like them to say?

   What difference have you made in their lives?

   What qualities or characteristics will you be remembered for?

   What outstanding or significant contributions would they mention?

2. In your life what gives you energy or when do you feel most energised?

3. When do you feel most alive?

4. With whom do you feel most alive? Why, in each case?

5. What would you really like to do with your life?

6. What do you feel are your greatest strengths?

7. How do you want to be remembered?

8. Who is the one person who has made the greatest positive impact on your life?

9. If you had unlimited time and resources, what would you do?

10. What are the three most important things to you?

11. How can you best contribute to the world?

12. Name an animal that you like or dislike – what are the characteristics that you like/dislike?

13. What gives your life meaning?

14. If you were to do one thing in your professional life that would have the most positive impact, what would that one thing be?

15. If you were to do one thing in your personal life that would have the most positive impact, what would that one thing be?

16. Who are the five people who have most influenced your life?

17. What outstanding characteristics or attributes do you most admire in these people?

18. Which three people in your life have had the most negative influence on your life?

19. What are the characteristics you most dislike about them?

Further questions

1. Which of the characteristics from Questions 16-19, in their positive form, would you feel important enough to include in your mission statement?
2. Make a list of the things you want to have that you feel are important (things may be tangible, e.g. house, or intangible, e.g. happy family). Choose the top five from your list.
3. When you daydream, what do you see yourself doing?
4. When you look at your work life, which activities do you consider to be of greatest worth?
5. When you look at your personal life, which activities do you consider of greatest worth?
6. What do you consider to be your most important future contributions to others?
7. What talents do you have, whether developed or undeveloped?
8. Are there things you should do even though you might have dismissed such thoughts many times before for various reasons? What are they?
9. Who has served as a positive role model for you and had a significant impact in your life? (List the people who come to mind.)
10. Why did each of these people have such a significant impact?
11. What qualities does each of these people possess that you would like to emulate?
12. What other qualities of character do you most admire in others?
13. You are at your best when . . .
14. You are at your worst when . . .
15. You are truly happy when . . .
16. You want to be a person who . . .
17. Someday you would like to . . .
18. Your deepest positive emotions come when . . .
19. Your greatest gifts and talents are . . .
20. When all is said and done, the most important things are . . .
21. Possible life goals for you are . . .
22. Write continuously for five minutes on 'the main thing in my life is . . .'. Free-associate – it doesn't need to make sense or be orderly.

Discerning your Personal Values

Your values are worth discovering. Values are what you are naturally inclined to and drawn to, or eager to do. Quite simply, values are the things you hold most dear in life, the things that give your life meaning and purpose. In a very real sense your values are about you in essence. For example, some people are natural explorers, they were at age 6 and still are at 40. They are still taking adventure trips. Identifying and honouring your values animates your life, brings you joy, connects you with yourself, makes you sparkle. Living your values is about achieving balanced living. Values are very much there and they make up who you are and how you live. Usually it isn't that you need to go and invent some values, they already exist, but you either haven't made the time to detect them or you have been so busy that they have fallen into neglect.

Failure to identify your values is likely to cause some lack of energy, lack of direction and certainly a gap between how you want to live your life and how you are living now. Hutcheson and McDonald (1997) go so far as to say that identifying and honouring your values can 'propel the difficult leap from the Stress Cycle to the Balance Cycle'. The Stress Cycle is driven by what lies outside of yourself and is often motivated by goals, wealth, status and other people's opinions. The Balance Cycle is always inner-directed. To be in the Balance Cycle you must have an internal sense of who you are and what you want in your life. While values run deep within, they resemble tortoises, because they hide themselves whenever danger is sensed. Danger is anything that gets in the way of values, such as weak boundaries, stress, needs and obligations. Given this list, it is no wonder values can remain hidden and unexpressed.

Step 1

Look through the following list of potential values. There are a lot of them so take your time to familiarise yourself and reflect on them. Add any values you like.

Potential Values

Achievement	Advancement and promotion	Adventure	Affection	Art	Authority
Accountability	Attractiveness	Challenge	Change	Closeness	Co-operation
Creativity	Caring	Coaching	Compassion	Community	Competence
Connected	Competition	Culture	Decisiveness	Design	Democracy
Ecology	Educate	Financial security	Effectiveness	Energise	Encourage
Ethics	Excellence	Excitement	Expertise	Energetic living	Fame
Financial gain	Freedom	Free others	Friendship	Growth	Development
Family	Helping	Altruism	Society	Honesty	Independence
Influence	Harmony	Inner harmony	Impact	Invention	Integrity
Ingenuity	Inspiring courage	Intellect	Involvement	Tranquillity	Venture
Loveliness	Peace	Knowledge	Learning	Location	Loyalty
Market	Meaningful work	Merit	Money	Nature	Openness
Order	Imagination	Stability	Conformity	Personal development	Orginality
Physical potential	Sex	Pleasure	Play	Power	Privacy
Public service	Purity	Quality	Recognition	Respect	Status
Religion	God	Reputation	Responsibility	Security	Self-respect
Serenity	Service	Sophistication	Stability	Sense	Stimulation
Supervise	Time	Truth	Wealth	Pressure	Working with others
Working	Love	Patriotism	Relationships	Wisdom	Leadership
Variety	Risk	Endeavour	Quest	Experiment	Exhilaration
Others					

Step 2

Select ten values that are essential for you and who you are.

Step 3

If you were forced to hold on to only five values at the core of your life, which five would they be?

Step 4

For each of these values you need to ask, Why is this value important enough to you to be one of your "true values"? If you can, write down three specific reasons for each value.

Step 5

For each of these values you need to ask, Who are you when you honour this value? How do you act? What do you think about? What motivates you? Write down specific examples.

Step 6

For each of these values you need to ask, How well are you honouring or expressing this value in your daily living? What are you doing in your life that permits this value to be free enough to express itself? Write down specific ways in which you are currently honouring each value.

Step 7

For each of these values you need to ask, In what aspects of your daily living are you not honouring or expressing this value? What are you doing that restricts, dishonours or does not give your value the room and nourishment it needs and deserves? Write down specific things you are doing which do not serve each of your values.

Step 8

For each of these values you need to ask, What changes could you make in your life in order to fully honour and express this value? Write down three specific changes to make in the next three months.

Understanding your Personal Needs

No matter how successful you are you can always become more self-aware if you have more information about yourself and understand how you tick. Finding out about your true needs is a little like finding out your hidden (vulnerable) hot spots. It is important to remember that each and every individual has hidden hot spots.

So what exactly is a need? Needs are what you must have to be at your best. It sounds so simple, and you're probably thinking 'what is so hard about that?' Our experience is that the needs you have are probably the things you would be embarrassed to come right out and ask for! A typically British example is being at a meal table and wanting the salt. Rather than asking for the salt someone might say, 'Have you finished with the salt?' People express the need indirectly. Would you, for example, be comfortable asking for 'recognition', if this was one of your identified needs? In fact, you may go around being careful *not* to show your need for recognition. In fact, most people have been well trained to think it is not appropriate to blatantly ask that their needs be fulfilled. The accepted behaviour is to pretend that you don't have any needs, that you are self-sufficient. The fact is that no one wants to feel needy, much less admit that they are, so it is not surprising that you have never learnt how to express your needs.

If you are not aware and alert to your needs then how can you get them met? Needs can't be ignored, they will be fed anyway. In fact the problem is that needs will 'drive and drain' you. Needs can run havoc and have a negative impact on your life. Your needs become the prism from which you see the world: they will skew how you see life, relationships, how you operate and how you choose your own satisfaction. They will be met consciously or unconsciously, so you may as well get your needs conscious and clarified. The aim is to get your needs met in a way that fuels you instead of robbing you of your ability to achieve. Your challenge then is to design ways to get them met.

Some facts about needs:

- Needs hold clues to who you are and what your vulnerabilities are.
- No matter how successful you are you still have needs.
- Once you know what they are you can protect them.
- You have many needs but some are more critical than others.
- You'll know the critical needs, they tend to rock your being – they have a Jekyll and Hyde effect on you.
- To get to what is great about you and to avoid being at the mercy of your downside, get your needs identified and met.
- You need first to identify situations where these needs are not met.
- What kind of boundaries do you have around those needs and those situations?
- You will need to practise ways of having and holding boundaries.
- Saying 'no' means building time for saying 'yes'. If you never say 'no' then what is your 'yes' worth?

Identifying your needs

Reflect on the following.

Step 1. Here is a sample of needs, which may help you to identify your own needs. Glance through them and think through which ones resonate with you. For example, is it the need to 'be the best' or the need to 'be respected'? Come on, keep on looking, if it hurts a bit you've probably unearthed a true need.

Examples of needs

Honesty	Achievement	Communicate	Loved
Excellence	Cared for	Recognition	Freedom
Power	Security	Noticed	Comfort
Acceptance	Quality	Control	Understood

Write down your list of needs.

Step 2. To help you reflect a little, imagine what others who care about you would say about your needs. Sometimes they can recognise your needs better than you can. It would be helpful if you could ask three people whom you know genuinely care about you what they see as your critical needs.

Step 3. Narrow down your list to three needs that are most critical to you. How are you getting those needs met currently? Do you get them met in ways that fuel you or drain you? How do you react when each need is not met or is denied? What feelings are present?

What systems do you need to put in place to help you to satisfy those needs? What resources can you surround yourself with to optimise your productivity and sense of fulfilment? On whom do you depend for what? A model of psychological health is to understand your needs and to spread them across a variety of well-chosen people and situations. It is dangerous to expect one person to fulfil all your needs for you and it is equally draining and pressurising for that person.

Benefits of getting your needs met

- You free up time and energy.
- You can move on and orient your life towards your vision.
- You have raised your own awareness of what you need to get to be at your best.
- This is a skill that will work well for you at whatever place in life you find yourself.

Meaning – Playing the Higher Game

In Jostein Gaarder's best-selling novel *Sophie's World* a 14-year-old Norwegian schoolgirl called Sophie arrives home from school one day to find an anonymous letter for her. Inside the envelope are two questions, 'who are you?' and 'where do you come from?' The novel is her adventure of discovery to find answers to these questions.

Gaarder highlights how school education does not teach people to ask the fundamental questions that are of most importance.

- Who are we?
- Why are we here?
- How was the world created?
- Is there any will or meaning behind what happens?
- Is there a life after death?

Gaarder suggests that a child's inherent sense of wonder that asks these questions is not nurtured and is quickly replaced by the habits of getting on with living. This means that many people have never invested serious time in their own investigations. What answers they have are often clichéd, second-hand sound bites from un-thought-through acquaintances or a far-from-unbiased media.

The question of meaning is the higher-level question of the Internal Compass Challenge. You may call it spiritual identity – how you see yourself in relation to the higher meaning of life. Remember your mortality is a 100% fact. So ask yourself:

- Beyond the biological realities what gives your life meaning?
- At core, what for you is the main thing in your life?

Some Things to Do

1. Increase your Self-awareness

At the heart of an internal compass is your self-awareness. 'Know yourself' is at the centre of effective leadership. All of the 18 Challenges of Leadership are designed to increase your self-awareness and, in particular, we would refer you to the section of the Insight Challenge that looks at emotional intelligence, the Influence Challenge, which looks at the way you impact people, and the Personality Challenge, which looks at how your personal preferences impact others.

As a summary of the work you have done on self-awareness through-out this book, why not précis what you know about yourself as if you were describing yourself to a stranger.

'Meet me – this is who I am.' (Describe all aspects of yourself.)

- What matters to you?
- What do others see when they see you?
- What do you see when you think of yourself?
- Where are the gaps between what you intend others to see of you and what they actually see?
- When the apples on a tree are ripe and you bump into the tree you get showered with apples. What do people get showered with when they bump into you?
- Do they get the same thing all of the time or does it depend on your mood or circumstances?

2. Try a visual version of self-awareness

Get a large sheet of paper. Try flip-chart paper if you can.

Draw a large circle on the sheet. Inside of this circle represents your inner world – the 'you' only you see. Outside of the circle represents the exterior you – the 'you' others get to see.

Collect a pile of magazines, coloured papers, textures and textiles. You'll also need scissors and glue. Cut and paste *inside* of the circle any picture, image, colour, texture or textile that represents how you see yourself internally. Cut and paste *outside* of the circle any picture, image, colour, texture or textile that represents how you see yourself externally or how you think others may see you.

3. Translating into behaviours

The Internal Compass Challenge only makes real sense when your identity (what you have discovered about yourself) is translated into action (your behaviours). Use this final section to summarise your discoveries about yourself and how they will translate into action.

Write down:

- Your main thing.
- Your vision of your future.
- Your values.
- Your needs.
- The absolute non-negotiables in your life.

Next write down the key ways these areas of behaviour will show themselves in your behaviour both immediately and over the next 6–12 months.

Ask yourself, if you were actually doing these things over the next 6–12 months:

- What would you see yourself actually doing?
- What would others see you doing?
- What would you hear?
- What would others hear?
- What would you feel?
- What would others feel?

The Final Question . . . What are you going to do now?
(See Appendix 1 for further development)

10

The

'Bigger and Bigger Challenge' Challenge

Continuously growing your skills base

A. Understanding this Challenge

The Skill Gap

Take this scenario. You get a degree in IT or computers, or accounting; you get your first job as a programmer or junior accountant; you do it well; you get promoted to team leader; you do that job well; you get promoted to department manager. The gap illustrated in Figure 10.1 is the 'Bigger and Bigger Challenge' Challenge.

Figure 10.1   The skill gap

Leaders face a constant demand to exceed the performance of the previous year regardless of the environmental factors: bigger numbers, larger roles, more responsibility, greater spans of management. People expect a skills gap for lower-level managers. You do not expect a new graduate or someone who is only a few years into their career to know all about the principles of:

Leadership	Influencing
Negotiating	Change management
Team leadership	Business planning
Budgeting	Management styles
Product cycles	Marketing strategies
Communication strategies	Project planning
Gantt charting	SWOT analysis
Force Field Analysis	Managing meetings effectively

Somehow, mysteriously, by the time someone metamorphoses into a position at senior-management level there is an assumption that they now have the full toolkit. From our experience this is a massive assumption. It is also a dangerous assumption. The problem is that it drives the skills and knowledge gap underground. For example, it is difficult to admit when you are marketing director of a large organisation that you have no idea how to write a business plan. So people remain silent and hope that their shortcomings are not found out. Forward-thinking organisations are matching the executive stretch of promoting people to new leadership roles and challenges with Executive Coaches to build in the support and development necessary to ensure people succeed well and learn, rather than survive (or not) with intellectual and emotional exhaustion.

Look at Figure 10.2 (the size of the box represents the size of the job). You may have an old role with old skills (not necessarily redundant skills). You shift to a new role and either meet the 'Bigger and Bigger Challenge' Challenge or end up in a new role with old skills (again, not necessarily redundant skills, but probably inadequate skills).

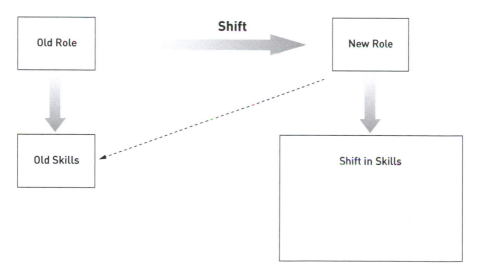

Figure 10.2 The 'Bigger and Bigger Challenge' Challenge

Our 'Bigger and Bigger Challenge' Challenges

When we started Executive Coaching all we needed was to be very good coaches, with consulting backgrounds, backed by solid experience and training in an aspect of psychology, bags of courage and a reasonable amount of intelligence. When we set up The Executive Coach as a company we needed also to know how to write business plans and create marketing strategies, develop sales pipelines, contracting and invoicing processes, understand account management, have legal awareness, employment and performance management skills, understand accounting, priority management, product development, become IT literate and so on.

When we created The 18 Challenges of Leadership on CD-ROM we knew absolutely nothing about software design and licence law. We do now! When we decided to create this book to support people's leadership development we knew little about the world of publishing. We know a little more now.

It would be easy to conclude that this challenge is simply about learning from experience. This is partly true but the fact is people are limited by what they do not know or do not know well. Experience is always playing catch-up and involves learning enough to get by rather than being proactive and learning enough to excel.

Encountering the 'Bigger and Bigger Challenge' Challenge

Apart from the skills listed earlier some of the ways you realise that you have encountered this challenge are:

- Increased hours.
- Increased responsibility.
- Increased authority.
- Increased budget.
- Increased consequences/implications.
- Increased expectations – overt and covert.
- Others.

Even when a person isn't looking for promotions it doesn't mean that more and more isn't expected of them!

The Challenge Is Two Jobs from Now

While you may be playing catch-up with your skills to meet the demands of your current role we would also want to encourage you to look beyond the present to one or two roles you might have in the next five years. What skills will you need to meet the challenges of the future? Set out to develop those skills now.

Example

Mike was UK manager of a global re-insurance company. He was highly effective in this role but knew that in eighteen months he would be offered a global role. He realised that there was a large gap between the more operationally and tactically focused leadership skills required to run a national operation and a global role which would require leadership skills that relied much more heavily on creating shared vision, high-level strategy, being much more political, and being a lot less 'hands-on'. He faced the 'Bigger and Bigger Challenge' Challenge early enough to invest in a skill base that would equip him for his next two jobs.

The ways to learn

- Some skills are learned in the classroom through training courses, seminars, e-learning, distance learning and correspondence courses.
- Some skills are learned on the job by doing a task.
- Some skills are learned through processing past experiences to look for learning for future situations and to identify learning gaps.
- Some skills are developed on the job but with the support of coaching. For example, we coach people to learn about how to think strategically or to create vision by using the current example of their team or division as the 'live' example.
- Some skills are learned through mentors. Mentors are people who have more skill and experience than we do in a given area and can be a source of advice and support and can stretch you in your learning.
- Using feedback from friends, a coach or colleagues reveals blind spots.
- Reading theories, biographies and case studies.

Understanding the importance of facing the 'Bigger and Bigger Challenge' Challenge

The implications of facing this challenge include good and bad. On the one hand, to face such challenges can produce emotional chaos; yet to avoid it can produce internal constriction, and dries up creativity and resourcefulness. The more implications of facing this challenge there are for you, the more that you have to invest towards moving to the bigger challenges.

Example

At 42 years of age Paul decided to step out of the fast track that his bank had him on in order to spend more time with his family and his out-of-work interests. Such was his credibility with his organisation that he was given one year's grace, but by the end of that year he had to make a choice – back into the succession planning or be sidelined in the organisation. He stepped back into the organisation's plan and went on to become a CEO.

Understanding the implications of why you chose not to face the bigger challenge

Sometimes it's OK to choose not to rise to the bigger challenge, but to make such a decision still requires you to face it and know clearly why you are not going to respond. Then it becomes a source of security, and it anchors you when others are telling you that you should 'rise to the challenge' and allows you to pursue your chosen path without guilt.

Example

At 52 years of age Jim decided that he only wanted to become assistant manager and not general manager. He faced the 'Bigger and Bigger Challenge' Challenge and was happy he could do the top job, that he wasn't running away from any issues and that he was making a constructive life choice. He was a high performer at that assistant level until his retirement.

B. Personal Reflection

How would you define this challenge for yourself?

Self-assessment of the 'Bigger and Bigger Challenge' Challenge

Read through all of the questions below and reflect on your work recently. Rate yourself in the box below on a scale of 1 to 10, where 1 = skill base doesn't match the needs of your current or next two roles and 10 = skill base matches the needs of your current or next two roles.

- Are you confident that you have none/some/all of the skills that you need to perform at a high level in your job?
- Have your professional and skills development kept pace with your increased responsibility?
- Do you feel that in order to expand your future job/career/role possibilities that there are significant areas of development that you need to pursue?
- Looking at the following list, do you feel that these are all areas that are either irrelevant or that you feel quite confident in?
    - Principles of leadership.
    - Strategic leadership (vision, strategic goals, strategy, etc.).
    - Influencing.
    - Negotiation.
    - Change management.
    - Matrix management.
    - Balanced Scorecard or other strategy implementation processes.
    - Team leadership.
    - Managing meetings effectively.
    - Mergers and acquisitions.
    - IPOs (initial public offerings – flotations).
    - Leading the board.
    - Managing investors and shareholders.

- Business planning and writing a business plan.
- Budgeting.
- Management styles.
- Product cycles.
- Marketing strategies.
- Communication strategies.
- Networking strategies.
- Project planning and management.
- SWOT analysis; Gantt charting.
- Force Field Analysis.

So where are you on the scale?

Challenge 10 – The 'Bigger and Bigger Challenge' Challenge

1	2	3	4	5	6	7	8	9	10

B. Developing the Skill for the Challenge of Today's and Tomorrow's Role

Choosing to Face the 'Bigger and Bigger Challenge' Challenge

We advocate that as leaders you choose to face this challenge and grow yourself in a changing world. It is easy to be reactive and wait or blame the current situation. Taking charge of your own future means you create personal vision for yourself at home and work and then discern what skills you will need to have to achieve the vision. There is a spectrum of choices you face in this particular challenge.

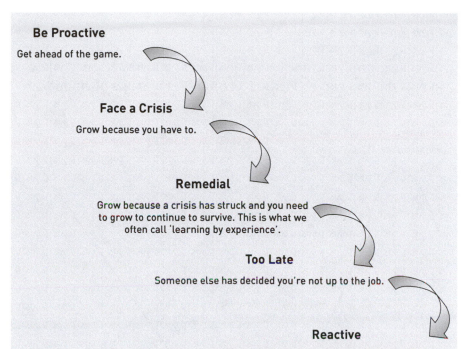

Be Proactive

Get ahead of the game.

Face a Crisis

Grow because you have to.

Remedial

Grow because a crisis has struck and you need to grow to continue to survive. This is what we often call 'learning by experience'.

Too Late

Someone else has decided you're not up to the job.

Reactive

Blame the boss, the changing environment, etc.

Figure 10.3   Choosing the 'Bigger and Bigger Challenge' Challenge

Responding to the Challenge: a Step-by-Step Process

Step 1. Recognise the reality

Look at your current role. Is there a shift taking place? Use these questions to identify what that shift is.

- What is shifting?
- What skills does someone in your position need?
- Do you have those skills?
- Who else would know what skills you might need?
- What is the next job you would like?
- What are the skills that this requires?
- Where will you need to learn these skills?

Step 2. Create a space

All change involves some loss, even if there is a greater gain. Take a look at the 'loss curve' (Figure 10.4) and see the stages of emotional response in processing a change.

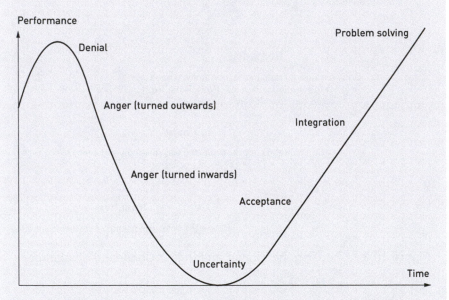

Figure 10.4 The loss curve – how people are affected by change

It may be that you are so busy that you remain in denial over the potential challenges that you face. What are you losing, what are you gaining? There needs to be a space to feel irrationally angry at the system, or the organisation/your boss for 'pushing' you into this challenge, or to face the anger at yourself for not spotting the challenge coming, or to face the uncertainty and anxiety that change provokes. You need a space to feel 'it's all too big'. You need a space because under such pressure your thinking will get cloudy or paralysed. You need a space to protest within yourself that you are 'too busy doing important things right now to deal with this challenge'. You need a space to think, to admit what you are feeling and to reach a place of acceptance as the platform for proactive influence in your development.

This links to the time management quadrant in the Proactive Challenge – see Table 10.1.

Table 10.1   Urgent v. important

	Urgent	Non-Urgent
Important	1.	2. The Bigger and Bigger Challenge
Non-Important	3.	4.

Leadership is focused on what is important, what achieves the vision and strategy you or the organisation have set. The 'Bigger and Bigger Challenge' Challenge is a Quadrant 2 activity. It needs to be planned for proactively and not left until it reaches Quadrant 1 – where it becomes urgent.

Step 3. Acceptance

You recognise that you are facing a bigger challenge or that there is potential for such a challenge on the horizon. Acceptance means that you have faced it, have allowed the space (Step 2) for an internal emotional roller-coaster, and now you are ready to face this new challenge. Alternatively, it means you have faced the issues and allowed yourself to work through the emotions and are choosing not to respond to the challenge. The choice to not 'skill up' is as much part of the 'Bigger and Bigger Challenge' Challenge as taking the challenge.

Step 4. Identify the gap

Using the list of areas in the self-assessment section, think through your own situation and ask what skills you currently have. Carry out your own skills audit (see Figure 10.5). You will be encouraged that you have more skills in your toolkit than you thought. Then ask what skills and experience someone in your new role has, and what skills you will need two years from now to be where you plan to be.

Figure 10.5   Identify the Gap

Step 5. Plan to influence

It may be helpful to revisit the Influence Challenge. You could also ask yourself these questions to think through your situation.

- As you look at your skills gap what can you influence?
- Is there someone you need to ask for help? Who?
- Is there someone you need to ask to be a mentor? If so, what area will you ask them to mentor you in?
- Is there someone you need to ask to be your coach?
- Is there a peer in another job/company/industry that you could learn from or shadow?
- Is there a training course you need to attend?
- Is there another job you need to get in order to gain experience for the job you really want?

Step 6. The eye of your storm

Sometimes it is helpful to look at your answers to assessing your skills gap and ask yourself what the nub of this challenge is for you right now. Sometimes there is an issue that underlies all the other issues.

The eye of the storm may be:

- **Emotional:** Your fear that you are just not able to learn these new skills at your age.
- **Physical:** You may have a specific disability that makes certain skills more difficult.
- **Motivational:** You may not want a job with more responsibility or more time away from home.

Step 7. Costs and benefits to you

There are benefits and downsides to many of your choices. It is important to weigh these up. Cost and benefits are not just 'hard', external rewards or costs; there are also emotional benefits and costs.

What would the benefit and cost be to you in rising to these bigger challenges? List them as we have illustrated in Table 10.2.

Table 10.2   Benefits and costs of challenges

Hard Benefit	Cost	Emotional Benefit	Cost
e.g. Raised salary	e.g. Longer hours	e.g. Fulfilled	e.g. Confusion and anxiety

Example

The shift from sole trader to limited company was one of those bigger challenges for us, especially as we had never set up a company, only been employed by them.

Some of the specific challenges were as follows:

- *Having to get into a lot of detail to start with.*
- *Harmonising processes.*
- *Having to get more efficient.*

- *Getting into legal work.*
- *Creating clearer procedures.*

We had to ask did we really want:

- *The extra hours.*
- *The extra burden.*
- *The extra responsibility.*
- *The extra effort.*

A Final Example

At 37 years of age Jane was asked by her divisional manager to come back to him with a medium-term career plan. She was reluctant to do so. As she faced the 'Bigger and Bigger Challenge' Challenge she noted that the job she currently did was one she felt comfortable in and equipped to do. Any future job she would want would be 'more of the same'; however, on looking a little further at this challenge she also realised that she was safe doing what she knew how to do, that if she entered into new areas of learning or new contexts of work she might not succeed and if she didn't succeed then the organisation would get rid of her. Better to stay where she was. Facing the 'Bigger and Bigger Challenge' Challenge meant exploring new possibilities and creating a strategy to set her up to succeed with all of the support necessary.

The Final Question . . . What are you going to do now?
(See Appendix 1 for further development)

11

The
Vertigo Challenge
Moving on from being stuck

A. Understanding this Challenge

A Working Definition

- 'I thought this was as far as I could go but I realise I've hit a ceiling made of glass.'
- 'I'm fearful of what the future holds in my job. I'm not sure how much further I can go.'
- 'This is as high as I want to go.'
- 'I've reached a stage where I'm scared to go upwards in this organisation and scared of the consequences of saying I won't.'
- 'Isn't the Peter Principle where you get promoted to the level of your incompetence?'

Leaders can reach a place in their careers where they are too scared and often feel ill equipped to go up but are also too scared and embarrassed to go down. The idea of 'leadership vertigo' was introduced to us by a chief executive of a City company that produces crucial software for leading banks around the world. What he meant by that expression was the feeling you get with vertigo – you freeze, you can't go up, down or on, so you just hang on for grim death. A paralysis in your career.

At the heart of vertigo is fear. In business terms it may be the fear of not being up to the next challenge, fear of getting the next decision wrong and undoing all of the progress your career has made up to this point. Fear of over-extending or under-extending yourself and making the fatal blunder that will see you facing redundancy, early retirement or the humiliation of a sideways move. Fear of the effects of moving upwards or downwards on your health, income or personal and family life.

Senior managers we have worked with cope in different ways. Some mark time until they receive their pension, others avoid risky decisions or let their companies lose their share in a competitive market by failing to make the crucial changes necessary rather than be exposed as incompetent because at heart they knew they were out of their depth. Some get quietly depressed and just cling to survival or look for early retirement with the same terror of someone with vertigo on the mountaintop.

A CEO's Story

I had a successful and adequate career as a senior manager in invest-ment banking which took me up to my late forties. Around this time the bank was taken over by a larger concern and in the turmoil a lot of us were head-hunted for other jobs. It was a time when the market was buoyant. I accepted a job as a CEO in an IT company that was just one company in a larger group. I wanted to make my mark and make this business a success. To start with the hard work was fun and we seemed to be making progress but then we failed to seal a crucial sale and it obviously affected cash flow. Fun became stress. We were now fighting to break gravity pull since it was proving a lot harder to make our sales targets than any of us realised. I worked more hours to just stand still and try to keep us floating but we reached a point where redundancies had to be made.

The internal battle was awful and I couldn't share it with anyone. I was the boss, I had to come to work with a smile and with vision and energy and belief that we were going to make this business work. People were relying on me. But on the inside I was eating myself up with anxiety and self-doubt. I kept feeling like I was out of my depth, that I just lacked the experience. The feeling was just like vertigo. I got to the place where I was too scared and lacked confidence to go forward, but it was too high a price to my ego to admit I needed to step down. I was stuck.

Eventually my body made my excuses for me. I started developing physical symptoms and went off sick. While I was off sick the group closed the company and I was given minimal pay-off. To have admitted to myself the vertigo challenge earlier was essential, but, to be honest, to do that I would have had to face a lot of internal questions about myself, what my life had been about up to that point, whether I was up to that level job, questions about my career and how much I was driven by making money. These are big issues to own up to voluntarily.

An example of a vertigo scenario is shown in Figure 11.1.

Figure 11.1   A vertigo scenario

In the introductory chapter of this book we highlighted the inner theatre or inner game (what is going on inside of you) and the outer theatre or outer game (what is going on in your behaviour or around you that is observable). The Vertigo Challenge is very much an 'inner game' challenge. It involves an honest confrontation with yourself. Some of the internal symptoms of the Vertigo Challenge are:

Fear	Uncertainty
Staleness	Anxiety
Constriction	Feeling squeezed
Concern	Malaise
Unease	Dissonance

The implication of having these feelings going on in your 'inner game' is that you will not think situations through. Its power is in holding you in an irrational, un-thought-through place where you feel you are trapped, up against the wall or a ceiling (real or glass), with no choice.

The Vertigo Challenge is easy to spot when someone has got 'stuck', paralysed or goes off sick but it is less easy to spot when it is developing or emerging. In the 'development' section of this chapter you will be shown how to plot the process of vertigo developing and then how to work with it in yourself and others.

B. Personal Reflection

What is your definition of the Vertigo Challenge?

Self-assessment of the Vertigo Challenge

Read through all of the questions below and reflect on your work recently. Next, rate yourself in the box below on a scale of 1 to 10, where 1 = feel stuck at this stage of your career and 10 = feel that you are moving freely through your career and able to make the choices that you wish to make.

- Do you feel like you are marking time until retirement or a better offer comes along?
- Are you living with the fear of being found out or seen as incompetent in your current role?
- Have you got stuck or stagnated at a particular level in the organisation?
- Do you feel you can, are able to, are clever enough to or are skilled enough to, progress in your career?
- Do you feel like you've been promoted to your level of incompetence?
- Do you feel like you are up against a glass ceiling in the organisation or in your career?
- Would you like a less stressful/pressured/responsible role but dare not tell anyone?
- Do you believe you can achieve a lot more than you are currently doing but another part of you is too scared to try?
- Does your career feel like it's in a state of inertia?

So where are you on the scale?

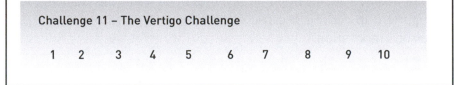

Challenge 11 – The Vertigo Challenge

| 1 | 2 | 3 | 4 | 5 | 6 | 7 | 8 | 9 | 10 |

C. Developing Movement throughout your Career Path

Spotting the Vertigo Challenge

In trying to spot where you might be facing the Vertigo Challenge the key thing to look out for are the '*shifts*'. These 'shifts' are periods of change or transition in either your work or private life or both.

Shifts occur when you move from one role to another, one job to another, one set of demands to another, one project to another, one team to another. On a personal level it may be children's life stages, periods of ill health (physical or emotional), divorce or similar relationship crises. Other shifts may be:

- Shifts from competence to perceived incompetence.
- Shifts from confidence to feeling less confident.
- Shifts from high-energy, potential, fully functioning self to low-energy, stuck, loss of self.

Understanding the Vertigo Process

This challenge (see Figure 11.2) starts by affecting someone internally (inner theatre) and then affects a person's outward performance (outer theatre). They begin by being actively engaged in their work, then for various reasons they start slowing down in their output or performance. Energy that was invested in the external tasks is now being withdrawn to handle the feelings going on inside of that person. In its extreme state the energy is largely focused internally in order to cope and in very extreme cases people seize up emotionally, mentally or physically. In general terms this challenge is important to address because of its effects on performance and a person's motivation.

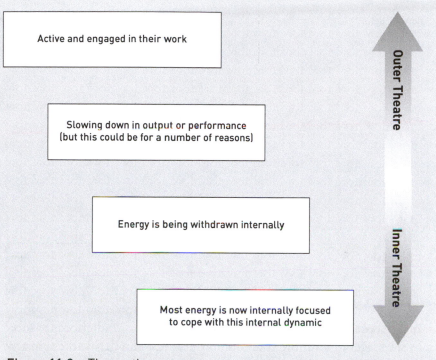

Figure 11.2 The vertigo process

Reflect on your career history

To begin the process of addressing where you are with this challenge we suggest that you reflect on your own career history. One way of doing this is by drawing a graph (see Figure 11.3) of your career history with upward arrows to denote times when you felt your career was advancing, downward arrows for when it was seemingly moving backwards and horizontal arrows for when it was in inertia.

Figure 11.3   Graph of your career history

A different way of reviewing yourself against this challenge is to look at the stages of your life (see Table 11.1). (You can define these in any number of ways you want.) Name them in terms of age and characteristics of what you were doing that made it a motivating or demotivating stage. What main emotions accompanied these life stages?

Table 11.1   Identifying the impact of stages of your life

Stage	Age	Characteristics	Motivating or Demotivating	Emotions

How will you know when you have reached your highest level within an organisation? First, define where you are now.

Defining the Challenge You Face

The next stage of working through the Vertigo Challenge is for you to define the particular challenge that you face. Here are two examples.

Example A

Sue is a consultant with a medium-sized consultancy firm. She almost exclusively does one-to-one work and rarely does training courses. She is only ever involved in training when she is supporting someone else, but never on her own. Whereas for many years it was easy to avoid training courses it has now become impossible to do this. Her fear of running these courses is in the way of her enjoying or developing further in her job. She is convinced that she needs to run courses to further her personal development, but fears failing. She knows the only way to gain confidence is to do them. She is stuck.

Example B

Eric is an area manager for a housing association. He is in a management team that, while friendly, is also stifling of creativity and initiatives. For the first few years in this role Eric felt like he was on a steep learning curve. It was scary but he knew he was developing priceless skills. Over the following years with the stifling of numerous projects he felt his enthusiasm waning. One part of him was desperate to leave the organisation and set up on his own but another part of him felt safe and comfortable and didn't want to jeopardise a good salary.

What is your story?

A Process

If you could self-coach yourself through this challenge then a process that might be helpful to follow is outlined in the following seven steps.

Step 1. Admit

Admitting to yourself or another person that there is an issue is a crucial piece of insight that will give leverage to change.

To yourself
- You feel stuck.
- You feel like you've hit a ceiling.
- You feel paralysed. You don't want to take the promotion but you fear for your job if you don't.
- You can see what you should be doing to lead the team/organisation but you just seem to avoid doing it.

To another
- Who can you talk to?
- Who has the influence?
- Who can do something for you?
- Who will do something for you?
- Who wants to do something for you?

What does it take to admit to vertigo? First, it takes *insight*. Insight that admits to yourself:

- Everything is not comfortable.
- Something more, something missing, some unease.
- Potential, performance and internal resourcefulness are shrinking or constricting.

Second it takes *courage*. There are often issues around your personal success, other ego issues or personal identity to confront.

Step 2. Explore

Think through your situation to gain a deeper and clearer understanding. A few questions you may want to ask yourself are:

- When do you feel this? (For example, always, sometimes?)

- Where?
- What is the source of the feeling?

Step 3. Need for a bigger 'yes'

The paralysis caused by vertigo can only eventually be broken by movement. This may be movement up or movement down or a liberated choice to stay where you are (as opposed to feeling defeated or trapped or paralysed).

What determines which way forward? Someone once said that the only way you could say 'no' to some repeating, self-defeating pattern is to have a bigger 'yes' for something else. For example, you may only say 'no' to working longer hours at work if your bigger 'yes' is to invest in your family. A bigger 'yes' is therefore something that you want *more than* the thing you currently choose.

Completing the Internal Compass Challenge will help you to be clear about your bigger 'yes'.

Step 4. Distraction

If vertigo is overtaking you then you can't help yourself. It needs supportive, involved management at this point. Ideally the manager will possess strong interpersonal skills, experience and wisdom, and can create a parallel path with you, the vertigo sufferer, for a while and be able to provide support and the expertise to create some tangible plan of action. While all of the challenges of leadership benefit greatly by having someone else involved in the development process, the Vertigo Challenge is one that definitely needs someone else involved. Why is this? If you have vertigo you need to be distracted for long enough to let go of the inner focus you are locked in to. Having vertigo is like holding your breath. You will need someone to help you to erect 'scaffolding' so that you can move up or down – because movement is the key to getting over the vertigo. Distraction is the first movement you, as a vertigo sufferer, must make to break the vertigo. This is an inner game movement that may not be seen in outward behaviour. You will need to be distracted long enough to reconnect to your bigger 'yes', or your internal compass.

One of the questions you may be stuck on is whether you are a failure if you admit you can't do something. You will need distracting from the fear long enough to reconnect with deeper questions around what is important to you in your bigger game plan for your life. Only when you reconnect will you either:

- Release the new potential that has been tied up until now so that you can make a plan to keep moving forward. Or:
- Redefine yourself confidently so that to step down, or sideways, or maintain your current position is felt to be a positive choice.

Ask yourself:

- What are the benefits of keeping going or continuing as you are?
- What are the risks of keeping going or continuing as you are?
- What are the benefits of stepping down?
- What are the risks of stepping down?

Step 5. Choice is the key

You have a choice. When you don't feel you have a choice then it is evidence of the paralysis of vertigo.

Recovering or discovering choice is crucial to getting some movement.

Ask yourself what choices you currently have. (However small or undesirable they may seem right now it is important to name the choices and to see that they are real choices.)

Step 6. Baby steps

Once there is an internal shift it is important to create small, baby-sized steps in the chosen direction. Small steps generally carry less risk and are a safe way to regain confidence and to rediscover what you know. Confidence in what you already know and lays the foundation for taking further steps into less known areas.

So, what needs doing?

Step 7. Redefine yourself

> Our deepest fear is not that we are inadequate. Our deepest fear is that we are powerful beyond measure. It is our light, not our darkness, that most frightens us. We ask ourselves, who am I to be brilliant, gorgeous, talented and fabulous? Actually, who are you NOT to be? You are a child of God. Your playing small doesn't serve the world. There's nothing enlightened about shrinking so that other people won't feel insecure around you. We were born to make manifest the glory of God that is within us. It's not just in some of us; it's in EVERYONE! And as we let our own light shine, we unconsciously give other people permission to do the same. As we are liberated from our fear, our pretence automatically liberates others! (Nelson Mandela's inaugural speech, 1994 – adapted from American writer Marianne Williamson)

There is a personal cost to the Vertigo Challenge. Everyone carries an image of themselves.

- It may be of a successful team leader or a chief executive or a world-class leader . . . and you may achieve this.
- It may be of a successful team leader or a chief executive or a world-class leader . . . and you may get nowhere near achieving this.
- You may see yourself as an 'average' manager and become an influential leader.
- You may see yourself as an 'average' manager and not competently run your team.

The point is that you may hold an image of yourself that may be accurate, or that may be unrealistically high or unrealistically low. The personal cost of the Vertigo Challenge is the readjustment you have to make to how you see yourself. It may be embarrassing; it may be humbling to have to readjust your image of yourself. There is comfort and security in your identity whether it be unrealistically high or low.

Here are some questions that may help you to reflect on how you see yourself.

- How have you always seen yourself?
- What is your optimum role at work?
- How do you know whether that is realistic or unrealistic?
- What would you feel if it were too high an image of yourself?
- What would you feel if it were too low an image of yourself?

Example

Mike had lived his life feeling that he was always a great number two, but was not able to be a confident number one – a good lieutenant to his area manager but never having the potential to be the manager himself. It was an encroaching depression that caused him to reassess his view of himself and to ask why he had written himself off.

Two Key Issues

Two further issues that are very important to think through are whether the organisation's agenda for you is the same as your agenda for yourself and how you assess your potential.

The Organisation's agenda v. your agenda

In succession planning the organisation has an agenda for you that is both an invitation and an expectation. They have assessed your current performance and their perception of your potential and decided that you are someone that they want to invest in for a future senior leadership role. Some organisations tell their employees whether they are on the succession planning list and some organisations keep it secret. If you are on the list, do you want to be? If you knew you were on the list would it make a difference to how you perform? If you don't want to be on the list will that affect how the organisation views you?

Do you feel the organisation's view of your performance and potential is:

- The same?
- Different?
- If different – why?

Potential

Crucial to the Vertigo Challenge is the issue of potential. It is also one of the key issues in organisations today. It affects appraisals, performance management and succession planning. How much potential does a person have? Someone may display excellent leadership skills over six people but seem to be out of their depth leading fifty people. Some people lead organisations of a hundred effectively but would not be able to lead organisations of five thousand. Some people have great potential in their work but choose to 'cap' this potential so that they can invest in other aspects of their life. Working mothers have always fought a battle between what they could do at work and their other priorities at home. The notion of a career break is acceptable in some companies for high performers who want to travel or have children. Whether we believe that potential is limitless and only hindered by interference (internal or external) we are convinced that people have a lot more potential than they believe themselves to have but that they put a glass ceiling in their minds as a limit to their potential.

Think these questions through for yourself (involve someone in a discussion if it helps you).

- How much potential does a person have?
- How do you assess potential?
- How do you rate your own potential?
- If you were to place a percentage rating on how much of your potential has been realised what would it be?
- What gets in the way of people's potential?
- What gets in the way of your potential?

Other factors from the 18 Challenges that will influence potential:

- The 'Bigger and Bigger Challenge' Challenge. (Your skills may have not kept pace with your responsibility.)
- The 'Life and Career Transition' Challenge. (Life stage can have an effect.)
- The Work–Life Balance Challenge. (You may be so focused on what you produce that you neglect the emotional, mental, physical or spiritual health that resources your ability to produce.)
- The Confidence Challenge. (Potential counts for little when confidence is low.)
- The Internal Compass Challenge. (Not having a bigger 'yes'.)

Leading Others through the Vertigo Challenge

It is worth spelling out what you need to do if you are in the position to help some of your staff through the Vertigo Challenge. What does this look like in a step-by-step process? Much of the process reflects those steps you have already looked at.

Step 1. Come alongside

Sometimes people keep their distance from those who seem to be struggling. One reason you may find yourself keeping your distance is a feeling of inadequacy in coping with another person's difficult emotions, in much the same way that people avoid those who are bereaved because they don't know what to say. Another reason for not coming alongside someone in the Vertigo Challenge is that you may be unable to separate your role as 'performance manager' from your role as 'coach' or 'support'.

Step 2. Empathy

Empathy is allowing yourself to acknowledge and sit with someone else's emotion without trying to cure, fix or convert them.

'I know just what you mean' is not an empathetic response; 'it sounds like you are a little fearful that you may be stuck in your career' is more likely to be empathetic. Empathy creates a space to allow people to acknowledge what they are feeling and not to be constrained to feel a certain way.

Step 3. Distract

One of the keys to dealing with resistance is not to Push (see the Influence Challenge) against it, as is often our instinct. Pushing against resistance creates further resistance. To distract someone is to get them to look at some other issue or some other area of the problem rather than the area they are fixed on.

Step 4. Not demanding they make a significant shift immediately in performance or decisions

Demanding immediate and significant change can create further anxiety and become a blockage to movement. Baby steps in the right direction are more important.

Step 5. Find concrete actions to point them in a safe direction

Specific, concrete actions are better psychological anchors than vague ideas, hopes or aspirations. People need something tangible to focus on and this gives them an easier way to encourage themselves when they see tangible results.

Step 6. Create a plan consisting of 'baby steps' in order to create some momentum

What are the baby steps the other person needs to take? Get them to take a pad of sticky 'Post-its' and write out all of the steps that they need to take to get from where they are to where they want to be. Put one action on each Post-it. Get them to put the Post-its in a chronological order of actions so that they end up with a rough plan.

Step 7. Plan slightly larger steps

When momentum is being achieved through taking a series of small, easier steps you can increase the size or challenge of the step. It is important not to do this too early because lack of success will have a demotivating effect on the person you are helping.

Step 8. When energy is returning into their outer game begin a supportive process of review for the longer term

When someone's performance is getting back on track, only then is the time to look ahead to longer-term performance goals.

The Final Question . . . What are you going to do now?
(See Appendix 1 for further development)

12

The
'Managing the Tension' Challenge
The art of delegation

A. Understanding this Challenge

As a leader you can't do it all on your own. This is an obvious statement. Even if you are tempted to or, worse still, think you can, the reality of your limited time and resources makes it impossible. Leadership is about bringing others into the vision. The challenge that follows is about releasing control and responsibility to others. Some leaders just can't let go and are suffocating the organisation or their team. Others just let go (give over all of the responsibility) and let people get on with the job and jeopardise the business. At the core of leadership is the discovery and vocalising of vision, values and strategy – whether within the organisation or in your own life. This is central to achieving success, or the future you are aiming at. But, in expanding organisations, as the numbers of people grow, the challenge is how to allow an increasing number of people more control and responsibility, while at the same time steering a dedicated path towards the vision and still living the values.

Do you let go? Do you hold on? Effective leadership recognises that this is not an either-or dilemma. The reality is that it is a tension that needs managing rather than something that can be resolved. This tension is played out internally within the leader as they struggle with their own desire to hold fast to 'their baby', their brainchild, the founding vision and values of their team and organisation. It is a struggle with the desire to hold on to the enjoyment of their abilities that have brought the team/organisation this far, a struggle heightened by the fact that no one does it better than they do given the finite time and emotional resources they have. The main external area where this challenge is played out within the organisation is in the area of delegation versus control, empowerment or disempowerment. Empowering others means letting go, but letting go involves the risk of losing focus, direction or performance. You may hear of leaders who are control freaks, through whom all decisions have to be ratified, who will not let go of any decisions, will not delegate any responsibility and want their fingers in all the pies. On the other hand, you may have experience of those who let go and delegate in a way that almost appears to be abandonment or disinterest.

If you track the rise and fall of organisations there is one key transition that gets little attention but the impact of which can at best stifle and at worst undermine an organisation. It is the transition from the entrepreneurial style of leadership that invents, creates, launches and pioneers a new organisation, process or system to the need to create a leadership team who can consolidate what has been achieved and then capitalise on that development. The usual solutions seem to focus on either telling these founding leaders to 'let go' or steeling them to 'hold on'. Little attention is given to the fact that actually there is a genuine tension between 'holding on' and 'letting go'. How does the founding CEO let go of authority, responsibility and power while ensuring that the energy and commitment to quality and innovation, processes and values are maintained and not watered down by the 'inheritors' of the entrepreneur's hard work?

A few of the challenges for the leader in managing this tension are:

■ Creating a strategic view that honours the past while planning for the future.
■ The emotional shift of power from 'your baby' to 'our baby'.
■ The loss of role and identity for the entrepreneurs.
■ Allowing the goal to remain the same while the style and appearance of leadership may change.
■ How people influence one another during key transitions.
■ The process of creating 'enhanced' rather than 'impaired' working teams.
■ Dealing with leadership vacuums and the emergence of secondary or competitive leaders and power bases.
■ Setting clear objectives that allow personal style differences to emerge.
■ Developing a high-trust culture in the leadership team.
■ Retaining buy-in and keeping everyone on board with the changes.

This is not a one-off challenge. You are likely to face it at a number of points in the evolution of your leadership role, particularly in growing or changing organisations. The painful analogy of boiling a frog by putting it into cold water and gently raising the temperature slowly comes to mind. The danger is that as your role develops or the organisation changes or grows you will add and add and add new responsibilities into your role and you will not face the impossibility of your task until the wheels come off in the form of illness or serious mistakes.

B. Personal Reflection

What does this challenge mean to you in your own language?

Self-assessment of the 'Managing the Tension Between Holding On and Letting Go' Challenge

Read through all of the questions below and reflect on your work recently. Rate yourself in the box below on a scale of 1 to 10, where 1 = I feel very ineffective at managing the tension between holding on and letting go and 10 = I feel very effective at managing the tension between holding on and letting go.

- Do you feel you are good at delegating tasks and responsibilities?
- Have you been given specific feedback that you are good at delegating tasks and responsibilities?
- Do you feel that you give away strategic responsibilities too quickly and people don't maintain the level of focus and commitment that you expected of them?
- Do you find yourself having to rescue or take the helm of projects that you had delegated?
- Do you hold on to power, control and responsibility too long so that people become too dependent on you?
- Do you feel that however long you stay in your role people don't seem to take on responsibility for themselves?
- Are you good at holding on to strategic vision, goals and responsibilities while at the same time helping your team to become proactive, responsible and creative in delivering their objectives?
- Do people call you a control freak?
- Have you created a strategic view which both honours the past and allows planning for the future?
- Have you facilitated a shift from the task/project/organisation being 'your baby' to being 'our baby'?

■ Is your personal sense of identity and role diminished by letting others take greater responsibilities and increased profiles in the organisation?

So where are you on the scale?

Challenge 12 – The 'Managing the Tension Between Holding On and Letting Go' Challenge

1   2   3   4   5   6   7   8   9   10

C. Developing the Ability to Manage the Tension between Holding On and Letting Go

The focus of this section will be on two areas of development. One area is to learn to manage this tension within yourself and the other is to learn to manage it externally through your management of others' performance.

Managing the Tension within Yourself

Creating a bigger 'yes' – a strategic approach

It has been said that the only way people can say 'no' to outdated priorities is to have something to which they attach a deeper sense of importance. In other words, you need a bigger 'yes' in order to say 'no'. For example, if you are to say 'no' to requests to solve everyday operational problems because that's what you have always done and what has always been expected, then you need to have something that you truly believe is more important than solving these problems. You need to have a conviction that your role is, say, strategic planning, and that if you say 'yes' to solving today's operational problem then you are saying 'no' to strategic planning. The bigger 'yes' is the conviction that if you are not doing strategic planning, then who is? Your bigger 'yes' is to make sure the organisation is facing in the right direction six months from now, while others deal with today's crisis.

So, what do you need to get a bigger 'yes'? First, you need to get clear about the following.

- Get clear on vision. (See the Vision Challenge.)
- Get clear on values. (See the Vision, Strategy and Internal Compass Challenges.)
- Get clear on strategic goals. (See the Strategy Challenge.)

Second, you need to create the picture of the future organisation. Michael Gerber in his book *The E Myth* (1986) encourages leaders and entrepreneurs to create a picture or organisational chart of what a mature, functioning team or organisation will look like. One way of doing this is to imagine creating a franchise of your team or organisation. Just as McDonald's, the hamburger chain, has everything down to a reproducible system, then what would the reproducible structure and processes be for your team or organisation if it were fully functioning? If you were to franchise your organisation or team what would the organisational template be? (See Figure 12.1.)

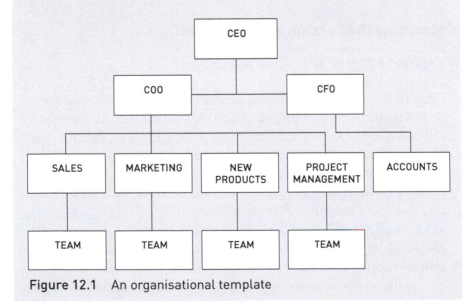

Figure 12.1   An organisational template

When you have mapped out the ideal future picture then place yourself within it as it is now (see Figure 12.2). To start with you will probably have more roles than you want to admit! That's quite normal.

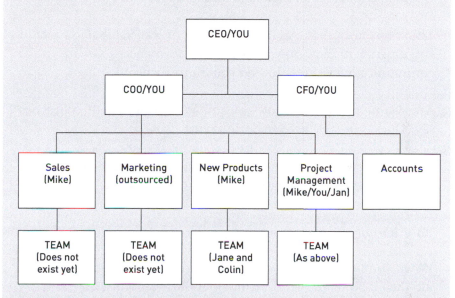

Figure 12.2 Current reality template

When you have a picture of the future and a picture of current reality overlaid onto it the next step will be look at the next 6–12 months. Ask yourself these questions:

- Who needs to fill the roles?
- How will you ensure that they are as clear and convinced (hearts and minds) about the vision, values and strategy as you are?
- What key performance goals will they need to have?
- How will you set performance goals for them?
- How will their performance be managed?
- What is stopping you from making the move? (Identify internal barriers to change.)

Make a note of the actions you need to take. You will need to bear these in mind when action planning for this challenge.

Assessing Your Current Approach

Leadership's First Commandment: 'Know Thyself'. (Harris Collingwood, editor, *Harvard Business Review*.)

Think seriously about your current style of leadership. How would you describe it? How do you manage performance? How are you at communicating vision? How do you motivate people?

Are you high-control or low-control? What would your colleagues say? Does your style need to be different?

Some other areas of self-awareness that have a bearing on this challenge are the following.

Your identity now

When you heavily invest your identity in particular aspects of your job then it becomes very difficult to let those aspects go.

How do you derive a sense of identity in your job?

Example A

Rob, an MD of a manufacturing company, was naturally very operational and loved solving problems. This is how he derived his sense of recognition within his role.

Example B

Hannah, a team leader in an insurance company, saw herself as the person everyone likes and would tell their problems to.

The supreme challenge for a leader is to change human behaviour, a formidable, if not impossible task. But the leader who is emotionally intelligent, who is aware of and comfortable with his own self, will have a far greater chance of changing the behaviour of others than a leader who is not aware of himself. Using the theories of the esteemed management thinker Peter Drucker, the author points out that the leaders who inspire are those who have resolved their own identity crisis. But that is much easier said than done, and the daunting nature of the task is encapsulated in Drucker's Challenge, which states that every human being has an emotional glass ceiling, a natural resistance to changing identity. (Abstract to Wieand, 2002)

Think about how your identity will need to change or how you will need to see yourself if you are to manage this tension between holding on and letting go differently.

Your use of time

If you are using 100% of available time on current tasks then there will never be any time free to invest in developing others to take over your tasks and free you up to do new ones. Take one simple aspect of performance management: helping people to become really clear about their objectives is an essential part of investing in high performance. If you don't have the time to help others become clear then even if you do devolve responsibility it may have a negative impact on their performance.

Your energy

How are your energy levels currently? If you are tired out then you will feel that it will take too much energy (that you don't feel you have) to change how you are doing things. When you are tired you often just cannot be bothered to shift out of unproductive working patterns.

Have you got the energy to step back, rethink your role and make the changes necessary to keep you and the organisation or team growing?

Your beliefs

How do you see people on your team? Do you see them as capable or not? If you got hit by a bus could they do the job without you? If the answer is 'no', then why not? If the answer is 'maybe', what else would they need for your answer to become 'yes'? If your answer is 'yes', what is stopping you from making some changes?

Your position

Do you feel secure in your position within the organisation? Some people hold on to responsibilities because if they delegated they may be viewed as not having enough to do. Do you feel that if you delegated some of your responsibilities people would regard you as surplus staff?

Trust

You will not delegate to people you don't trust.

- If your trust of others is too low to delegate, why is this?
- What would need to be different within you for you to trust them more? How would you need to be different?
- What would need to be different in them for you to trust them more? What differences do you feel you need to see in others? What can you do to influence this?
- If you don't feel that you have the right people then how do you get the right people?

Emotional cost

What is the emotional cost to you of letting go or of holding on?

Negotiating Within Yourself

To move from high control or low control to being able to recognise when to hold on and when to let go, you need to change within yourself. How could you conduct an internal negotiation with yourself to change? Figure 12.3 describes a process that you could coach yourself through.

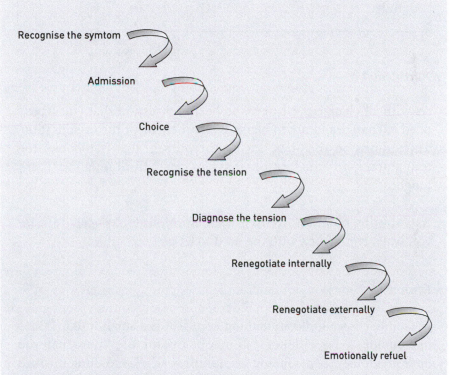

Figure 12.3 Negotiating within yourself

Recognise the symptom

How would you recognise the symptoms of too much control or too little control within yourself and within your organisation? Use Table 12.1.

Table 12.1   Recognising the symptoms of control

	Within yourself	**Within the organisation**
Too much control		
Too little control		

Admission

As with all change there needs to be an admission that you have a need to change and not to blame it all on 'them' or the organisation. This admission might be saying to yourself 'this is too big; too tough; too hard' or admitting that you can't afford to ignore it any longer.

As a starting point ask yourself what emotions are triggered off for you when confronted with the need to let go.

Choice

Make the choice to do something even if it is a small thing. Taking five minutes a day with key staff may be five minutes more than you have previously spent. Taking ten minutes each day to think through what your leadership priorities are and what tasks need to be delegated may be ten minutes more than you normally spend.

To reinforce the choices ask yourself, 'What is the concrete evidence that you have made a choice to make some changes?'

Recognise the tension

The key to this leadership challenge is to recognise that holding on or letting go is not an either-or but a tension that needs managing.

Thus the key to your development will be recognising the tension. To do this, ask yourself these questions:

1. Externally
   - What do you need to hold on to?
   - Why?
   - What are the benefits of your holding on to this?
   - What are the dangers of your holding on to this?
2. Internally
   - Where do you feel the tension? For example, in your head, in your body?

Diagnose the tension

Having spotted the tension you need to understand it or diagnose what this tension means for you. What kind of issue is it? Is it a letting-go issue? Is it a holding-on issue? Exactly what are you letting go?

What is the issue around?

- Responsibility.
- Power.
- Authority.
- Values.
- Vision.
- Strategy.
- Ego.
- Tasks.
- Visibility.
- Ear to the ground.
- 'You're a nice, friendly person.'
- 'You're the cool, calm, distant person.'
- 'You're the tough, rough person.'
- 'You're the problem solver.'
- Recognition.
- Satisfaction.
- Something else.

Who or what is the issue with? In what situations does it arise?

Renegotiate internally

Describe a picture of yourself in this new role. What will you be doing, saying, feeling? How will you organise your time and priorities? Who will you be managing? How will you make decisions? Which decisions will you make and which will you not make?

Renegotiate externally

What needs to change in your behaviour and in how you organise yourself, your time, your office, your team? What is your strategy for moving towards this new role or reshaped job? Who needs to be clear about the impact of these changes on their role? Who needs to be kept informed of the changes?

Emotionally refuel

It is easy to underestimate how draining these shifts are to make. That is why it's easier just to continue to control or abdicate responsibility. So, if you are responding well to the changes needed to be effective in this challenge, what are you doing to refuel emotionally? What structures are you putting in place to support the changes? What structures are you putting in place to support you?

Managing the Tension through Performance Management

Having looked at what needs to change inside of yourself to respond to this challenge let's now turn to the more external side of the challenge. If you are to lead effectively it will be through others. As you turn your attention to your leadership priorities the work still needs to be done. In this section we will take you through a basic process for delegation and managing performance.

As you look through these steps it is quite possible that you will think you don't have time for all this stuff, that you pay people just to get on with it. If you have these concerns consider the following two questions.

1. What value do you add to the organisation?
2. What value do you add to your staff?

The important point here is that in leadership you have key tasks to focus on, i.e. vision setting, strategy, aligning your bit of the organisation with the whole, achieving key objectives. You also have to achieve this through others. Investing in others is a key leadership task. Having the time to invest in your people's performance is a leadership issue, not a distraction from it.

Step 1. Who you are

The key to this challenge will always be who you are before what you do. To explore this in more depth revisit the Internal Compass Challenge.

> Once an organization understands that who a leader is as a person speaks more powerfully than what he or she says, the connection between identity and communication becomes clear . . . a truly authentic leader knows that his or her identity is based on values, not emotions. (Wieand, 2002)

Step 2. The shared vision you create

All delegation or holding on relies on the shared vision of the leader and the team. A leader's tacit vision isn't enough, it needs to be communicated with and shared by the team. (See the Vision Challenge.)

Step 3. The clarity of the high-level goals you set

Out of the vision fall the agreed strategic goals, the high-level areas that you must all focus on if the vision is to be realised.

Step 4. The clarity of the individual goals you set

Once the team's or organisation's vision and strategy are shared you have a foundation from which to manage people effectively; without it people management falls into the realms of instinct and *ad hoc*. The key investment with individual delegation is to get people really clear about their own goals. A lot of goals that we see in individual appraisals are very generic and too broad to produce high perform-ance. Excellent goals are those that are clear, agreed and expressed in language that is understood and meaningful to the individual they are intended for.

Step 5. The clarity of outcomes, measures and milestones

Once the goals are very clear then the next step is to agree what each goal will look like when it is achieved, how you will recognise success when you see it, how it will be measured and what the key milestones are along the route that will ensure that you will achieve success in the timescales agreed. At the risk of overstating the point, the role of the leader in performance management is first to get their staff really, really clear. The purpose of clarity is twofold. First, clarity creates focus and people can marshal their own energy and creativity to pursue a goal. Second, if you are confident that someone is very clear about goals, outcomes, measures and milestones then you have the basis for confidently letting go and allowing them to get on with it.

Step 6. The clarity of what style of management each person requires

The next key to good performance management is to agree what kind of support a person needs. For a fast and effective lesson in this it is worth reading Blanchard et al., *Leadership and the One*

Minute Manager (1987). In this book they talk about the need to agree with each person, whether you will be using a 'tell' style, a mentoring style, a coaching style or a more delegational style of leadership with them, and specifically which goals you will be using which style with. For instance, there may be some things you can let a person get on and do because they have a high degree of experience and a strong track record in a particular area, but in other areas they may need some hands-on help and direction, a more 'tell' style of management. If you agree up-front which style you will be using with your individual staff then they will not feel abandoned when you are letting them get on with the job or smothered when you are coming alongside to give them specific instructions.

Step 7. The clarity of people's development needs

Do an analysis of each member of your team, board or direct reports. Ask yourself this question. If you got hit by a number 13 bus which of your tasks could each person do right now without your help? Then ask which tasks they could do with some support from you. Then ask yourself which tasks they could potentially do, given some training. Finally, ask yourself which tasks each individual could never do. If they can already do certain tasks why aren't you letting them? If they can do them with training input then set out a plan to get them the training.

The Final Question . . . What are you going to do now?
(See Appendix 1 for further development)

13

The
'Life and Career Transition' Challenge
Change across the whole lifespan

A. Understanding this Challenge

Transitions In Life

> Midway in life's journey I found myself in a dark wood, having lost the way. (Dante Alighieri, *The Inferno*)

One of the gaps in most approaches to leadership development is treating people as static beings, assuming that people will be the same at 52 as they were at 22. The key behind this challenge to leadership is the recognition that people change as they grow and develop. In some fundamental respects we would say that people are the same person at 30 as they were at 20, and the same person at 40 that they were at 30 and so on; however, people change in many respects over the decades. Research and experience have identified a number of changes and transitions across the career and lifespan.

Daniel Levinson, Professor of Psychology at Yale and previously Harvard, outlined some key transitions from his research. They are as follows:

Early adult transition: consolidating your identity as an adult, moving into the world of work, creating a social context more among adults than adolescents, making initial choices in love, peer relationships, values and life style, exploring possibilities and keeping options open.

Age 30 transition: if you are to change your life – if there are things you want to do, or modify or exclude – you must start now or it will be too late; women become more aware of the biological clock ticking and the choices this forces them to make between career and family. If the structures a person chooses at this stage don't match the 'grain' of their personality, emotional development, aptitudes and abilities then a crisis of some kind may occur.

Mid-life transition: becoming the person who you are meant to be is important. Up until this point there has been practice, experimenting, being a novice adult – but now there is a sense of the finiteness of time. Are you doing what you want to do? Are you making it? Are you where you want to be? What have you done with your life? What do you really get from and give to your wife, children, friends, work and community? Some people emerge from this period with a new or renewed vision and focus for the coming years and some emerge disheartened, discouraged and resigned to the future.

Age 50 transition: a time of modifying the decisions and choices made in the mid-life or a potential time of crisis where this work has not been done.

Late adulthood transition: preparing for and settling into the challenges of a life with less or no formal work or limitations and new possibilities. (Daniel J. Levinson, *The Seasons of a Man's Life*, 1978).

Implications for Work Life

The issue for your work life is that these transitions happen within you but also while you continue to do your job. One of the life transitions that has had most publicity is the mid-life transition and in particular the mid-life/mid-career transition. Mid-life often coincides with mid-career. Leadership is at its most demanding at the same stage of life as when the ignored parts of yourself are demanding some long overdue attention.

Mid-life is part of a continuous series of transitions spanning from the mid-thirties to the early fifties. The issues of mid-life and mid-career are both personal and professional. Personal, in that some key gearshifts in personal development take place during this period of life. Professional, as expressed by one director who told us that 'if you haven't got your top job by 40, then it won't happen', or by a Chief Executive lamenting over a glass of wine that at 55 most of his peers in the City of London are taking their pensions and getting out. Suddenly that thing called 'work' which has sapped the life out of you for thirty-five years is ending and you are left wondering what the next few years will bring, what have you actually achieved in the previous thirty-five years, was it worth it, at what cost and with what effect on the future or future vocation? A further example is of a sales manager who at 43 lamented to his boss 'the only time I'm in the house with my children is when they are asleep and I've had enough'.

Mid-life Crisis?

A life crisis usually only becomes a crisis when you don't take the work needed for the transition seriously.

We asked the CEO of a leading debit card company about this issue of mid-life and mid-career. From his forty years of experience he shared with us four different scenarios.

Scenario 1. Steady as you go

This is the type of person who is no high-flyer. They are often content with the regularity of their work: they do a good day's work, they are the salt of the earth. No business can manage without this type of person. They are not overly ambitious and they do not get great satisfaction from their work. It's a job that they do well. They do not like hassle or change and above all crave a quiet life. The steady-as-you-go person probably gets their main life satisfaction from their home, their family, their friendships, their hobbies or sport, or their faith. They use their career as a means to an end.

Scenario 2. Missed the boat

This type of person starts their working life with a focus on 'career' and with great ambitions. It is probable that they over-estimated their potential. Now they are in a management role but frustrated because they do not appear to be moving upwards very quickly. They do not enjoy their work. Sometimes they are bitter and anti-establishment. They are often a frustrated individual who could well be getting grief at home from a partner who is disappointed with their lack of progress. All in all, they are not happy souls. They may or may not have hobbies or relationships outside of work, and even these are often a source of discontent.

Scenario 3. Onward and upward

These people are doing OK. They are bright and recognised as such. They receive regular promotions. They can move from job to job with confidence. They've done well. They look to the future and it's bright. Maybe an early retirement beckons – they have earned it, they can afford it. They are often self-satisfied and possibly lost in their work. Home life is minimal – but they don't really care. They are providing generously for the family – so they shouldn't complain.

Scenario 4. The Chief Executive's own story

In my early twenties I was identified by the bank as a potential executive. I was placed in a wide variety of challenging jobs. Life was good and rewarding. The future looked good. However, my challenge was one that questioned the application of my faith in my work. My view of work changed to focus more on the wider 'mission' of being in the City. I still enjoyed my work, but by the age of 37, because I wasn't prepared to sell myself totally to the bank, I knew that I wouldn't reach the top. But I worked on the balance of work and vocational activity and have enjoyed contentment and reward. If I had undergone a review of my life at that stage, some twenty years ago, what changes, I wonder, would I have made?

These are the reflections of one Chief Executive. The purpose of The 18 Challenges of Leadership is to get leaders to think proactively about the scenario that they want to create. Do you want to keep going as you are? Are you aiming to survive? Are you aiming to maintain the status quo? Are you aiming to excel? What is the game you want to play out in the organisation you are part of?

Two things are certain. You are changing whether or not your career is developing. Alternatively, your career is developing but maybe personally you are not. Either you stagnate as a person or the job stagnates, or both. The possible scenarios are shown in Figure 13.1.

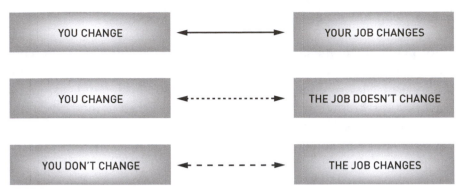

Figure 13.1   Creating a work–life scenario

Furthering Your Understanding

James Hollis in his excellent book *The Middle Passage – from Misery to Meaning in Midlife* (1993) outlines what is probably at the core of life and work transitions. He says in childhood people have a *real* identity and also create a '*provisional personality*' that learns to adapt and respond and shape itself around what is going on at home or in the surrounding relationships. The crisis comes when the inner reality of an individual personality (who you really are) does not match the external or adapted personality they have had to create (what you have had to become to get to this place in your career). This gets played out across the whole of life.

A Client's Story

I wanted to be a doctor at 16 years old. Why? Because I hadn't got a clue what I wanted to be, many of my family were involved in medicine in some shape and my elder brother was noted at my school for his excellence in the sciences. So I took science A-levels. About two months in I had a crisis – I realised with great pain that the subjects I was studying were not the ones I wanted to be studying, they were not a reflection of who I was. I wanted to be doing English, History and Art. I went to my tutors and told them what I was feeling and they said it was too late to change. I finished the courses and did badly – neither gaining the right grades to be a doctor nor a different set of subjects that better fitted who I believe I was. I took a college course that fitted with my exam results and it went on from there. From first job to late thirties I did a job where I always had a nagging sense of 'bad fit'. At the worst points I felt like 'I'm dying here, in this job'. Finally, around the age of 37 or 38 I made a radical shift and changed career. I couldn't have carried on doing what I was doing but it is only with the benefit of hindsight that I can see just how much I was only ever firing on three cylinders.

Many people just fall into the jobs they are in by a convergence of a whole host of factors. To start with this is usually fine but as you move through the key transition stages of life you have the opportunity to re-evaluate who you are and what job would be the best expression of this. If you ignore the signals of these transitions and don't develop at a personal level then the result can be a crisis *in the job* or *in yourself* or *both*. The famous mid-life crisis is often a mid-life transition that people ignored. Transitions in life or career, according to Hutcheson and McDonald in *The Lemming Conspiracy* (1997), are not usually a single point in time but usually spread out over one to three years. They signal periods of heightened awareness. Everyone faces transitions during their adult working lives: about one every seven to ten years; they don't even stop at retirement! There are about eight in all (see Table 13.1). At turning points the strands of people's lives tend to unravel slightly and they decide to weave them together again. In all transitions people make decisions that affect the course of the next seven to ten years of their lives for better or for worse. Hutcheson et al. say that during transitions people are aware that they have become less like their true selves. The life they have no longer expresses who they are and they become increasingly aware of that fact. At all turning points people will start looking for answers and trying to find something new.

Table 13.1   The eight turning points of adult life

Age 17–18	High school to college, first career decision.
Age 20–25	College to work. 'How do I get into the adult world?'
Age 28–33	Age 30 assessment. 'How far can I go?'
Age 38–45	Mid-life transition. 'OK, that was fun, now what?'
Age 50–55	Age 50 assessment. 'Is there a way to integrate my life?' 'How do I finish?'
Age 60–65	Pre-retirement transition. 'I'm not dead yet.' 'What next?'
Age 70–75	Age 70 assessment. 'How can I be creative?' 'What can I give back?'
Age 80–85	Senior transition. 'How can I stay connected to others?'

The Dangers of Ignoring this Challenge

The unconscious life is not worth living. (Aristotle)

- If you ignore the little nagging voice it eventually mounts an insurrection and demands your attention in the form of a crisis.
- You need to live a conscious life if you are to have a full range of choices in life.
- If you are bored in the job it is probable that you are underperforming.
- If your job is not a good match then it will demand more of your resources and increase stress. It takes more energy to do a job that you don't enjoy.
- How much of yourself do you bring to work? If the sense that 'this job isn't you' is increasing it may be evidence that this challenge needs some immediate attention.
- If you didn't score well on the 'Bigger and Bigger Challenge' Challenge or the Vertigo Challenge it may be evidence that this challenge needs attention.
- The job you chose at 23 and were thoroughly enjoying may not be so energising at 43. You can outgrow a job or the job can outgrow you.

B. Personal Reflection

How would you define this challenge for yourself?

Self-assessment of the 'Life and Career Transition' Challenge

Read through all of the questions below and reflect on your work recently. Rate yourself in the box below on a scale of 1 to 10, where 1 = I haven't paid any attention to how I have changed or developed over the course of my life and career, and 10 = I have paid a lot of attention to how I have changed or developed over the course of my life and career and have made the right adjustments.

- Have your priorities within yourself shifted significantly over the years but they are not reflected in your job/your role/how you spend your time?
- Do you feel that you have missed the boat in your job and that younger people seem to be taking over?
- Do you feel like you've lost the plot in your career?
- Do you feel like you've lost yourself somewhere along the way in your career?
- Do you feel you are facing retirement with a terror of how you will spend your time and how your relations will cope with your being around more?
- Do you feel a sense of malaise, feel 'down', slightly depressed, unfulfilled, listless?
- Would you like to reinvent yourself and start again doing something totally different?
- Do you feel your work dreams have passed you by, that you have had the best that you will have, that it's downhill from here?
- If you stopped and did an honest review of your life right now, are you living the life you want to live?
- Are you aware of changes in your values, personality preferences, priorities and are you rewriting your personal job/life script to reflect these changes?

So where are you on the scale?

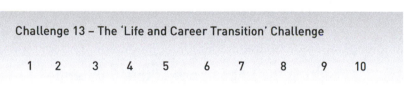

Challenge 13 – The 'Life and Career Transition' Challenge

1   2   3   4   5   6   7   8   9   10

C. Developing a Constructive Harmony between Life Transitions and Career

So what are the key steps to developing a response to the 'Life and Career Transition' Challenge?

Step 1. Going Back to the Start

With a notebook by your side to jot down your thoughts, take some time to reflect on these questions.

- Why did you choose this line of work?
- What influenced you to choose this career?
- What was important to you at the time?
- Are the same things still as important to you now?
- What has changed?
- Has this change been reflected in your career/work choices?
- Is this where you expected to be right now at this stage of your life?
- Where did you expect to be?
- If you are not where you expected to be, what changed or what has happened?
- Where do you plan to be at the later stages of your career?
- What needs to change now in order to get there?

Step 2. Accepting the Importance of this Challenge

Have you accepted with more than a passing academic interest that this is a real challenge? The key to working with this challenge is to understand how you, as a leader, consciously manage yourself in order to go on developing at a personal level (the inner game) and find a relevant expression for who you are in your career (the outer game). This is a dynamic process because you are changing all of the time and your circumstances are changing all of the time. The difficulty of working with this challenge is that a disconnect between how you are developing yourself and the job you do can be hard to recognise initially unless you are aware of the potential implications of personal change. An indication of the need to accept this challenge is that you 'feel' it as an unease or malaise in yourself.

Step 3. Plotting Your Career

Plot the significant or key stages of your career to date (see Figure 13.2). Now, over the top of this (in a different colour) plot the significant phases of your life as you see them.

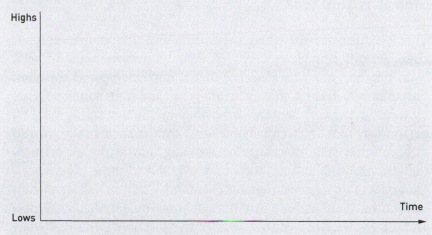

Figure 13.2 Plotting your career

When you have done this, look at the graph. What do you notice? Any insights? For example, were there any points where your life and career stages had a bearing on each other?

Step 4. Where Are You Now?

Reflect on who you are and where you are in this stage of your life.

- On a scale of 1 to 10, how happy are you in yourself as an individual at this stage of your life?
- On a scale of 1 to 10, how happy are you in your career?

Step 5. Is There a Gap?

Is there a gap between the personal and career scores? Ask yourself, what is the issue(s) here – in your career and/or in your life?

Step 6. 'Is This You?'

This is a difficult issue where personality and developmental theorists have differing views. Our view is that a person's sense of 'self', 'who they are', has a core essence that is unchanging and constant. For example, feeling that 'you are you' and not someone else. However, a person's sense of 'who they are' is not static. While a person may remain essentially the same over the years they are also in a constant state of change or evolving due to the experiences they live through and the ways they respond to these experiences. Examples of experiences that our clients have told us had significant impacts on them include parenthood, bereavement, divorce, illness and success. So, when you ask yourself the question 'is this me?', your focus needs to be on thinking about whether who you feel you are at this stage of your life matches the career or job you are currently in. For example, a lot of work is now being done to help people to examine their own values and then the organisation's values and to ask whether they are compatible (Williams, 1999).

- What are the aspects of your job where you can see 'this is you'?
- What are the aspects of your wider life where you can see 'this is you?'
- Is the job more compatible with who you are or less compatible with who you are?
- What do you like about your life right now?
- What do you not like about your life right now?

■ What makes you happy/satisfied/feeling like you are making a contribution or a difference?

There is a difference between enjoyment and competence. You may be good at something and successful at something but it doesn't mean you enjoy it or feel that it is a best fit in terms of who you are.

Step 7. Look at Your Tolerations

What do we mean by toleration? Imagine you have a light bulb that keeps flickering on and off in your bathroom. You promise yourself that you will change the light bulb. The flickering goes on for a month and every day for a month you keep meaning to change the bulb. You *tolerate* the flickering bulb. At the same time that you are tolerating something (like the flickering light bulb) you are often also irritated by it and it saps your energy and time. Then one day the bulb pops and gives out and you have to change it. There are things you want to change or know need attention but you tolerate them until they reach a crisis point, and then you act. A very real example for us as we write this book is that we are sitting here tolerating a power cable into the computer that is faulty and needs changing!

So what are you tolerating?

■ Physically (e.g. sleeping on an uncomfortable bed; being over-weight).
■ Emotionally/socially (e.g. slight anxiety attacks; getting in touch with someone that you keep on putting off phoning).
■ Financially (e.g. running up an overdraft; not having set up a direct debit).
■ Spiritually (e.g. issues around personal meaning and purpose in life).

What else?

- What are you tolerating in your team?
- What are you tolerating at work?

With toleration there is always a temporary but often negative benefit. For example, you can keep on moaning with others and feel like you all share the same emotion or you can avoid dealing with a conflict in the team because there is a short-term relief of avoiding unpleasantness. However, not addressing your tolerations leaves you where you are. It ensures that nothing changes.

What Issues Do You Need to Address?

Organisations are crying out to engage the hearts and minds of their employees.

At Work

- Career – where do you want to go in your career?
- Skills.
- Position and power.
- Restoring relationships.
- Building relationships.
- Personality – structuring the job to work with the grain of your personality rather than against it.
- Hygiene factors – money, working conditions, bad chair, bad office lighting, ventilation, working hours.
- Visibility – how do you manage your image with integrity?
- Which of the four scenarios outlined in section A do you most identify with?

Personal

- Personal development.
- Emotional development.
- Physical condition.

- Spiritual development.
- Intellectual development (are you developing your mind regularly, not just exercising it?).
- Financial development.

Clarify Your Optimum Future

This means clarifying what it will look like if *your career* and *yourself* are *synchronised*. It means knowing this is who you are, who you really are, in the job you are doing.

Set a point in the future (e.g. three years' time).

- Where do you want to be in your job/career?
- Who do you want to be – what will be true about you/what do you want people to say about you?
- What do you need to be aware of?
- What is working well for you in your current 'Life and Career Transition' Challenge?
- What are you having difficulty with?
- What do you need to stop doing? And by when?
- What do you need to start doing? And by when?

The Final Question . . . What are you going to do now?
(See Appendix 1 for further development)

Further reading

This is a crucial area of leadership development. However, we are aware that this challenge can be experienced at many levels. For those of you who want to take your development further we strongly recommend any or all of these books.

Bolles (2000), *What Color Is My Parachute?*, Ten Speed Press.

Williams (1999), *The Work We Are Born to Do*, Element Books.

Levinson (1978), *The Seasons of a Man's Life*, Ballatine Books, New York.

Hollis (1993), *The Middle Passage – from Misery to Meaning in Midlife*, Inner City Books.

Patenaude (2003), *Too Tired to Keep Running, Too Scared to Stop*, Vega Books.

Hutcheson and McDonald (1997), *The Lemming Conspiracy*, Longstreet Press.

CHALLENGE

14

The
Loneliness Challenge
Creating networks to
maintain integrity

A. Understanding this Challenge

The Challenge

Loneliness is a part of leadership that can derail the best of leaders unless managed well. Sir Ernest Shackleton was a model of a truly effective leader. Of all his exploration trips it was the remarkable Antarctic expedition of 1914–16 that won him his greatest acclaim as a leader. One of Shackleton's key observations whilst reflecting on leadership is:

> Leadership is a fine thing, but it has its penalties. And the greatest penalty is loneliness. (*Shackleton's Way*, Morrell and Capparell, 2001)

Colin Powell similarly came up with a number of lessons on leadership drawn from his experience in the US army. One of these lessons was:

> Command is lonely. Truman was right. Whether you're a CEO or the temporary head of a project team, the buck stops here. You can encourage participative management and bottom-up employee involvement but ultimately, the essence of leadership is the willingness to make the tough, unambiguous choices that will have an impact on the fate of the organization. I've seen too many non-leaders flinch from this responsibility. Even as you create an informal, open, collaborative corporate culture, prepare to be lonely. (*www.littleafrica.com/career/powell.html*)

Leadership can be a very lonely journey at times. Whether in commercial, public or voluntary arenas, leaders carry enormous responsibilities for many people, vast budgets and important outcomes. Leaders are called to redefine the future, to create new destinations and new paths to get there. They are called to lead change so that the organisation is positioned and relevant for the future, but as Machiavelli said about leadership and change management:

> There is nothing more difficult to plan, more doubtful of success, nor more dangerous to manage than the creation of a new system. For the initiator has the enmity of all who would profit by the preservation of the old institutions, and merely lukewarm defenders in those who should gain by the new ones.

Leaders are then expected to make the right decisions and carry the consequences of these decisions. Not too many shareholders actually want to know or care that the Chairman, CEO or department manager is quietly terrified, feels out of his or her depth, is sleeping badly, doesn't know what to do next or to whom they can turn for help. And it's not just the leaders in the commercial sectors that are affected by the Loneliness Challenge. We have seen leaders in the medical field be abandoned by the silence of their colleagues when unjustified complaints have gone to the British Medical Association. We have seen leaders in the voluntary sector organisations in communities being ground down by the fact that every part of their life including finances, marriage and children is open to the scrutiny of the public around them.

The Dangers

The negative pay-off for loneliness in leadership is that isolation leads to vulnerability. This can lead you in a number of possible directions which all share a desire to seek out the '*feel better*' factor. M. Scott-Peck's writing on the subject of loneliness for Chief Executives says:

> There's an old adage that it's lonely at the top. This loneliness poses a temptation associated with power that has not yet been considered. The temptation is to seek relief from that loneliness in a form that can be destructive. (Scott-Peck, *A World Waiting to Be Born*, 1993)

The first route is a *private* road of solace; be it with mistresses, drugs, financial irregularities or mild depression, the destination is one of either decreased performance or bailing out of the job altogether.

The second route is an *organisational* one. The Chief Executive may form alliances with their board or their staff. She or he becomes identified with one particular group or clique who 'feel' like or behave as if they are the CEO's cronies. As Scott-Peck points out, 'The lonely reality is that the CEO cannot identify themselves with any part of the organization; their loyalty must be to what is right for the organization as a whole.'

The third route is around *personal judgement*. This is where vulnerability leads to the exposing of deeper insecurities. When people's insecurities get uncovered and they feel the rawness of that kind of exposure, then they can freeze. In reality this translates into the potential for making irrational decisions, seeking to be liked and so compromising on key decisions or failing to address the performance challenges of their teams or line responsibilities.

The challenge is to identify the areas of your own loneliness and to put in place key external relationships and points of accountability to support you.

B. Personal Reflection

How would you define this challenge for yourself?

In your job do you ever get times of feeling lonely?

Take a moment to reflect, in the past ten years of your career have you had moments or experiences of feeling lonely? When were these? What situations? How often?

How do you know you are lonely? (What symptoms or evidence tells you?)

Examples

- *There is so much going on it feels like you've got it all on your shoulders. Where is everybody else?*
- *Conflict situations where you've been under attack.*
- *When you realise that your colleagues have different values/agendas.*
- *Carrying a burden of confidentiality that you can't share with anyone else.*
- *Tired and working late too many evenings.*
- *No one sees it like you do.*

Mary, a service manager in local government, felt trapped in the Loneliness Challenge. Her boss was aggressive and abusive to her and made comments that constantly undermined her confidence, but he never made these comments when anyone else was around. 'No one will believe me; who can I tell? Senior management will surely support my boss.' Mary felt isolated and trapped.

A quick sanity check

- The more successful you are the less needy you are? True/False
- The more successful you are the less lonely you are? True/False
- The more successful you are the more fulfilled you are? True/False

---

Self-assessment of the Loneliness Challenge

Read through all of the questions below and reflect on your work recently. Rate yourself in the box below on a scale of 1 to 10, where 1 = I feel very ineffective at owning and managing my loneliness as a leader and 10 = I feel very effective at owning and managing my loneliness as a leader.

- Are you very aware of the loneliness of your leadership role?
- Is loneliness something that never occurs to you in your leadership role?
- Are you able to make tough, unambiguous decisions that have an impact on the team/project/organisation?
- Are you aware that your need for people to like you compromises or waters down some of the decisions you make?
- Are you aware of the vulnerabilities in your personality and the effect that loneliness has on them?
- Do you find yourself seeking out quick-fix and feel-good behaviours when you are lonely that could compromise the integrity of your leadership?
- Do you feel that when you are under pressure in your leadership role you have no one that you can talk to?

- Has loneliness in leadership led you to seek refuge in an affair, drugs, financial irregularities, depression or decreased performance?
- When you feel under pressure in your leadership role do you feel that you have a selected network of people you can call at any time?
- Do you find yourself forming unhelpful alliances with your board/staff/team to compensate for feelings of loneliness in your role?
- Do you feel that if you were under extreme pressure through the loneliness of your role you have people you could phone and be totally honest with about the situation and temptations you face to make yourself feel better?
- Have you found yourself behaving irrationally or making irrational decisions when you've been trapped in your loneliness as a leader?

So where are you on the scale?

Challenge 14 – The Loneliness Challenge

1	2	3	4	5	6	7	8	9	10

C. Developing Support for the Loneliness Challenge

Part One – Four Key Steps

Step 1. Identify Needs

We have quoted the *Harvard Business Review* on the golden rule of leadership, but it is worth repeating – '*Know thyself*'.

Everyone has needs. You may not think about your own needs until they are not being met. When you are tired or under pressure and stressed your needs are very exposed but you are less likely to consciously pay attention to them because you are too stretched coping. These needs are like a hook waiting to catch hold of something that will meet the need (the solution). If you are unaware of the need then you can easily be caught up by an inappropriate solution to the need. You can take the need to the wrong person or respond with the wrong behaviour. The result of this potentially is that it not only makes you more vulnerable in the business but also reinforces the loneliness. Figure 14.1 illustrates this process.

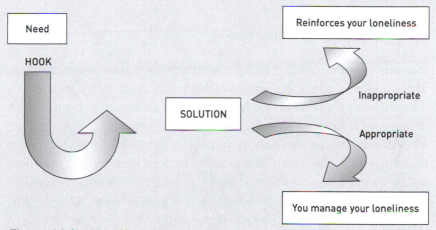

Figure 14.1   Identifying your needs

What are your needs? Your needs fall into a number of categories:

- 'Deep needs' like love, security, significance, meaning, purpose.
- 'Pathology needs' – the left-over issues from your childhood taken into adulthood.
- Relationship needs – friendships, a listening ear, a sports partner.
- Exercise needs – to build up stamina and to break down stress.
- Intellectual needs – to keep on developing an active mind.
- Competitive and/or achievement needs.
- Situational needs – for example, when you are working away from home and you are stuck in a hotel room on your own.

What other needs are you aware of in yourself?

What happens when needs are ignored? You may become open to quick-fix or inappropriate solutions.

The unhelpful pattern in the loneliness process is shown in Figure 14.2

Figure 14.2   Negative loneliness process

Step 2. Building Relationships

No one person can meet all of your needs. It is wise to spread your dependencies across a number of different types of relationships. One of the problems is that leaders can be too busy to build in the support mechanisms that they need so that when a crisis hits either they don't have the motivation to seek out help – which increases the loneliness – or they don't know who to turn to for help. For instance, as a senior manager you are going to be under tremendous pressure. At some point you will probably need a person who can help you process your business activity in order to increase your performance – invest time now in finding a good coach so that you are ready. Many senior managers suffer from the symptoms of prolonged pressure and these sometimes break out in things like depression or anxiety attacks. The time to locate a good therapist is now, before you actually need to see one. Find a therapist and set up a one-off meeting to introduce yourself so that the relationship is in place for when you need it. It is likely that you will be faced with challenges that you know others must have faced before you. The time to locate a good mentor in your field is now, before the need becomes critical.

Porlock Hill in Somerset is so steep that on the left-hand side of the road, at regular intervals, are little 'escape roads' made of deep sand. They are places where you can crash in safety if your brakes fail. You need to put escape roads in place in your life to effectively respond to the Loneliness Challenge. The potential consequences of not putting escape roads in place may be far reaching. Witness the now infamous example of Nick Leeson at Barings, who found himself caught in something he couldn't admit to anyone else and as such was unable to handle a situation that got out of hand. In one organisation that I (Trevor) set up, because there was no existing structure, I established a 'council of reference' of three older, wiser men and made myself accountable to them. I gave them permission to ask me difficult questions.

Who is it that you need to set up relationships with? (see Table 14.1.)

Table 14.1   Setting up relationships

Role	Who?
Coach	
Therapist	
Mentor	
Friend	
Business adviser	
Best source of wisdom	
Most honest source of feedback	
Others?	
Someone to be accountable to	

Step 3: Set up your networks

As well as setting up relationships for specific needs it is good to think through who you would go to in specific situations (see Table 14.2). The key is to invest in the relationships and build the networks before the problem arises so that you can pull the ripcord before you hit the ground!

Table 14.2   Who to go to in specific situations

Situations	Who?
In a crisis of confidence	
Business crisis	
Legal crisis	
Financial crisis	
Personal crisis	
Moral crisis	
Ethical crisis	
Other	

Step 4. Maintain your networks

People move, situations change, you get busy, they get busy. You need to keep maintaining the relationships and networks as an important non-urgent priority (see the 'Bigger and Bigger Challenge' and the Work–Life Balance Challenges).

Review these needs: love, security, significance, meaning, fun, 'pathology', business, creativity, sports-partner, confidant(e), friendship, childcare/other practical needs, intellectual stimulation, movement, comfort, competition, being cared for.

Review these people: partner/spouse, coach, friend, mentor, therapist.

Review who you need to make a phone call to.

Part Two – Uncontained People

> Individuals are often isolated from others and from parts of themselves, but underlying these splits is an even more basic isolation that belongs to existence – an isolation that persists despite the most gratifying engagement with other individuals and despite consummate self-knowledge and integration. (Irvin Yalom, *Existential Psychotherapy*, 1980)

Loneliness isn't just a problem to solve. It is part of human existence. The second dimension, when you have ensured that you have your networks in place and they are healthy (and not as an excuse to avoid this!), is to look at how you learn to live with the uncomfortable feeling of loneliness and isolation that is part of the job. Like the times when:

- The buck stops with you.
- You can't tell anyone.
- You have to make the decision.

How do you live with your loneliness?

Step 1. Admit it

Sometimes you just need to say to yourself 'I feel lonely. It is lonely.' Just observe the feeling without ignoring it or trying to solve it. Keep the awareness in front of you without becoming obsessed about it or losing sight of it.

Step 2. Self-coach

Figure 14.3 shows a well-known model used in coaching conversations. It is called the TGROW model. The model provides a map for a conversation typically between two people in team facilitation.

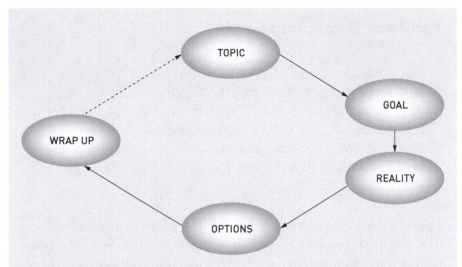

Figure 14.3 TGROW model

You can use this model to support yourself when life is getting challenging by having a conversation with yourself, about yourself, based on asking yourself five simple questions.

- Topic. What's the issue you are faced with right now?
- Goal. What do you need to go away from this conversation with?
- Reality. Expand. What are the issues? What have you tried? What is the core of the issue?
- Options. What options do you have? Brainstorm without judgement. What are the benefits and downsides of each option?
- Wrap-up. So, what is the best option? What is your plan of action? Who/what/why/when/where/how?

Out of the TGROW exercise you will need to write down a clear action plan with dates.

Step 3. The gestalt way

The gestalt way is based on a field of psychology with the same name. It is very useful when you need a more active, 'out-there', concrete way of thinking through your challenges. In the gestalt way you act out the conversation or situation by yourself rather than just thinking about it. It is like a drama with you playing all of the parts. If you do it in your study or at home no one will think you are a crank. You can get a close friend or partner/spouse to play a role if this helps.

This may seem a little odd to start with, but you need not tell any one!

Get two chairs facing each other. You sit in one and have the empty chair situated facing towards you as if someone else were to sit in it. Decide in your mind who it is that you need a conversation with and then imagine them in the opposite chair. Have a conversation out loud or in your head with this other person in the opposite chair and be as honest as you dare about your thoughts and feelings on the particular challenge that you face. As you say what *you* think or feel, remain in the chair you started in. When you've finished this, then move to the opposite chair and see what you would say to yourself if you were this other person talking to you. You will be surprised what you will gain from just living out someone else's viewpoint on your situation and having the relief of 'sharing' your thoughts and feelings.

Note down what you noticed or learned.

Step 4. Longer-term therapy

This may seem a little drastic but in the right situation it makes total sense. People who grew up in a healthy parenting relationship will have internalised the love and security their parents provided which created a mechanism inside that is able to cope with difficult feelings and situations. For those people who had less than 'good enough' parenting this internal support mechanism is under-developed – either partially or seriously. The result in adult life is that when difficult situations or difficult emotions come along they do not have the internal support mechanisms to contain the emotion, and so the emotion spills out. This is where people feel compelled to tell someone confidences that they should just hold on to themselves. Or they burden their loved ones with the weight of emotion because they cannot carry it on their own. Or they burst out with anger inappropriately because they are struggling to hold on to difficult emotions inside. We have worked a lot with people in high-stress jobs like pastors and teachers and it is interesting how their partners ended up with the nervous breakdowns.

Therapy provides a longer-term relationship that allows you to develop something of the internal resource that was not developed in childhood.

See the Pathology Challenge for further insight.

Part Three – Other Loneliness Factors

Personality

Your personality has a bearing on how you handle and experience loneliness. For example, if you work in a highly extrovert team or organisation and have an introverted preference you may feel quite isolated. Or if you are in a team of analytical, rational, left-brain people and you are a 'feelings-based' person you can feel lonely because everyone may seem to be making decisions in a very different way from you. (See the Personality Challenge.)

Organisational culture

One thing we get to notice as consultants visiting many organisations is how different they all are. Consider an HR specialist who worked in a manufacturing environment that was very friendly, team-based and supportive. She had people popping in and out of the office all of the time asking for advice or just being friendly. She then moved into a commercial sales environment where all of the desks had high barriers, the office floor was almost totally silent and no one seemed to need her help at all. After six months she was so lonely that she just couldn't wait to get a new job.

Job roles

There are certain roles where you just cannot afford to be as close in friendships to work colleagues or customers as in others. Obvious examples of this include many of the professions. The higher up in the organisation, the less people there are to talk to as a peer.

In an organisational context one way that can help is the notion of 'hats'. If you regard each role that you have with people as wearing a different hat – for example, your manager hat, your coach hat, your friend hat – then you can clarify with people what hat you are wearing in each situation to manage their expectation of you.

Moving across cultures

More and more people are moving globally with their jobs. Moving to a new culture with a different language, culture, operating norms or processes all lead to the newcomer feeling potentially isolated and lonely.

If you moved to a new job abroad what support mechanisms would you put it place to ensure that you minimised the risks of loneliness?

The Final Question . . . What are you going to do now?
(See Appendix 1 for further development)

15

The
Personality Challenge
Understanding your impact
on others

A. Understanding this Challenge

People's personalities and how they differ from each other play a key part in management styles and 70% of performance improvement comes as a result of improving the relationship between managers and their staff. (See the Further reading list at the end of the chapter.)

You express your life through your personality; in other words your personality speaks for you. Your personality is integral to who you are and how you deal with life. All leaders have different ways of motivating themselves, processing problems, making decisions and dealing with life. Managing your personality among people with different personalities is a core leadership skill.

The following observations about personality are worth noting.

- It is neither good nor bad.
- It comes out clearly under pressure.
- It is tied up with Emotional Intelligence and how you manage yourself.
- It is tied up with how you manage your excitement, your stress, change and leadership.
- It affects how you do everything.
- There are advantages and disadvantages to all personality types.
- There are parts of your personality that you will like in yourself more than others.
- Knowing how your personality operates under stress is essential for good management.

Defining Personality

When someone studies for their MSc in Counselling Psychology they look at about eight theories of personality and how it develops. So the subject is not a straightforward one. However, the playwright Arthur Miller provides an excellent definition:

> Nobody wants to be a hero – but in every man there is something he cannot give up and still remain himself – a core, an identity, a

thing that is summed up for him by the sound of his own name on his own ears. If he gives that up he becomes a different man, not himself. (*New York Times*, 8 August 1958)

Often the part of the work equation that people are most unaware of is themselves. Yet everyone takes themselves to work every day. One of the most frequently used models of personality in the workplace is the Myers-Briggs Type Indicator (MBTI). This looks at four dimensions of personality. For the purpose of illustration in this assessment and development process this chapter will look at just one of those dimensions, the dimension that looks at where you get your energy. The introverted types get their energy from their inner world of thoughts and ideas. When faced by a leadership challenge they will often go quiet for a moment to process internally the situation, think it through, challenge or question, in order to find out what they think about the situation. They will then deliver their findings back to the team or individual. The extroverted types will generally get their energy from the external world of people and their environment. Where the introvert preference is 'thinking it through', the extrovert preference is saying 'let's talk it through'. They will form their ideas through discussion and interaction. The extrovert preference types may be thinking the introverts are disengaged and too quiet and the introvert preference types are wishing the extroverts would be quiet long enough for them to think and allow them, when ready, to get a word into the conversation!

A lot of issues of underperformance that senior managers identify in different members of their staff are the result of personality differences of which both are unaware. *I'm not crazy, I'm just not you* (Pearman and Albritton, 1997) is a book based on the MBTI and encapsulates how leaders need to understand and manage their own personalities as well as those of others'. Daniel Goleman's (1998b especially) research into Emotional Intelligence, which includes this level of self-understanding, shows that effective leaders have high Emotional Intelligence at a two to one ratio against the other factors – skill levels and IQ. In other words, leaders have got a high IQ and they obviously have a high skill level, but twice as high as each of these is their Emotional Intelligence: their level of self-understanding and transparency around how their personality affects those around them.

Why Is This Challenge Important?

- **Personality and stress** – how you respond to other people when you are under pressure will be a crucial influencing factor.
- **It's the 'you' people meet each day** – your personality is how people experience you because it is the 'you' that you present to the outside world.
- **Management style** – your style of adding value to your staff will be shaped by your personality preferences.
- **Influencing style** – your preferences in personality may not correspond to those of the people you seek to influence.
- **Managing change** – structured personalities handle change in very different ways from unstructured ones; those who manage change by analysing the right path handle change differently from those who are more concerned about how values or people are impacted.
- **Motivating style** – personality has an effect on how people get their energy.
- **Difference and diversity** – understanding personality is important in managing people who are different from you.
- **'Pressure points'** – understanding personality is important in managing people who 'push your buttons'.
- **Emotional Intelligence** – highly effective leaders have twice as much EQ as IQ and skills.

B. Personal Reflection

The key to self-assessment on this challenge is your level of self-awareness. You need to consider the following questions.

- What is your personality?
- What is your impact on others?
- What is your strategy for managing this impact?

Self-assessment of the Personality Challenge

Read through all of the questions below and reflect on your work recently. Rate yourself in the box below on a scale of 1 to 10, where 1 = I feel very unaware of my own personality strengths and weaknesses and their effect on others and 10 = I feel very aware of my own personality strengths and weaknesses and their effect on others.

- Would you rate your level of self-awareness as very high?
- Have you had feedback from an assessment centre or personality profiling (MBTI, OPQ, FIRO-B, etc.) that has helped your self-understanding?
- Are you aware of how your preference for introversion or extroversion affects how you get energy or are motivated in your job, how you handle yourself in meetings and how you communicate with people?
- Are you aware of how your preferences for focusing on the future can affect the need of your team/organisation/direct reports to deliver immediate results?
- Are you aware of how your need for facts, details and focusing on the present can affect the need of your team/organisation/direct reports to be more visionary and strategically focused?
- Are you aware of how your detached, analytical style of thinking can impact on people's feelings and values?
- Are you aware of how your values and people-focus can sometimes obscure your judgement in making certain decisions?
- Are you aware of how your need to leave things open or to the last minute can affect the people you seek to lead and influence?
- Are you aware of how your need for structure can lessen the effectiveness of some of your team's enjoyment, spontaneity and creativity?

So where are you on the scale?

Challenge 15 – The Personality Challenge									
1	2	3	4	5	6	7	8	9	10

C. Developing Greater Leverage from Your Personality

Part 1. Developing Personal Insight

Describe your personality

People spend most of their lives just 'being', and when questioned they say 'well, it's just me, it's just how I am'.

To increase your awareness of 'who you are' write some paragraphs or keywords to describe yourself. Here is a list of examples of the sort of words that people sometimes use to describe their personality:

Energetic	Planned	Detailed	Controlled
Structured	Reflective	Warm	Outgoing
Reserved	Competitive	Fantasist	Dreamer
Passionate	Cold	Committed	Intuitive
Responsible	Analytical	Feeling	Emotional

Describe the personality of your team

It isn't just individuals that have personalities. Teams have a collective personality when they are together. If you have a personal profile that is opposite to that of the team then it can be a difficult environment to perform well in. For example, to be a very people-centred or value-centred person within a very rational, analytical team can be very uncomfortable. Or a reflective, thoughtful individual can find it difficult to thrive in a team whose overall personality is more outgoing, fast-moving and verbal.

Take a moment to reflect on the personality of your team.

Who knows you well?

So, many influencing issues can arise out of the mismatch between your perception of yourself and your impact and how others perceive you. For example, Trevor's wife gets cross when he doesn't respond to her questions when, from his perspective, he was reflecting on the question before giving an answer. It is no accident that high-performing individuals and teams have a good culture of giving and receiving feedback. Ask someone who knows you well at work to describe your personality and write down his or her perspectives.

Sub-personalities

The idea behind sub-personalities is that while you may be just one 'you', you are different versions of yourself in different situations. Some people may see you as a fun, joking person while others may only get to see the serious, analytical person. In certain situations you may display the very caring side of your personality but others may view you as slightly detached, objective and sometimes even hard.

So who are you in what situations?

Look at Table 15.1. In the horizontal column write down the situations you are most frequently in; for example, work, boss, coach, family. Try to alternate between situations where you are known well and those where you are not known well. Ask yourself the question, 'Which parts of my personality do I bring out/express and with whom?'

Table 15.1 Which sub-personalities do you use in which situations?

Personality	e.g. Work	e.g. Boss						
e.g. warm								
e.g. dynamic								

An exercise in Personality and Organisations

You have a choice as to whether you express different parts of your personality in different places.

Think this through: an organisation has complained that someone is less than effective in their job because they are cold, aloof, distant or dispassionate.

- What might be a 'good' personality for this organisation?
- What personality types might be rewarded in this organisation?
- What personality types are rewarded in the organisation that you work for?

Intention and effect

Most people, consciously or not, have an intention behind what they do. For example, you may have some or all of the following intentions.

- An intention to raise performance.
- An intention to improve quality.
- An intention to show an interest in your direct reports.
- An intention to be open and approachable.
- An intention to develop your team.

However, experience and feedback often reveal that the effect of people's behaviour is not what they intend.

Consider Figure 15.1. You start with intention. This is the effect you desire to have on someone. You then exhibit behaviours. These are the actions you take, both verbal and non-verbal. Then there is the effect. This is seen in how the person experiences your behaviour and perceives your action.

Figure 15.1   Intention and effect

A crucial aspect of Emotional Intelligence is being able to answer the question, 'Does your behaviour reflect your intention?' For example, if you intend to convey warmth, what are the behaviours that demonstrate warmth, and are these the kinds of behaviours that others read as warm? The only way to develop integrity between intention and effect is through the process of feedback (see Figure 15.2). Feedback tells you that your *intended behaviour* is having the *intended effect.*

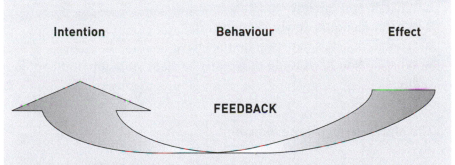

Figure 15.2   Feedback is the route to checking your intent against others' perception

Getting feedback

If you have never had feedback on your personality, then now would be a good time to get some.

- Ask someone you know well at home (partner/sibling/child).
- Ask someone you know well at work.
- Ask someone at work who has only recently met you.

Ask them to:

1. Describe your personality.
2. Describe how your personality comes across to them.
3. Describe how your personality is affected by being under stress.

Analysing your feedback

What matters most to you about your personality? Is what matters most coming through to others?

Choose one area of your personality where you have had feedback that reveals your intent is different from the effect and ask yourself these questions:

- What do you intend?
- What behaviours do you demonstrate?
- From feedback, what effect do they have?
- What do you need to do differently to align your intention with effect?

The Myers-Briggs Type Indicator

One of the instruments most frequently used by organisations for developing insight into leaders' personalities is the Myers-Briggs Type Indicator (MBTI). Based on Jungian theories around personality it looks at people's preferences.

For example, pick up a pen and write your normal signature. Now put the pen in your other hand and do your signature again. Which hand did you use for the top line? This was probably your preferred hand. How did it feel? Usually it is instinctive, natural, effortless, without thought, smooth and easy. How was it when you tried with your less preferred hand? You were probably able to produce a signature, but often it feels awkward, requires effort and concentration, feels uncomfortable and unnatural.

Everyone has preferences in their personality – preferred behaviours and ways of working. You do these things without any thought; they are just 'how you are'. You are able to behave in ways that are not your preference, but they will take a lot more conscious effort and feel unnatural to you.

The MBTI looks at four sets of preferences in people's personalities. You can do both of the preferences in each set, but one will be more natural to you.

- **Where you get your energy from:** internally, thinking through, reflection *or* through the outer world of people and things.
- **How you process all the inputs that come your way throughout the day:** through facts, data, details and reality *or* hunches, possibilities, theories and meanings.
- **How you make decisions about all of this information:** through analysis, logic, critique and reasoning *or* personal values, appreciation and sympathy.
- **How you orientate yourself to life:** by being organised, planned, decisive and systematic *or* flexible, spontaneous, open to change.

As a next step, ask your training/HR/personnel manager or department to run the MBTI questionnaire on you (it takes about 30 minutes to fill in) and get them to give you the feedback from the results to gain maximum benefit. If there isn't a licensed person in your organisation ask them to put you in touch with someone who is. (Most organisations will have consultants or assessment centres that will do this for you.)

Part 2. The Challenge of Personality in the Workplace

This section will take a brief look at five areas of work where personality has a direct impact.

1. Personality and your line reports or team members

Many managers manage instinctively; that is to say they do not take time to consciously think through the personality types on their team and work out how best to manage them. Without consciously thinking through the personality needs of your line reports you will end up with a 'one size fits all' or 'this is my management style – like it or lump it' approach. Take time to think through each of your line reports or each member of your team and consider these questions:

- How would you describe each of their personalities?
- What would be the most effective management approach for each person?

2. Personality: Leading Change

How do you respond to change? The stress of change has an effect on personality. Introvert preferences become more introverted; extrovert preferences become more extroverted; sensing personalities want more facts, details and information; intuitive preferences want more blue sky and more possibility thinking; thinking preferences need to do more analysis; feeling preferences feel more deeply the anxiety of others; perceiving preferences find it harder to come to decisions or closure; and judging preferences create more rigid structures.

There is much helpful material on this subject, but for a good summary of how the MBTI relates to how your staff best contribute to the organisation, their preferred leadership style, preferred work environment, suggestions for development and potential pitfalls read Krebs, Hirsh and Kummerow, *Introduction To Type™ in Organisations* (1994).

3. Personality: Handling Conflict

People handle conflict in different ways. Think about your response to conflict by working through the following questions.

- What examples do you have of how you respond to people who are similar, different or very different from you?
- Rate your level of acceptance of people who are different from you.
- Do you find some people too vague and impractical and find it hard to follow their ideas? What positives can you find in this? (For example, do they bring vision, help prepare for the future and offer new ideas?)
- Do you find some people too negative and nit-picking in their response to new ideas? What positives can you find in this? (For example, do they bring reality, facts and 'ground' vision?)
- Do you find some people over-emotional and illogical? What positives can you find in this? (For example, do they bring out the people and values side of things?)
- Do you find some people critical and insensitive? What positives can you find in this? (For example, do they bring good analysis, make tough decisions and weigh up the pros and cons?)
- Do you find some people too cool, quiet or withdrawn? What positives can you find in this? (For example, do they bring reflection and add depth?)
- Do you find some people too loud, intrusive and superficial? What positives can you find in this? (For example, do they bring energy and action and broaden people's networks?)
- Do you find some people too disorganised and irresponsible? What positives can you find in this? (For example, do they bring adaptability and an openness to change?)
- Do you find some people too rigid and inflexible? What positives can you find in this? (For example, do they bring organisation, structure and completion to tasks and projects?)

(There is a link between this challenge and the Influence Challenge in the sense that difficult personalities stretch our influencing skills.)

4. Personality: Structure and motivation

An area of motivation that is often overlooked is the area of structured and non-structured working environments or cultures. Structure means order, knowing what to do, when to do it and how to do it. Our experience is that if you put a highly structured person in a non-structured environment it affects their performance. They need structure to enable them to perform to their best. Likewise, if you put a very non-structured person in a very structured environment it affects their performance because they feel hemmed in and constrained from bringing their uniqueness and energy to the challenges. Furthermore, if you are very structured and 'sensing' (like facts, information, data, detail, here-and-now reality), as you move higher up an organisation you are likely to be confronted with a greater need to focus on:

- The intuitive function (future-focused, designing a system, theory or vision, speculating and possibility thinking).
- The perceiving function (less structure – in fact it will be your job to live in an unstructured world and create structure for others).

Some managers start to struggle when they reach senior levels because they have progressed through an organisation that has provided the structure for them to perform to a high level, but in a senior position they encounter a lack of structure because *they* are now the person whose job it is to create the structure for others. The gear change required for top leadership positions may need some planning to ensure that you know how to handle your personality in these new roles. If you do not learn to handle the difference that the context has on your personality then it may very well have a negative impact on your performance.

5. How can you bring all of yourself to work?

One final question concerns how much of 'yourself' you bring to work. Do you sit at your desk feeling like only a small percentage of who you really are, or that your potential is actually being used by your job? Are there other whole areas of potential, energy or resourcefulness that you make available when outside of work, which simply don't get used inside of work? One piece of research (Spencer and Spencer, 1993) suggests that you have up to 27% of your individual effort at work in your own hands. This means that while there is up to 73% of your effort that the job demands of you, there is still 27% more effort available if you choose to use it. Write down a percentage figure for yourself. What percentage of yourself do you bring to work? What hinders the bit of you that doesn't get to come to work?

- Do you feel you have to moderate, minimise or alter your personality to come to work?
- What gets in the way of bringing all of yourself to work?
- What can you put in place to lessen these interferences?

Part 3. 'Healthy' Personality

Imagine a situation where the natural grain of your personality is that you prefer to re-energise through having space, listening to music, reading or doing a quiet hobby, but you are in the job of sales representative for an insurance firm meeting people all day long. The emotional toll of this situation is self-evident. The issue is not necessarily 'are you in the right job?' but more 'are you investing enough time in re-energising activities?' To ignore your personality is to set yourself up for higher levels of stress and potential burnout.

How do you nurture and nourish your personality? What are the ways in which you restore your personality after a hard day at work? Examples of restorative activities may be music, sport, socialising, writing, walking or cooking. As you consider how you can nurture your personality it is important to refer to the Work–Life Balance Challenge.

Nourished or exhausted?

There are two major consequences of neglecting to nurture personality:

1. You give people the stress reactions from your personality (the irritated, short, terse, unfocused reactions).
2. You bring a very diminished resource from the huge potential within your personality to the challenges you face.

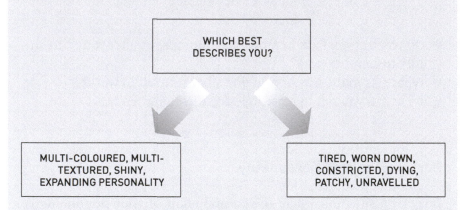

Figure 15.3   Nurturing a healthy personality

One of the key skills of an effective leader is their ability to create space. Some people call it 'blue-sky thinking time' or 'strategic time'. Whatever you prefer to call it the important point is that they do not live with a jam-packed diary. They create the space to lift up their heads and decide if they are still on track and whether it is still the right track. So the conclusion is simple: *build a reserve of space and time.*

The challenge of this challenge: inner game and outer game

Remember the theme of the inner game of work and the outer game of work that was discussed in the Introduction? The inner game is what is going on inside of you as you greet the leadership challenges. The outer game is the visible side of what you actually do. The effective management of your personality is an inner game–outer game issue. To be proactive in leadership (outer game) takes time and energy (inner game). The challenges you face (outer game) create all kinds of tensions for you (inner game). The more the leadership role and challenges grow (outer game) the more it puts pressure on your inner game. You need a reserve (inner game) within your personality to undertake this leadership role (your mind sharp, your emotional reserves topped up). To have a reserve (inner game) to draw on requires space, time, refreshing relationships, exercise, plus the other activities you identified for yourself earlier (outer game).

The choice within leadership is to grow your personality where you see potential being fully realised, or to diminish your personality where you feel internally smaller, tighter, more monochrome and within limited responses. If you are serious about being more effective as a leader you have to be willing to address the less effective dimensions of your personality – and this will require an investment of time.

The Final Question . . . What are you going to do now?
(See Appendix 1 for further development)

Further reading

For further research on the effect of management style on performance read:

Spencer (1995), *Reengineering Human Resources,* New York: John Wiley and Sons, Inc.

Spencer and Spencer (1993), *Competence at Work: Models for Superior Performance,* New York: John Wiley and Sons, Inc.

Spencer (1986), *Calculating Human Resource Costs and Benefits,* New York: John Wiley and Sons, Inc.

Litwin and Stringer (1967), *Motivation and Organization Climate,* Harvard Business School Research Press.

McClelland (1984), *Motives, Personality and Society,* Praeger.

Boyatzkis (1982), *The Competent Manager: A Model for Effective Performance,* New York: John Wiley and Sons, Inc.

16

The
Pathology Challenge

Managing the effects of your blind spots

A. Understanding this Challenge

This is a bit different! So what is this challenge about?

Can you think of some examples where:

- You were out of order?
- Your response to a situation was out of proportion to the event?
- Certain people push your button?
- You have certain behaviours – loud or quiet – that you know have an unhelpful impact on others?

So what is 'pathology'? This is one of the deeper psychological issues of leadership that is of vital importance and yet receives little attention. Because it is a deeper issue and can sometimes be a little scary to look at, the aim here is to examine it on a number of levels.

At a basic level

All leaders have blind spots and repeating patterns of ineffective behaviour, which, if not rightly processed, gets worked out, in and through their organisations.

On a slightly deeper level

Everyone brings baggage into their roles at work that has to do with their past, early life development issues and childhood issues that they bring into adulthood. For example, an elder child often has a lot of responsibility and therefore in adulthood takes responsibility when it's not necessary, with the consequence of frustrating their team or colleagues who are saying 'trust us' or 'let go' or 'we're fine, let us get on with it'.

A little deeper still

Many of your basic behaviour structures and attitudes are laid down by as early as 2 years of age. If you had good enough parenting you will have developed a reasonably secure sense of who you are, which will provide a foundation and a resource for much of your adult life. However, no one had a perfect developmental track record when they were growing up. To the extent that you missed out on 'good enough' parenting you will have found ways of reacting as a child that compensated for this, or developed survival strategies to defend and protect your emerging sense of yourself. As you grew up the reason for the behaviours, attitudes and defences will have been further and further buried out of conscious view. What you are left with are patterns of behaviour. However unproductive these behaviours may seem to you as an adult they made sense at an early age, the problem being that why they made sense is out of sight.

Someone has defined insanity as 'if you keep on doing what you have always done you will keep on getting what you have always got' and, as this book has already mentioned, Albert Einstein said that a problem cannot be solved at the same level at which it was created. This is where the problem comes at work. You have habits in your behaviours or attitudes that you or others see are unproductive, but you keep on doing them anyway.

Why is responding to this challenge so important?

- Leaders shape organisations around themselves. Just as dog lovers are meant to end up looking like their dogs, so organisations invariably end up being shaped around the profile of their top leaders.
- Integrity is recognised as foundational to leadership. Integrity is not about being perfect but it is about being integrated and genuine. Without integrity there will be little trust in the organisation, team or department. Without trust, relationships will be affected and consequently performance will be affected.
- The Introduction to this book spoke of the crucial aspect of leadership called Emotional Intelligence. To understand and deal with your pathology is a key application of Emotional Intelligence.
- Loneliness is a leadership challenge. When the going gets tough the resource you rely on is you. You need to know that 'you' is a reliable resource.
- Pathology creates blind spots. Leaders need to eradicate as many blind spots as possible. When Nelson held his telescope up to his blind eye he

is famed for saying 'I see nothing'; your pathology will lead you to see nothing when there is something there, or something when there is nothing there or a distortion of the real picture.

■ Your pathology, if not managed appropriately, will certainly weaken your leadership and when mixed with the potent cocktail of power can make you dangerous as a leader.

Let us assume that you accept that your primary care-givers (parents, guardians, foster parents) did their best, with the best of intentions (though this isn't always the case!) and that you do your best in caring for your own children. In the adult world of organisations where you work it is your responsibility to update (or redefine or fine tune or elaborate) what was useful or made sense to you as a child, into what is now useful and productive in the current adult context you are working in.

Personality Or Pathology

A difficulty in this particular challenge is separating what behaviour or attitude is the result of your personality and what is the result of your pathology because when you present yourself to people you present as a package – personality and pathology are wrapped up together.

Example

Jim, a senior manager in a biotechnology company, has a personality that is very structured so that all ideas and information are shaped by him into clear structures, outcomes and hypotheses with only three possible options, a, b and c. The pathology dimension is seen in his inability to respond in any other way, in any other situation, and in the way he always attacks, criticises and puts down members of his team when they try to persuade him that there are other ways of looking at data, individuals' behaviours and strategies.

Work environment supports or exposes your pathology

If you have an environment at work that is conducive to your pathology then it may not be a problem and it may even work to your advantage.

Without naming names there are certain companies that we work with that have very aggressive cultures where Jim's (example above) pathology would not be noticed as out of the ordinary. But take the example of Mike.

Example

Mike was in the Army for fifteen years before taking a management job in an export company dealing with auto parts. For fifteen years people had simply obeyed his requests. If they had a problem with the request they would resolve it by barking orders further down the chain of command. The problem now was that when he asked a team member to do something they might challenge him, disagree or be half hearted in their response.

'How do you respond to these staff?', I asked?

'In my body language', he replied.

'Tell me more', I continued.

'I stand there when they sit down so that I convey a quiet sense of intimidation, or I get up close into their personal space or I use enough verbal put-downs or other forms of what I now realise are seen as aggressive or bullying behaviour.'

Examples, Examples, Examples

Take the example of the leader who has grown up with a fear of close relationships. They design their leadership in such a way as to keep everyone functioning as individuals; they are more focused on the task than the relationships between the people doing the task. They keep team meetings down to a minimum or meetings are non-existent and they only see their direct reports on a one-to-one basis rather than together.

Another example is that of the CEO who has a very fragile sense of their self. This is well hidden behind patterns of high task focus, driving organisational skills and high achievement. Closer colleagues will see evidence of this pathology in the fact that they are never asked for feedback. In fact this type of CEO avoids ever getting any and becomes very defensive and angry when anything like feedback is given to them.

Take the example of Mike, a director in an investment bank. Part of his pathology is his personal insecurity, seen in his inability to put himself forward in situations where he will be publicly disagreed with. In board meetings he will redden and use all of his positional authority and power to beat his more junior opponents into quick submission.

A final example is that of Doreen, who is PA to the director of a Primary Care Trust. While she is efficient and seems to get on well with her boss she doesn't speak to anyone unless she is spoken to, doesn't even greet people as she enters the office in the morning, eats lunch generally at her desk and never says a word at meetings. The generous-hearted say she's shy, but most people regard her as just plain rude.

The point is everyone is a little or a lot dysfunctional and you need to know what shape it takes for you and how you can manage it in order to maximise your effectiveness and the effectiveness of those around you (or, in the case of the CEO, the whole organisation).

B. Personal Reflection

There is more that can (and will) be said on this subject, but first, consider your own definition of pathology.

Self-assessment of the Pathology Challenge

Read through all of the questions below and reflect on your work recently. Rate yourself in the box below on a scale of 1 to 10, where 1 = very ineffective in responding to this challenge and 10 = very effective at responding to this challenge. The key to self-assessment

---

on this challenge is your level of self-awareness. Are you able to answer the following questions?

- What shape does 'pathology' take for you?
- What is your impact on others?
- What is your strategy for managing this impact?

If you are really clear and have done a lot of personal work on this, you will score nearer 10 on the scale. If this is all really quite new to you and you haven't got a high level of awareness and strategies for managing it then you will be nearer to 1 on the scale.

Here are some questions to help you self-assess.

- Are you aware that you have insecurities that affect how you behave at work?
- Do you see patterns of anger in yourself at work that you know have an unfair effect on people you deal with, especially when you are under pressure?
- Is it true that people see you as very calm and confident on the outside, but you know that this just hides a conflicting range of emotions inside of you?
- Do you see patterns in how you deal with conflict that has roots in how you dealt with conflict as a child?
- Have you made an investment in coaching/counselling/therapy/ EQ to deepen your understanding of your own baggage and how it affects you and those around you?
- Are you aware that there are different versions of yourself that seem to exist at different times? For example, sometimes confident, sometimes sick or terrified?
- Are you always wrong or never wrong?
- Do you always admit to being wrong or never admit to being wrong?
- Do you consistently read situations at work in ways that are inaccurate by everyone else's viewpoint, but which seem very accurate according to your viewpoint?
- Do you seem to manage to avoid ever getting feedback from your peers/boss/team?

■ Are you consistently defensive when people challenge your ideas?
■ Are you terrified of being out of control in your role at work?
■ Can you see how the culture of the organisation is being shaped around your personality?

So where are you on the scale?

Challenge 16 – The Pathology Challenge									
1	2	3	4	5	6	7	8	9	10

C. Moving Forward with the Pathology Challenge

How Does Your Baggage Get Played Out in Your Leadership of an Organisation?

This is a new and growing area of leadership development, so the aim is to provide you with as much help as possible as you think through this question for yourself and for the leaders that you work with. Manfred Kets de Vries, one of the leading writers on the Pathology Challenge, takes the personality types outlined in the definitive psychiatric text for diagnosing the different manifestations of pathology and translates them into some key descriptions of how they might apply to leadership pathology. What follows is a summary of his thinking (but we suggest you read the full text – *The Leadership Mystique* (2001) – if you are interested in pursuing this challenge a little deeper).

Look at each type and ask:

■ Can you think of anyone like that?
■ Is there something of this in you?
■ How might this affect how you/they lead others and influence the character of the organisation?

1. The narcissistic personality type

They need the admiration of those around them and know how to manipulate or use people to get what they want.

2. The paranoid personality type.

They are hyper-vigilant, distrustful of others and always on their guard for others' 'real' motives to suddenly pop out and bite them.

3. The obsessive–compulsive personality type

They are conscientious, orderly perfectionists. While very obliging on one side they can also be very inflexible on the other.

4. The histrionic personality type

They are very dramatic; their life is full of crises, high highs and low lows. An outwardly personable nature can shield a self-centred person.

5. The dependent personality type

They always need approval; they like to be under strong dominant leaders who provide much-needed protection.

6. The depressive personality type

Their glass is always half-empty and life doesn't have much joy in it. They feel useless and worthless.

7. The schizotypical personality type

Relationships with others and social situations are difficult; they sometimes appear a little odd or different.

8. The borderline personality type

They keep their distance from others and often appear indifferent to praise or criticism. Their range of emotions seems limited. There is a kind of emptiness, deadness or boredom inside of them that others may sense.

9. The avoidant personality type

Insecure in social situations, they are risk-avoidant and slightly withdrawn. They desire closeness to others but find it difficult to achieve.

10. The schizoid personality type

They have no desire to be in close relationships and therefore will be introverted, aloof and reclusive, and definitely avoid the office socials!

11. The antisocial personality type

They have an underlying frustration and act in ways that are anti-authoritarian. Irresponsibility, unreliability and untrustworthiness are sometimes their characteristics.

12. The sadistic personality type

Intimidating and abrasive, they are often very opinionated and use personal or role-based power to control others.

13. The masochistic personality type

They beat up on themselves, run themselves down; they are self-effacing, self-denigrating and self-sacrificing.

14. The passive–aggressive personality type

They fail to carry out their promises because 'yes' is their habitual response to wanting to say 'no'. They may come across as unbelievably nice when everyone is understandably angry or frustrated.

15. The cyclothymic personality type

Their moods fluctuate. Their highs can engage those around them.

Pathology is an invested habit. This means that there is a lot of *you* in that habit, behaviour or attitude. It is much more deeply embedded than a bolt-on. Awareness of the need to change will occur when you have had feedback that your behaviour isn't working for you or isn't acceptable any more.

The choice is to keep your personality but to reshape your pathology or at least understand it and its impact on others and to put in place ways of managing it to reduce the negative effects. Outlined here is a process for developing around this challenge.

Developing around the challenge

Step 1. Identifying your baggage

You may be familiar with arriving at some foreign destination and going down to the baggage reclaim hall and waiting around a carousel until your particular flight is unloaded. At that point you develop very sensitive vision to one set of luggage – yours. Out of the entire luggage moving around the carousel you look out for distinguishing colours, shape and labels so that you can say with confidence 'that's my baggage'. Pathology is a type of personal baggage that you carry around with you and it has your distinguishing marks on it (see Figure 16.1).

Consider the following questions:

- What is your pathology?
- What do you think are some of the evidences or symptoms of your pathology?

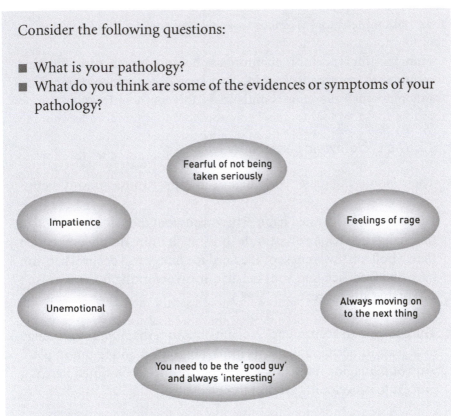

Figure 16.1 Identifying your baggage

Step 2. Drawing a blank?

If you can't think of any areas within yourself then try these further questions:

- What patterns of behaviour/attitude/emotions have you observed in yourself throughout your career?
- Are there self-defeating habits that you notice in yourself?
- If you were to describe the 'shadow' side of your personality and how it shows itself at work, what would you say?
- Do you observe high levels or outbursts of anger, irritability and anxiety in yourself at work?

Get some feedback from close friends, colleagues or your partner using some of the questions already outlined in this chapter.

Step 3. Context

Give examples of a context where you notice yourself behaving or feeling like this. For example, using the illustration in Figure 16.1 of the type of baggage you may identify, consider when and where in the work context you feel a need always to be moving on to the next thing. Or, when and where in the work context are you impatient?

Step 4. 'Button pushers'

The phrase 'they really push my button' is often used when certain people trigger unhelpful emotional responses.

Who pushes your buttons in your family? Note the feeling and emotion.

Now bring this into the work situation. Who pushes your buttons in your team, office, among your clients or customers?

Step 5. Critical stakeholders

Is anyone on your list of 'button pushers' a critical stakeholder in your job/strategy/project? Focus on these relationships as you work through this challenge. If you have the luxury to do so then start with the easier relationships.

Example

Charles, a team leader in a local engineering company, described his boss – an older, strong, clear-thinking, kind supportive man (like an elder brother or father figure). Charles had also seen the other side of his boss on occasions that provided evidence of his ruthless use of logic to annihilate people who crossed him on certain issues.

So for Charles the challenge was how to deal with his boss's anger. On occasions when he had confronted his own father he had always come out badly. If he challenged his boss would he come out badly? The stakes were high, because his boss gave him support and affirmation – something he had never been given by his dad – but he realised that decisions were being compromised and avoided in order to keep things 'happy'.

Warning

You must be very careful not to change pathology too fast. Pathology involves personal structures that you need deeply. You therefore need only to deconstruct at the same pace as you reconstruct new and supportive structures or behaviours.

Step 6. Needs

At this point it is worth pausing to recap.

- You have identified some attitudes/behaviours/habits.
- You have noted some of the contexts in which these occur.
- You have noted which people are particularly involved.

Looking at each of the contexts you have noted, what are your main needs in each context? As you consider this the following examples of needs may help you in your thinking.

Recognition	Stimulation
Certainty	To be heard
To be liked	Secure relationship
To be thought interesting	Closeness

What Do You Do with This Insight?

1. Awareness is the key to new choices

The main step in working with the Pathology Challenge is awareness. With awareness comes increased choice. This is why much of this chapter has been spent on awareness raising.

Examples of some new choices we've seen clients make are:

- Choosing to make more use of the people they are managing to confront difficult relationships.
- Counting to ten!
- Meeting the person face to face (maybe with a third party).
- Walking away and planning the feedback that needs to be given rather than 'shooting from the hip'.

Feedback or Lies, Manfred Kets de Vries (2001) has a wonderful subtitle in one of his chapters on pathology. He called it 'A World of Liars'. He looks at the problem of lying at high levels in organisations and how the higher you climb the less people tell you the truth. He quotes an estimate that only 10% of executives accurately assess themselves! He says, 'In hierarchical situations people have a tendency to tell those above them what they think they want their superiors to hear' *(p. 89)*. We are very aware, as consultants, that people dress up their feedback to us to such an extent that the passionate conversation with us in the corridor has no resemblance to the conversation we then overhear them have with the boss in their office.

The danger this underlines is that the Pathology Challenge is one that needs to be taken seriously at a personal and organisational level. One of the most important tasks for an organisation is to develop the right climate and relational trust in order to get feedback. People need to feel safe in dealing with leaders at senior levels. One of the features of the narcissistic personality is just the opposite of this – they create relationships to make themselves feel better by getting you to tell them how great they are.

2. Healing route

There are different views about whether pathology can be changed. Our view is that significant healing at a fundamental level can be achieved through the safe relationship provided by therapy. Therapy allows you to examine some of the deeper knots that create your pathology and to create a safe place to rework some of the internal dilemmas.

3. Management route

On a basic level, once awareness is developing coaching is probably the best way of creating strategies for managing your pathology. This is because the strength of coaching lies in helping you to develop strategies that are appropriate for your pathology, personality and individual situation. Coaching will help you to develop new patterns of thinking and behaving which will maximise your support while seeking to create the most helpful ways of impacting those around you.

The Final Question . . . What are you going to do now?
(See Appendix 1 for further development)

17

The
Confusion–Complexity –Chaos Challenge
Performing through uncertainty

A. Understanding this Challenge

While confusion, complexity and chaos are three different things, for leaders they share some common themes: mess, shades of grey, not knowing, lack of role and identity. You may be happier with one of this trio than another; for instance, some people enjoy complexity but hate to be confused. The key point is that leadership is not just about knowing and organising, it is also about the ability to live with complexity, uncertainty, chaos and confusion. Some leaders believe that if they are doing a great job then everything should be working well and running smoothly. This is, of course, a myth. Yet, however much you know this, it doesn't help you in countering the deeply scripted feelings of panic, anxiety and stress that can be induced by confusion, complexity and chaos.

What do these words mean to leaders?

1. Confusion

This is where the leader's mind is drawn in so many directions at once, often about the same issue, that the mind becomes locked and clear thinking becomes blocked. Your thinking goes round and round in circles; your thought patterns are unproductive and exhausting. Usually the answer lies in doing whatever it takes to get clarity of information through clear lines of communication, but sometimes when that strategy doesn't work it suggests that there may be a creative process going on. It is at times like this that you need to acknowledge and live with the confusion as a crucial part of the process.

2. Complexity

There is now a body of theory around complexity. At its simplest level it is learning to recognise that two or more perspectives may well be true at the same time. While the best strategy to overcome complexity is to search for simplicity (not to be confused with being simplistic!), sometimes you will need to acknowledge the creative tension that exists between different perspectives, points of view or understandings. The challenge here is to hold, enjoy and play with a number of different perspectives at the same time.

3. Chaos

The antonym to chaos is organisation. Organisation is there to mitigate chaos. However, sometimes reducing chaos by organisation leads teams to become impaired in their functioning, creative energy to be restricted and new solutions to be undiscovered. In *The Different Drum* (1990) Scott-Peck underlines that chaos is absolutely crucial as a stage in groups and teams discovering real synergy. It was Nietzsche who said 'one must still have chaos in one to give birth to a dancing star'. The importance of chaos is that it allows many thoughts and emotions to have space together so that something new or different can emerge.

Like the Vertigo Challenge, the Confusion–Complexity–Chaos Challenge is very much an inner-game challenge. It is also linked to the Personality Challenge. Using the language of Myers-Briggs (see the Personality Challenge) some people with a structured approach to life don't want too much confusion, whereas someone with an open, flexible approach to life may see confusion as an energising part of how they work. Perspective, therefore, is the key to whether people see confusion–complexity–chaos as something to be embraced or avoided.

> We should make things as simple as possible – but not further.
> (Albert Einstein)

Six Reasons Why this Challenge Is so Important

1. Builds Emotional Intelligence

As the Introduction outlined, research has highlighted the link between effective leadership and Emotional Intelligence. Leaders know what they feel, understand something of their personality and pathology, are aware of their impact on others and have the ability to manage an internal dialogue or to process these emotions, attitudes and beliefs to maximise their influencing relationship on others. To learn to make space for chaos, complexity and confusion and to manage these in a way that unlocks creativity, potential and performance is to go a long way in developing Emotional Intelligence. You need to know and manage yourself well to respond effectively to this challenge.

2. Builds high-performing teams

Many organisations have grown up with a team-building model from Tuckman (1965) – Forming, Storming, Norming and Performing. Scott-Peck, in *The Different Drum*, develops this idea into a more dynamic model of building community or synergy in teams and stresses the importance of this in creating a learning environment or organisation. Scott-Peck's stages are Pseudo-relationships, Chaos, Emptiness and Real relationship or Community. In his rules for maintaining low-performing, deficient or impaired working teams, Scott-Peck highlights the ways people avoid chaos by not saying anything that might offend someone else. If they do offend, annoy or irritate someone, that person pretends they are not bothered in the least. If signs of disagreement appear, they change the subject as quickly and smoothly as possible. The basic pretence of pseudo-community in teams is the denial of individual differences and the essential dynamic of pseudo-community is chaos avoidance.

3. Releases energy for creativity and innovation

When you keep chaos, confusion or complexity at bay, it takes up mental and emotional energy. The use of this energy inhibits your levels of awareness, your understanding of the full range of choices available to you and the possibility of coming up with the best creative solutions. In simple terms, imagine playing with a beach ball in the water. When you push the ball under the water it takes a lot of focus and energy to get it under and then hold it under. The energy that it takes to keep the ball out of view is energy that is not freed up for playing with the ball.

4. Increases the options

Albert Einstein said that a problem couldn't be solved on the same level on which it was created. Insight and awareness are crucial for creating new solutions or options. If you don't allow chaos, confusion or complexity on to your radar screen then you will be limited to old understandings and therefore old solutions. Allowing chaos, confusion or complexity on to your radar screen is like throwing all the balls up into the air to see new configurations or patterns. Seeing even the familiar in a new way will be the key to new options being created.

5. Builds confidence

Allowing chaos, confusion or complexity into your mental and emotional world increases awareness. As awareness increases, so choice increases. You allow many more alternatives than you previously did. As you shift from feeling that something is so overwhelming that you don't want to go there to being able to see a little light or a new way forward, then your confidence increases. You will feel power returning – moving from a place where you are disempowered to one where you are empowered (see Figure 17.1).

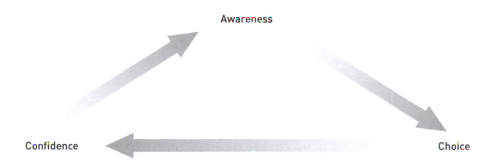

Figure 17.1 Building confidence

6. Releases potential and therefore increases performance

How much of you do you bring to work? How much of you or your team's potential effectiveness is realised at work? Dr Huseman in his presentation to the Linkage Coaching and Mentoring Conference in 1999, in London, quoted from his research with JRI Databank on the question, 'If you wanted to, could you improve your effectiveness on the job?' In answer to this question, 37% said they could be 10% more effective, 31% said they could be 25% more effective and 11% said they could be 50% more effective. Your actual performance or effectiveness at work is related to how much interference – both internal and external – gets in the way. Making space for chaos, confusion or complexity and working with the challenge it presents releases the potential that has been locked up in your inner game and then your outer game.

How do you spot Confusion, Complexity or Chaos?

Here are four possible sets of symptoms.

1. It may be the emergence of conflict, high energy, increased anxiety levels or your becoming mentally distracted.
2. You may spot them when you lack engagement with a task or situation, where you don't feel 'present' or involved. It may be that creativity or involvement feels like too much of an effort.
3. You find yourself making contradictory statements. An example of this would be acknowledging that you want to do something and then saying you are not sure if it is a good choice for you. The result of the contradictions is a paralysis of thinking or action.
4. You see it in 'brain lock'. This is where the mind suddenly or slowly locks up or feels too full or too tired.

B. Personal Reflection

Self-assessment of the Confusion–Complexity–Chaos Challenge

Read through all of the questions below and reflect on your work recently. Next, rate yourself in the box below on a scale of 1 to 10, where 1 = very ineffective in responding to this challenge and 10 = very effective at responding to this challenge.

The key to self-assessment on this challenge is how well you manage the three Cs to create better outcomes at work. To score a 10 is to make space and work with the three Cs to create better outcomes. To score a 1 is to avoid the three Cs altogether. If you are really clear and have done a lot of personal work on this, you will score closer to 10 on the scale. If this is all really quite new to you and you haven't got a high level of awareness and strategies for managing it then you will be closer to 1 on the scale.

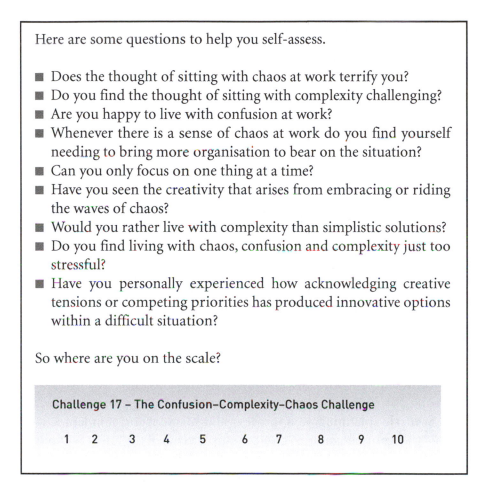

Here are some questions to help you self-assess.

- Does the thought of sitting with chaos at work terrify you?
- Do you find the thought of sitting with complexity challenging?
- Are you happy to live with confusion at work?
- Whenever there is a sense of chaos at work do you find yourself needing to bring more organisation to bear on the situation?
- Can you only focus on one thing at a time?
- Have you seen the creativity that arises from embracing or riding the waves of chaos?
- Would you rather live with complexity than simplistic solutions?
- Do you find living with chaos, confusion and complexity just too stressful?
- Have you personally experienced how acknowledging creative tensions or competing priorities has produced innovative options within a difficult situation?

So where are you on the scale?

Challenge 17 – The Confusion–Complexity–Chaos Challenge

1   2   3   4   5   6   7   8   9   10

C. Developing Your Ability to Perform through Uncertainty

F. Scott Fitzgerald once said that first-rate intelligence is the capacity to hold two opposing ideas in the mind at the same time and still function.

In the assessment you have taken a look at your general effectiveness at managing this challenge. The aim of this chapter now is to equip you for the challenge by helping you to work it out in four different areas. They are:

1. Your business.
2. Your team.
3. Your staff.
4. Yourself.

Your Business – Creating Multiple Futures

In the business context a more familiar expression for the Confusion–Complexity–Chaos Challenge is 'managing uncertainty'. Rather than re-invent the wheel we suggest that a book like *Profiting from Uncertainty* by Paul Schoemaker (2002) will provide you with an excellent process for thorough planning around uncertainty in your business. The author also outlines an extensive range of tools essential for managing confusion, complexity and chaos in business. These include:

- **Scenario planning** – a process that focuses on fundamental variables or outcomes to create multiple views of the future without trying to reduce their number in order to reduce complexity.
- **Analogies, history and reference cases** – these look at the stories of other companies and seek to learn from their experience (and mistakes!).
- **Contingency planning** – basically this is about looking at all of the key processes and creating a plan B, in case of failure of plan A.
- **Extrapolative forecasting** – looks at past and current trends to predict the future.
- **Sensitivity analysis** – looks at what happens when you change one little factor and keep all of the other factors the same.
- **Management flight simulators** – a flight simulator seeks to give you a very realistic experience of a situation and its risks without the cost of getting it wrong. A simulator reproduces your business in every way and then will add random factors into the picture to see what or how you will deal with them.

- **Monte Carlo simulation** – based on crunching numbers, it seeks to work out the probability of outcomes by adding uncertainties into complex and strategic initiatives.
- **Core competency analysis** – analyses the business's skills, resources and capabilities. The aim is to create flexibility in order to create new ways of working or to redeploy old skills in new ventures.
- **Corporate venturing units** – these involve creating new businesses or new technologies so that there are safety nets in place or new initiatives in the starting blocks in case an existing project fails.
- **Decision analysis** – a rigorous process for looking at a decision and working out what other alternatives are available and what the outcomes might be.
- **Insurance and risk management** – this is a traditional method of assessing risks and creating strategies to cover these risks. The creation of 'hedge funds' in the financial markets is an example that arose out of looking at investment risk.
- **Net present value** – this takes a project, looks at its current value, then looks at what it may be worth against certain risks, and then looks at it against how its value will change over a period of time.
- **Portfolio analysis** – this involves taking an area of your business and portfolio and analysing it against some key variables such as risk and opportunity.
- **Real options analysis** – this involves taking a project and looking at all of the possible decisions or opportunities that may occur along the way. This creates flexibility and creativity as the reality emerges.
- **Knowledge management** – systems and processes for collecting and collating what we personally, the team or the organisation know. It covers how to retain and manage what you already know and how to handle new knowledge as it occurs so that it is readily available to create new ideas and avenues of thought and action.
- **Consumer and market research** – surveys, focus groups and so on comb through the internal and external environment for trends and data that may help assess the risks and opportunities in your market.

- **Organisational benchmarking** – compares business against business especially in the area of processes.
- **System dynamics modelling** – dissects organisations' processes in complex business environments. The use of influence diagrams is a key part of this process. Uncertainties can be introduced at random into the picture to model how these will affect relationships.
- **Games theory** – thinks through how one set of decisions may be affected by the opponent's actions.
- **Fuzzy logic and artificial intelligence** – an example of the artificial simulation of intelligence is neural nets that seek to mimic the human mind as it seeks to handle complex and random data.
- **War rooms and opportunity centres** – visually gather vast amounts of complex information and organise it in ways that are easily understandable.

Your Team – Impaired or Enhanced?

How do you create high-performing teams? This is a crucial question for most managers and all businesses. There are a number of models around effective team development. One of the better known of these is Tuckman's (1965) model around teams needing to go through four stages of development: Forming, Storming, Norming and Performing. The chaotic, confused stage is the 'storming'. The model this book uses is a development of the idea by M. Scott-Peck and is worth reading about in *The Different Drum* (1990) and *A World Waiting to Be Born* (1993).

Scott-Peck has worked with countless groups in organisations of all shapes and sizes to try to understand and facilitate the move from impaired or ineffective functioning teams to highly effective teams. It will come as no surprise that the critical factor is what goes on between people in a team. Scott-Peck talks about building community in teams. Some people may regard this word 'community' as a bit soft or Californian but his intent is clear. Teams are as good as the relationships between their members. Scott-Peck defines community as 'a way of being together with both individual authenticity and interpersonal harmony so that people become able to function with a collective energy even greater than the sum of their individual energies' (1993). The other word that is used in organisations is *synergy*.

A group is just a bunch of individuals joined together by a common interest. A group doesn't necessarily need to be a team. A team shares a common objective or task and its members need to work together to achieve it. A problem is that for all kinds of reasons you may not feel able to bring all of your experience, skills, wisdom, perspectives, personality, gender and so on to the table. One of the biggest limiting factors to 'how much of you does your team get?' will be how safe it is to bring all of you to work. If you only bring 50% of 'you and your potential' then the team is diminished in realising its potential. Multiply this by the number of people in the team and the effect is obvious.

The essential issue that needs addressing in creating high-performing teams is:

> How do you bring all of you to work? And how do you help others bring all of themselves to work? And how can you all bring all of yourselves to work so that you all can create something together that is even bigger than the sum of all the parts?

So, how do you create synergy or community in teams? Scott-Peck has distilled a model with four stages but it is a dynamic model and recognises that a team never 'arrives' although its effectiveness can be dramatically increased. (Before going any further we wish to acknowledge our huge debt of gratitude to Ivan Sokolov for his work in translating Scott-Peck's work into some helpful diagrams.)

The four stages Scott-Peck talks about are outlined below (see also Figure 17.2) on page 316.

1. Pseudo-relationships or community

What is it? This is the usual level at which people start relationships. This is the time of 'How are you?' 'Fine, thanks.' It is the stage of surface relationships and acquaintances rather than friendships. As a social convention this is very normal and acceptable for Western-type teams, but if a group of people involved in meaningful tasks remain at this same level of communication and relationship over time then it is likely to reduce the effectiveness of the team.

2. Chaos

What is it? This is where personal differences begin to appear: different views on how to do the project, what the key objectives are; different personalities emerging as stronger or weaker; voices demanding to be heard; toys being thrown out of the pram; old wounds surfacing; unhelpful alliances surfacing; subgroups emerging. Chaos doesn't necessarily break out in observable energy and conflict. A key sign of chaos emerging is when the energy levels of the team go down, when the team loses focus on the task or when people begin to disengage or 'check out'.

The typical movement when chaos breaks out – whether it be outward and noisy or quiet withdrawal – is to move back into pseudo-relationships and make everything better or to reorganise the team (reorganisation is the easy antidote to chaos) or allow secondary leaders to emerge (you're not doing a very good job, she or he could do better). People often cycle back and forth between pseudo-relationship and chaos. The problem is that there are two key issues that will undermine the development of a high-performing team. The first is that pseudo-relationships deny individual differences. 'We all think the same really, don't we?' 'We all believe the same, don't we?' The truthful answer is 'No, we don't.' A team is made up of people from different age groups, different sexes, different personalities, different life experiences, different skills and different pathologies and development issues. For a team to mature there needs to be a space where people can be very different and find a way of putting all of the richness of their differences to work together on an issue. Community or synergy creates a space where people can bring all of themselves to work; pseudo-community shuts down the space so that people all behave in a certain way. The fear of chaos is that you will not get the job done, so the team resorts to organisation. However, organisation will not build synergy. The second key is that the essential dynamic of pseudo-community is conflict avoidance, the belief that if you keep everyone happy then you will keep the team functioning well. Not necessarily. The result can be conformity but lack of engagement and motivation. If there isn't room to bring 'all of you' into the team then you will find a place outside of the team or work to express who you are. Conflict avoidance actually weakens relationships and creates the very vulnerability and insecurity for a team that it was so keen to avoid.

3. Emptiness

What is it? The uniqueness of Scott-Peck's model is in the identification of this stage. This is where the team stops trying to avoid the chaos and confusion on one side by maintaining a pseudo-community and also the team members stop trying to convert each other to their beliefs, point of view or perspective. In emptiness people identify their own preconceptions and stop labelling others with them; they identify their own expectations and stop expecting others to meet them; they identify their own prejudices and start to withhold judgements about others; they stop trying to heal, fix or convert and they suspend their need to be in control. This stage is characterised by meaningful silence, a lot of listening and seeking to understand, and an acknowledgement of how hard it is for such a diverse bunch of people to work together. It also involves a commitment to each other and to finding a way of working together. What the emptiness does is create the space for you to bring all of you to work.

4. Synergy or community

What is it? Now there is space for a group of people to be fully present, and although very different they can start using their differences to solve the problems and come up with very creative solutions that before would have been impossible (see Figure 17.2).

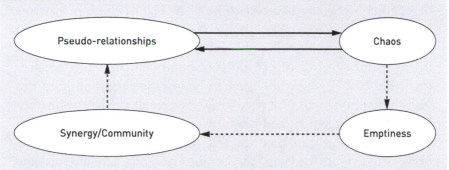

Figure 17.2   Creating synergy/community in teams

Successfully embracing and managing chaos and confusion is essential to the development of high-performance teams.

Here are some questions to think through.

- What stage of development is your team in?
- Do you personally avoid or embrace chaos?
- Does the team avoid or embrace chaos?
- How do you or the team avoid the chaos?
- How do you facilitate your team through the chaos?
- Does the team deal openly with issues that are painful, threatening or deeply buried?
- Does the team consciously face individual judgements, prejudices and beliefs or ignore them?
- Does the team seek to build on diversity?

Steps to working through chaos in building high-performing teams

Step 1:   Teach the Scott-Peck model of team development to new teams or teams embarking on new projects together.

Step 2:   The team needs to be focused on its interpersonal process as much as achieving the task.

Step 3: Building the relationships around the questions outlined above is seen as a legitimate agenda item each time the team meets.

Step 4: Team leaders learn to spot the stages and facilitate the team through them or know when they should be using an external facilitator to achieve the task while also building the team.

Your Staff – Managing Diversity

What does 'diversity' mean in this context? R. Roosevelt Thomas (in *Harvard Business Review*, 2001b) defined it as 'the process of creating and maintaining an environment that enables all participants to contribute to their full potential in pursuit of organisational objectives'. Why is diversity a part of the Confusion–Complexity–Chaos Challenge for leaders? Because in leading people you are not leading a monochrome group of people – you are leading males and females, different gender identities, different colour skin, different cultural backgrounds, different religions, different values, different locations, different abilities and disabilities, different ages, different social backgrounds and so on. There is a book called *Building with Bananas* (Copley and Copley, 1978) and you can't get anything more difficult than trying to construct a building with bananas. Managing diversity is like building with bananas! Leading a diverse workforce is no longer a challenge to be acknowledged by the few; the global market isn't out there somewhere – it exists within every office and team. It is now a challenge for every leader.

> Often when companies have achieved maximum levels of scale economy in their production process through expert systems, such as information technology and advanced logistic strategies, they turn their attention to their Human Resources. Fully utilising their Human Capital helps to raise the level of efficiency, competitiveness and the necessary innovation to retain leadership positions.

An outstanding feature that identifies this era is the diversity of the global marketplace. Diversity in gender, demography, age, religion, culture, knowledge level, and disabilities. Organisations are microcosms of this new socio-economic environment.

By managing diversity, organisations may increase corporate profits by enabling every employee to fully contribute and develop to his or her professional potential, that is, in line with corporate objectives. (European Institute for Managing Diversity, *www.iegd.org/English/ FrameHomePage.htm*)

The European Institute for Managing Diversity outlines six areas that need attention if diversity is to be taken seriously. We have adapted those areas for you to evaluate how you are doing with your team.

1. Evaluate

What are the diversity issues in your team/project/organisation?

- Gender.
- Demography (where people live).
- Age.
- Religion.
- Culture.
- Knowledge level.
- Disabilities.
- Language.

2. Diversity Programme Design

What is your strategy for an inclusive climate for all your employees?

3. Communication

What is your internal and external communication plan to achieve this?

4. Training

What training do you, the team or individuals need to give support to your diversity programme?

5. Measurement and Evaluation

How will you measure and/or evaluate the economic and non-economic results of your diversity programme?

6. Auditing and Accountability

What measures need to be in place to ensure accountability and continued development of your approach to managing diversity?

Yourself – Sorting out Your Head

Some examples:

- You have potentially got four or five different markets and you just don't know which ones to go for.
- You have got two or three new products you could develop.
- The business is growing – what do you keep and what do you let go of? Do you hold on to it all? If you do you will feel like you'll burst!
- Which direction should your career take?
- Which way do you go in this market?

Step 1. Create a space

Creating a space means creating some time in your diary. This doesn't just apply to this challenge. It is a basic tenet of good leadership that you have regular space in your diary to reflect, to think strategically, to create wisdom out of experience, to maintain your personal resourcefulness and to gain insight.

- Block out the time in your diary.
- Put a ring fence or boundary around it by getting away from your phone. (Go and work at the coffee shop for half an hour. Or hide yourself in a dedicated meeting room.)
- Ask yourself whether it is the right time to be doing this or would you be able to give it more of your attention at a different time?

Step 2. What's the issue?

What are the issue(s) that you feel are confusing, complex and chaotic? What is it at work that is occupying your attention so much right now?

When a car gets stuck in the mud its wheels just spin round however hard you press the accelerator. What is it that you are 'spinning wheels' with in your head at two in the morning?

Step 3. Emptying your head

You need to get all that is in your head out on paper where you can see it. It is important that you capture all of the ideas, distracted thoughts, contradictions and things that you are unable to resolve. Here's the problem. You have to carry all of this inside your head. A key part of this challenge is to externalise the chaos, confusion or complexity and then, by spreading it out in front of you, you can begin to look at it and think it through rather than having to hold on to it.

The brain can only retain three to seven blocks of information at a conscious level. The rest has to be stored at a pre-conscious or unconscious level. At these levels you feel the weight of it all but don't have enough access to the issues to think through it all. What you end up with is constipation in the head! It is a weight on your mind. You feel full in your head because your head *is* full. In constipation digestion is held up and the digested material won't come down.

We suggest two ways of emptying your head.

The first is the '*dump box*'. Just literally dump every thought on to a blank sheet of paper.

The second method is '*mind-mapping*'. Mind-mapping involves writing the problem in the middle of a blank page. As a new thought about the issue occurs to you draw a new line or artery from the centre and name it with the issue. For every new issue draw an artery but if a thought is related to an existing artery then draw a new line off the artery. Figure 17.3 is an example that Shenaz drew out when coaching Trevor on a business issue.

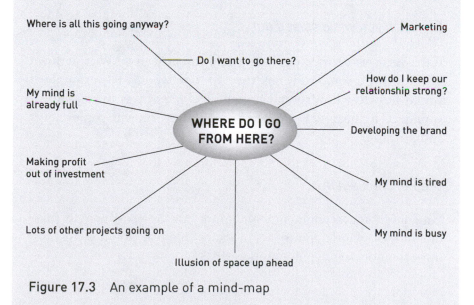

Figure 17.3   An example of a mind-map

Your turn! Map out the complexity of a current business issue.

Step 4. Be kind to yourself

When you begin to download the confusion, complexity or chaos it can often feel worse. It would be easy to think this is why you didn't face all this stuff before – now it feels as bad as you thought it would. At this point you need to validate the feelings: validate the confusion, complexity or chaos.

Acceptance and validation is an important part of the process. It is OK to feel that it is this complex. There is a subtle pressure you can put on yourself that you should be more 'sorted' as a leader than you are, that this shouldn't be as difficult as it feels and that you shouldn't be as tired with the issues as you feel.

Life is messy. You cannot reduce it into neat comfortable bundles, boxes or packages. When you have downloaded the issue it may be important to step back, sleep on it and try not to rush in and sort it out too quickly. Trust the process!

Step 5. If you were sorted out . . .

If this issue were sorted out how would you be feeling? Write it down in the first person, i.e. 'I' not 'they' or 'one would'. For example, 'I would feel clear headed and I would feel like it was manageable. I would feel lighter and I would feel I could move on with some energy and purpose.'

Step 6. Look again

Look again at everything in your 'dump box' or mind-map. Is there one of these words, comments or issues that you would say is most important or needs your attention first?

For example, from the mind-map in Figure 17.3, knowing the endgame or 'where this is all going' stood out as the most important issue.

If it isn't immediately obvious, then use the pie diagram method. Create a circle and then create a separate slice of the pie within the circle for each element of the puzzle. Figure 17.4 is an example of what Shenaz wrote down when coaching Trevor on the business issue we highlighted earlier.

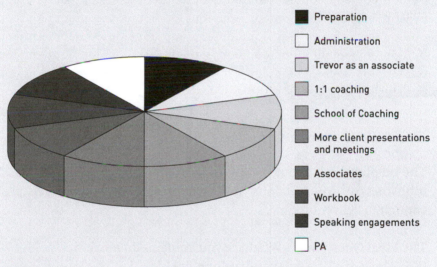

■ Preparation
□ Administration
▨ Trevor as an associate
▨ 1:1 coaching
▨ School of Coaching
▨ More client presentations and meetings
■ Associates
■ Workbook
■ Speaking engagements
□ PA

Figure 17.4   Pie chart method

When you have constructed your own pie chart rate each segment in terms of importance to you. As we worked on the example above we asked:

■ Which segments produce a direct income?
■ Which segments are crucial to achieving the vision and mission of the company?

Our observation is that leadership is an integrated activity and mindset. Leadership involves integrating vision, wisdom and your internal compass. It is vital that you keep having a conversation with yourself and your team about these issues in order to navigate your way through the Confusion–Complexity–Chaos Challenge.

Step 7. Focus

Decide where you need to put your focus. If you had to give up one or two chunks from your pie chart, which ones would have to go?

If your vision, mission and values dictated that there was one area you definitely could never give up, which area or chunk from the pie chart would that be?

- Make a decision on which areas to focus on.
- What are the gains and risks of this focus?
- Prioritise a course of action.

Step 8. Set a time frame for the action

The helpful thing about setting time frames is that it focuses the robustness of your actions and ensures that they are practical enough to deliver on time.

The Final Question . . . What are you going to do now?
(See Appendix 1 for further development)

18

The
Work–Life Balance Challenge

Getting results whilst living a
satisfying life

A. Understanding this Challenge

In this challenge let us start with a question. Do you think you have a good work–life balance?

How should work–life balance be defined? Some people's definitions are:

- Time to just kick the leaves.
- To be home by 5.30 p.m. three times a week.
- To move from a 65-hour to a 50-hour week.
- To fit in lunch.

Our definition is this: the laws of demand and supply in life (or input and output in your life) are balanced. People are in balance when they feel that they are working from reserves rather than running on empty. They are in balance when they have recognised their needs and are not getting bent out of shape by trying to meet them. Work–life balance for leaders is like in-flight refuelling for planes – taking in while giving out. Stephen Covey (1989) talks about 'P/PC balance', where P = Production or what is being given out and PC = Production Capability or the ability to keep on giving out.

Abraham Lincoln is reputed to have said that if he had eight hours to cut down a tree (Production) he would spend several of these hours sharpening his axe (Production Capability).

We asked a CEO in early January how his Christmas break had gone. He said it was OK, but there were so many pressures at work that the temptation was to come into the office and fix it all. 'So did you?', I asked him. He paused and then said, 'No, I was so tired before Christmas I decided that the law of diminishing returns meant that even if I had come into work I wouldn't have got that much done.' On another occasion I was told about a very senior manager in the automotive industry who has never worked a weekend so that his family gets his emotional and physical involvement in a way that he can never give it during the week. These are good examples of emotional objectivity and the value people put on family life and how they balance that with their working environment.

A sad example was evident in a leadership team to whom we suggested, as a kind of warm-up exercise, that they share with the person sitting next to them what was the best book they had read in the past six months and why. Their responses suggested that they thought we had committed an indecent act. These were a group of leaders in their mid-thirties to early fifties who all had a university education but now confessed that during the last six months they had had no time to read books.

From the language of the casino, work these days is like being on a perpetual roll, but the challenge is how to maintain it. You keep on giving out but what attention is being paid to putting something back in?

Work–life balance involves:

- Intellectual stimulation to maximise the brain's potential as the most under-used organ in the body.
- Physical exercise, keeping in reasonable shape and not undertaking anything to excess.
- The emotional and social intercourse with friends and family and with people who give rather than deplete energy.
- The emotional and social investment in those who work with you and for you so that they remain people rather than objects: build trust rather than feel used.
- A spiritual dimension that includes anything that gives life a higher sense of meaning and purpose above and beyond the mundane.

In an interview with *Daily Mail* writer Derek Lawrenson, golfer Nick Faldo reassessed his past 20 years. 'Faldo admits that he lifted his head for the first time two years ago and like a child in a toyshop, stared in wonderment. He said, "for 20 years I put the blinkers on, my career first, and got on with it". Interestingly, the date of that interview turned out to be the day whole cultures within society asked themselves what the higher meaning of their life was beyond the working world – Tuesday 11 September 2001.

To ignore the investment in work–life balance is to be so focused on productivity that you neglect to develop the capability to be productive.

B. Personal Reflection

What is your definition of work–life balance? What is your life-partner's or significant other's definition? Is it similar to yours? (If not, where do they differ?)

Self-assessment of the Work–Life Balance Challenge

Read through all of the questions below and reflect on your work recently. Rate yourself in the box below on a scale of 1 to 10, where 1 = very ineffective in responding to this challenge and 10 = very effective at responding to this challenge (i.e. work and wider life are very much in balance; you are investing as much in your ability to maintain long-term productivity as you are into short-term work goals).

- Do you live to work or work to live?
- Do you believe that 'it's better to burn out than rust out'?
- Do you regularly exercise your body?
- Have you had a full physical or medical check-up in the past 12 months?
- Have you enough relationships that you find nourishing and refreshing to counterbalance the emotional drain you find in some of your work relationships and situations?
- Do you read and continue to stretch your intellectual and mental capability?
- Was college the last time that you were mentally and intellectually stretched?
- Have you invested time in understanding who you are and what life is about, and what gives your life meaning?
- Do you monitor your physical, emotional, mental and spiritual reserves on a regular basis?
- Are you currently working some weekends, many weekends or no weekends?
- Do you feel close and connected with your partner/children/key friends?

■ If this were the last day of your life would you be happy that your priorities had been right recently?

So where are you on the scale?

Challenge 18 – The Work–Life Balance Challenge

1   2   3   4   5   6   7   8   9   10

C. Developing Greater Work–Life Balance

Specifically when are you in and out of balance? Score yourself on each dimension of the work–life balance wheel, where 1 is out of balance and 10 is very much in balance (see Figure 18.1).

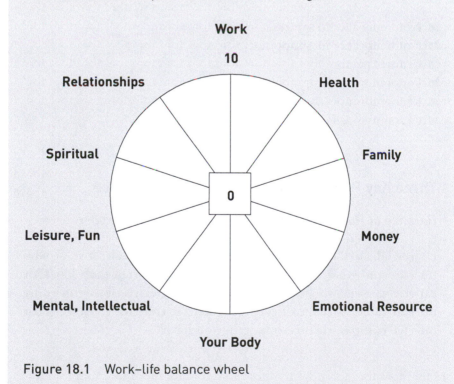

Figure 18.1   Work–life balance wheel

Imagine balance to be like a smooth wheel.

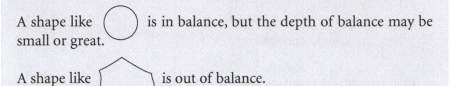

A shape like ◯ is in balance, but the depth of balance may be small or great.

A shape like ⬠ is out of balance.

If health is out of balance, and emotional reserves are very low, then you will feel the 'bumps' in the wheel at those points. The 'bumps' are simply where you feel you are most vulnerable to the imbalance.

Inner/Outer Challenge Question

Having mapped out your levels of balance or imbalance, what are the external obstacles to you getting back in balance? What are the internal obstacles to redressing the balance?

- Not being able to say 'no'.
- Not being able to disappoint others.
- Control needs.
- Perfection needs.
- Recognition needs.
- Certainty needs.

Three Key Principles behind Work–Life Balance

Balance of Purpose – Develop a clear sense of purpose

Highly effective leaders have a clear compass, a clear sense of who they are and what they are about that is bigger than their job. Our experience suggests that many people have been so busy investing in their career that they have not taken the time to develop a clear internal compass. Is this something you have?

See the Internal Compass Challenge for developing this sense of purpose. How do you know when you have got a good internal compass?

Balance roles and relationships – what are your roles and relationships?

All people have many different roles in life – not just their work role. Even at work they often have a number of different roles. These can be divided into personal and professional roles. For example, these may include husband/wife, mother/father, brother/sister, uncle/aunt, team leader, CEO, friend, peer, supervisor.

Take time to identify the different roles in your life. Once you have named your roles ask yourself these questions for each one.

- Which roles are most important to you? Score them on a scale where 1 = important and 5 = least important.
- How much time approximately do you spend in each role?
- In reality who gets most/least of your time?
- Looking at the roles listed above, which do you want to focus your time on?

Reflection

You are looking for inconsistencies between each role that you have, that you intend to have or that you desire to have, and the actual investment you make in each of these roles. Change requires people to face up to realities. For example, if you say your role as a father is most important and you reflect that the total amount of time spent with your child(ren) in the past week totals only minutes then you have clear evidence of imbalance.

People often desire that a role be most important but in reality it isn't. We play mind games with ourselves to make ourselves feel like we are actually doing what we intend or desire to do. Change needs us to face up to realities.

What are your goals?

One way to shift your behaviour is, having identified the role to then identify a goal or two for that role. In Table 18.1 there is a work and a personal example. Consider three of your roles and identify goals for each role.

Table 18.1   Roles and goals

Role	Goal for each role	Initiatives
Manager	To develop your line reports to their best potential while they work for you. To ensure that each member of your team is totally clear about their objectives, how they will be measured and what support they need from you to achieve them.	To meet with line reports once per quarter for an extended coaching session lasting 45 minutes.
Uncle	To be the person your nephew can turn to if he feels his parents are unapproachable.	Make a weekly phone call to your nephew. Book a trip to football with him.

Balance of Time – Diary control: Putting in the big rocks first

Stephen Covey (1989) quotes Goethe as saying:

What matters most should never be at the mercy of what matters least, so the next step is to plan the most important initiatives into the diary.

There is a great activity you can do with a group. You need a Perspex goldfish bowl, a bag of pea shingle sufficient to fill the bowl to the brim and half a dozen different-sized small rocks. Each rock represents a key area of your life, areas that are important and that you must invest in in order to realise your mission and vision (this is true of work or your whole life). The pea shingle represents all of the little things or urgent, but not important, things that crowd our lives (things that demand our attention but add no real value to our work or whole life mission or vision). Fill the bowl up with the pea shingle and then try to get six rocks into the bowl. It can't be done. The only way you can do it is to empty the bowl of all the small stuff and put the big rocks in first. The pea shingle can then only fit around the big rocks. And some of the pea shingle, the small stuff, will have to be left out altogether. The point is that your key goals need to be in the diary first. They are priority. These are the things that must be in place if you are to achieve your personal mission. When they are in place you will have to make decisions not to do certain things. In your diary, write in where you will be actioning your key goals identified in the previous section.

Don't sweat the small stuff – assessing urgent v. important

You determine as important those things that you must do in order to achieve your mission and vision. Something may be demanding your attention as *urgent*, but it is not *important*. The key is to plan as much into the *important, non-urgent* category. For example, investing time in children should largely be in the *important, non-urgent* category, but if you get a call at work to say they have been rushed to hospital that would obviously fall into *urgent, important*.

Analyse your past week and decide where your time has been spent, i.e. important, non-urgent or urgent, not important. What do you notice? Where do you need to target some actions? What will those actions be?

…rt of Success

Rob Parson's best-selling book (2002) outlines Tom Murray's Seven Laws of Success. These could be called seven laws for work–life balance.

Law 1: Don't settle for being money-rich, time-poor.
'I'm happy for you that your work is going so well. I just think you should know that you have become the most boring man I know.'

Charles Handy's wife

Law 2: Believe that the job you do makes a difference.
'I am still looking for the modern-day equivalent of those Quakers who ran successful businesses, made money because they offered honest products and treated their people decently, worked hard themselves, spent honestly, saved honestly, gave honest value for their money, put back more than they took out and told no lies.'

Anita Roddick

Law 3: Play to your strengths – find your x factor (your gift/ability/strength).
'God made me fast and when I run I feel his pleasure.' Eric Liddell

Law 4: Believe in the power of dreams.
'Those who say it can't be done shouldn't get in the way of those who are doing it.'

Law 5: Put your family before your career.
'Few people who have led successful lives have also achieved the most important success of all – taking part in the joys and extra dimensions that a close relationship with one's family can give.'

Sir John Harvey-Jones

Law 6: Keep the common touch.
'If . . . you can walk with kings . . . nor lose the common touch . . . you'll be a man, my son.'

Rudyard Kipling

Law 7: Don't settle for success: make a difference – strive for significance.
'What does it profit a man to gain the whole world, yet lose his soul?'

Jesus Christ

How do you view time?

In the film *Mr Holland's Opus* there is a core image around people's view of time. Do you, like the teacher in the film, see time as hours and minutes that you have to spend or do you see time in terms of purpose, values and investment? The key mindset of a balanced life is one of 'investment' not 'spending'. Mr Holland had seen his life as a teacher in terms of resentment over the time 'spent' with his pupils and 'wasted', not composing his life's opus. It took many years before he could see the investment he had made in the lives of countless young people who were now adults.

Time management is a leadership issue. If you are driven by others' agendas, unbalanced demands or your own demons, then you are not setting a clear agenda for yourself or proactively organising your time to achieve it. This is the difference between the compass and the clock.

Managing your response to time is a leadership issue. It is directly linked to the Proactive Challenge, where you are author of the script of your life, and is also linked to the Internal Compass Challenge where you have a purpose in life that is bigger than the job you do.

Performance and Balance

Tim Gallwey (2000) has highlighted a crucial dimension of how to maintain high performance. He points out that sustained high performance needs to facilitate both an individual's learning or development from this performance and enjoyment of their performance. 'Enjoyment' and 'development' are easy to say but the fact is people give so little attention to either of these as key performance indicators.

Map your own levels of performance, learning and enjoyment in your current job (see Figure 18.2).

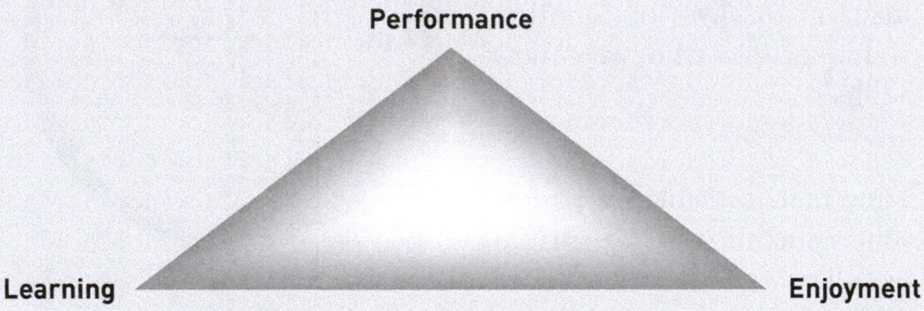

Performance

Learning **Enjoyment**

Figure 18.2 Performance/learning/enjoyment triangle

Consider the following questions

- What three examples do you have to confirm your current level of performance?
- What three actions could you take to improve your current level of performance?
- What three examples do you have to confirm your current level of learning?
- What three actions could you take to improve your current level of learning?
- What three examples do you have to confirm your current level of enjoyment?
- What three actions could you take to improve your current level of enjoyment?

Investing in Balance

The dashboard of a car is expertly designed to provide crucial information, expressed in very simple ways, available to the driver at a glance. For example, in a moment you can see by looking at a dial whether you need to stop soon or immediately for more petrol. Bill Hybels (co-author of *Leadership by the Book*, Blanchard et al., 1999) came up with the idea of four dials people can monitor for work–life balance (see Figure 18.3).

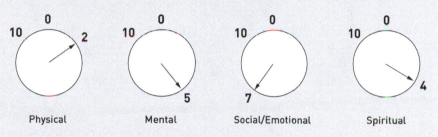

Figure 18.3   Dials for work–life balance

Each dial can be explained as follows:

Physical   This relates to the limits of your own physical/health range. How fit and well are you? Have you had a full health check this year? Are you feeling in good shape? Are you overweight or under-weight?

Mental   This relates to how much you are stretching and developing your mind right now. The brain is the most under-used organ in the body. Are you reading to develop your brain? Are you reading to develop and widen your interests? Are you reading for pleasure? Are you fulfilling your mental potential? You can be busy and stressed but not developing.

Social/Emotional   Are you feeling in good shape with your relationships? Feeling emotionally full or running on empty? While you may have many conversations at work that are draining emotionally are you investing at least equally in conversations and relationships that give you energy and that you enjoy?

Spiritual Given that life is short and that death is the ultimate statistic, what gives your life a bigger meaning? Are you clear about what this is and are you investing in it?

Exercise 1. Put an arrow where you think your 'tank' is. On the dial 10 is full and 1 is virtually empty. Looking at your dials (see Figure 18.4), which ones need urgent attention, which ones are in need of some attention and which ones are currently going well?

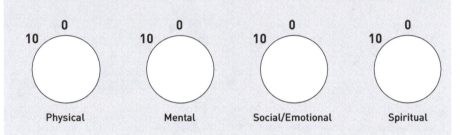

Figure 18.4 Monitor your work-life balance

Exercise 2. For each dial, list specific actions you need to take to invest in that particular area: e.g. for the physical dial it might be something like *'exercise three times this week'*.

Exercise 3. Take a reality check – reflect on your use of time. Rate yourself on a scale of 1 to 10 as to how well you think you are managing time (1 = managing time badly and 10 = excellent time management).

Exercise 4. Earlier in the chapter you were encouraged to identify the key roles in your life, their importance to you, the time you spent on each role and which roles you would like to invest more time and energy in. If you have not completed this exercise, then do so now. You may find it helpful to reflect also on the following questions:

- Which roles take up most time?
- Which roles get neglected?
- Where do you need to recover more time?

- From where can you best recover this time?
- Which roles give you most satisfaction?
- Which roles drain you most?

A Vision for a Balanced Life

If you were brought before a court and accused of poor work–life balance would there be sufficient evidence to convict you?

Take time to consider what a balanced life would look like for you. The following questions may help you in creating your vision for a balanced life.

- In your balanced life what roles would you be focusing on?
- What is your current view of these roles?
- What would you be thinking, feeling, seeing and hearing if you were living according to your vision?
- What actions do you need to take to achieve this? Be very specific.

Challenging Yourself to Change

OK so you may have a problem here. There may be an area or areas where you can see that you are out of balance.

What do you do now? Challenging yourself to change involves examining your choices.

- What were the choices you made that made you become imbalanced?
- Why did you make those choices?
- What were you compromising by doing this?
- Was it worth it? What were the benefits of the choices you made?
- What was the cost of the choices you made?
- Brainstorm here all of the possible alternative choices, however difficult or improbable they may have seemed at the time.
- Which ones in hindsight were the better choices?
- What constrained you from making those choices at that time?

Ask 'why?' four times. Why didn't you do that? Then take your answer and ask again, 'Why didn't you do that?'

If for some reason you said 'no' to the better option, then you need a bigger 'yes'. In other words, your reason to say 'yes' to the new choice must be bigger than your reason to say 'no' to it. What would the bigger 'yes' need to look like? What do you need to do to create this bigger 'yes'?

> Things which matter most must never be at the mercy of things which matter least. Goethe

> The main thing is to keep the main thing the main thing.

The Final Question . . . What are you going to do now?
(See Appendix 1 for further development)

APPENDIX

1

The final question –
'What will you do now?'

Each challenge chapter ends with the same question, *What are you going to do now?*

The reason why this is so important is that while we believe raising your awareness or increasing your understanding is a crucial first step, to truly add value to the organisation and yourself in terms of growing your leadership this has to be translated into actions and into different ways of doing something. Rather than repeat ourselves at the end of each chapter, here are some keys to action planning.

Key 1. Set a goal for your development

People often ask us whether coaching is an effective way of developing leaders. We frequently reply that a person's development is as effective as the goal they set is clear. So a key step is to help you to define what being a higher score might look like. For example, if you scored yourself a 6 in the assessment then what might it be like if you were an 8? What would you be doing differently? Turn that into a specific goal.

Key 2. Identify what is working well

However high or low your score was, describe specifically what positive behaviours you currently display that would give you the score that you gave yourself.

Key 3. Identify what is working less well

However high or low your score was, describe specifically what is missing in the behaviours you currently display that prevented you from giving yourself a higher score.

Key 4. Create a clear picture of the future

If you scored yourself a 5 on the Proactive Challenge, describe a picture of how you would behave, feel, act or think if you were to score yourself 8. One way to anchor this picture of how you want to be is to see it in terms of your senses.

See
What would I *see* you doing that was different?

Hear
What would I *hear* you or others saying about you?

Feel
What would it *feel* like to you or others if you were being this '8' by Christmas (or whenever you set your focus)?

Key 5. Set a time scale

We could tighten up your goal setting for development in this challenge by putting a rough time frame on development. Can we put a time scale on this next stage of your development?

For example, if it's October now and you scored yourself a 6, what would you want your score to be in three months' time?

Key 6. Identify how you will measure success

How will you measure whether you have improved in this area within your stated time frame?

An example of a measure in the Vision Challenge is that you would have a clear and shared vision in your team three months from now. If this is a good measure we should be able to ask you and the team what the vision is and how much you all buy in to it.

Key 7. Take baby steps

Decide a number of small actions to get you going in the right direction. Break the elephant down into manageable spoonfuls or you will get discouraged by lack of progress.

Key 8. Creating momentum

What will you do to create some momentum for change? Do you need to explain what you are doing to someone else to create some accountability?

Key 9. Supporting you

Is there someone you need to speak to? Do you need a coach, a mentor, a therapist, to talk with your line manager, your HR manager, a friend, attend a training course?

Key 10. Link it to your Performance Review

Whatever your organisation calls it – performance review, appraisal, coaching for performance, annual review – link your actions from working with the 18 Challenges of Leadership to the existing goals high-lighted in your review.

Key 11. Just do it!!!!!

Just begin somewhere. A little change will produce new results but, as the saying goes, 'If you keep on doing what you've always done, you will continue to get what you've always got.'

APPENDIX

Getting feedback on your influencing behaviours

(To be used with the Push–Pull model outlined in the Influence Challenge.) Below are 20 different behaviours that people use to influence their line reports, peers or managers. Rate the level of effectiveness of these behaviours for either yourself or the person who has asked you to complete this form. The rating is on a scale of 1 to 5, where 1 = very ineffective and 5 = very effective. Under each behaviour is a space to make comments that would be helpful to this person in becoming more effective. Please be specific in your comments.

Behaviour	Rating
I/They make clear and helpful suggestions Comment:	1 2 3 4 5
My/Their advice is relevant and timely Comment:	1 2 3 4 5
I/They give clear and constructive feedback Comment:	1 2 3 4 5
I/They are usually directive rather than non-directive in my/their management style Comment:	1 2 3 4 5

Behaviour	Rating
I/They are assertive without being overbearing or controlling Comment:	1 2 3 4 5
I/They persist in making points without lapsing into aggression Comment:	1 2 3 4 5
I/They give clear and logical arguments when making my/their point Comment:	1 2 3 4 5
I/They state my/their point of view clearly Comment:	1 2 3 4 5
I/They state what I/they want clearly and effectively Comment:	1 2 3 4 5
I/They are most often on my/their own agenda rather than on those of others Comment:	1 2 3 4 5

Behaviour	Rating
I/They state my/their feelings about a situation clearly without being overly emotional Comment:	1 2 3 4 5
I/They listen effectively Comment:	1 2 3 4 5
I/They are most often on others' agendas rather than my/their own Comment:	1 2 3 4 5
I/They are usually non-directive in my/their management style Comment:	1 2 3 4 5
I/They look to create a shared picture of the future Comment:	1 2 3 4 5

Behaviour	Rating
I/They effectively summarise others' views in conversations Comment:	1 2 3 4 5
I/They recap other people's points of view before presenting my/their own Comment:	1 2 3 4 5
I/They are effective at paraphrasing others' comments and ideas Comment:	1 2 3 4 5
I/They explore others' points of views and arguments Comment:	1 2 3 4 5
I/They look for common ground in discussions with others Comment:	1 2 3 4 5

Behaviours 1–11 fit into the Push side of our influencing model and behaviours 12–20 fit into the Pull side of our influencing model

© The Executive Coach Ltd

APPENDIX

3

The Complete Assessment Summary

	Self-assessed Score 0–10 Where am I now?	Goal Setting Score Where do I realistically want to be?
Challenge 1.	0 1 2 3 4 5 6 7 8 9 10	0 1 2 3 4 5 6 7 8 9 10
Challenge 2.	0 1 2 3 4 5 6 7 8 9 10	0 1 2 3 4 5 6 7 8 9 10
Challenge 3.	0 1 2 3 4 5 6 7 8 9 10	0 1 2 3 4 5 6 7 8 9 10
Challenge 4.	0 1 2 3 4 5 6 7 8 9 10	0 1 2 3 4 5 6 7 8 9 10
Challenge 5.	0 1 2 3 4 5 6 7 8 9 10	0 1 2 3 4 5 6 7 8 9 10
Challenge 6.	0 1 2 3 4 5 6 7 8 9 10	0 1 2 3 4 5 6 7 8 9 10
Challenge 7.	0 1 2 3 4 5 6 7 8 9 10	0 1 2 3 4 5 6 7 8 9 10
Challenge 8.	0 1 2 3 4 5 6 7 8 9 10	0 1 2 3 4 5 6 7 8 9 10
Challenge 9.	0 1 2 3 4 5 6 7 8 9 10	0 1 2 3 4 5 6 7 8 9 10
Challenge 10.	0 1 2 3 4 5 6 7 8 9 10	0 1 2 3 4 5 6 7 8 9 10
Challenge 11.	0 1 2 3 4 5 6 7 8 9 10	0 1 2 3 4 5 6 7 8 9 10
Challenge 12.	0 1 2 3 4 5 6 7 8 9 10	0 1 2 3 4 5 6 7 8 9 10
Challenge 13.	0 1 2 3 4 5 6 7 8 9 10	0 1 2 3 4 5 6 7 8 9 10
Challenge 14.	0 1 2 3 4 5 6 7 8 9 10	0 1 2 3 4 5 6 7 8 9 10
Challenge 15.	0 1 2 3 4 5 6 7 8 9 10	0 1 2 3 4 5 6 7 8 9 10
Challenge 16.	0 1 2 3 4 5 6 7 8 9 10	0 1 2 3 4 5 6 7 8 9 10
Challenge 17.	0 1 2 3 4 5 6 7 8 9 10	0 1 2 3 4 5 6 7 8 9 10
Challenge 18.	0 1 2 3 4 5 6 7 8 9 10	0 1 2 3 4 5 6 7 8 9 10

Setting Your Agenda for Leadership Development

Immediate Attention (Score 1–3)	The . . . . .Challenge
	The . . . . .Challenge
	The . . . . .Challenge
	The . . . . .Challenge
Important Attention (Score 4–7)	The . . . . .Challenge
	The . . . . .Challenge
	The . . . . .Challenge
	The . . . . .Challenge
	The . . . . .Challenge
	The . . . . .Challenge
	The . . . . .Challenge
	The . . . . .Challenge
	The . . . . .Challenge
	The . . . . .Challenge
Effective but maybe set a stretch goal (Score 8–10)	The . . . . .Challenge
	The . . . . .Challenge
	The . . . . .Challenge
	The . . . . .Challenge

Bibliography

Adair, J. (2002) *Inspiring leadership – learning from great leaders,* Thorogood. Excellent link between famous leaders and key areas of leadership

American Management Association (2002) Survey on corporate values, *www.amanet.org/research/pdfs/2002_corp_value.pdf*

Bannister, D. (1971) *Inquiring man: the psychology of personal constructs,* Penguin. Introduces George Kelly's theory of personal construct psychology which we found very useful in forming our concepts and models

Beck, A. T. (1991) *Cognitive therapy and the emotional disorders,* Penguin

Belbin, M. R. (1995) *Team roles at work,* Butterworth Heinemann

Bennis, W. (1989) *On becoming a leader,* Addison-Wesley. Looks at 28 leaders to understand what makes them effective. Good for general understanding and Reality and Wisdom Challenges

Bennis, W. and Nunus, B. (1985) *Leaders,* Harper Perennial. Looks at what makes leaders effective. Good for Influence, Wisdom and Strategy Challenges

Bennis, W., Spreitzer, G. and Cummings, T. (eds) (2001) *The future of leadership,* Jossey-Bass. 'Renowned leadership gurus speak to the next generation.' Eighteen excellent essays covering the whole domain of leadership

Blanchard, K. (1999) *The heart of a leader,* Honor Books. Influence, Insight, Wisdom and Internal Compass Challenges are all covered in this short reader

Blanchard, K. and Bowles, S. (1998) *Gung ho!,* Morrow. Influence, Wisdom and Strategy Challenges

Blanchard, K. and Johnson, S. (1983) *The one minute manager,* Fontana. Worth reading as part of 'Bigger and Bigger Challenge' Challenge

Blanchard, K. and Lorba, R. (1989) *Putting the one minute manager to work,* Fontana. Worth reading as part of 'Bigger and Bigger Challenge' Challenge

Blanchard, K., Carew, D. and Parisi-Carew, E. (1993) *The one minute manager and high performing teams,* Fontana. Worth reading as part of 'Bigger and Bigger Challenge' Challenge

Blanchard, K., Hybels, B. and Hodges, P. (1999) *Leadership by the book,* HarperCollins. A good story that combines 'Life and Career Transition', Work–Life Balance and Internal Compass Challenges

Blanchard, K., Zigarmi, P. and Zigarmi, D. (1987) *Leadership and the one minute manager,* Fontana. A good perspective on leadership styles. Important for the Influence Challenge

Bloch, S. and Whiteley, P. (2003) *Complete leadership,* Pearson Education. Some practical insights into some key leadership skills. Good access to current research

Block, P. (1981) *Flawless consulting,* Jossey-Bass/Pfeiffer. A must!

Bolles, R. (2000) *What color is my parachute?,* Ten Speed Press

Boyatzis, R. (1982) *The competent manager: a model for effective performance,* Wiley

Bridges, W. (1992) *The character of organizations – using Jungian type in organizational development,* Davies-Black. Applies Personality Challenge to an organisation's character

Briggs Myers, I. with Myers, P. B. (1995) *Gifts differing,* Davies-Black. Personality Challenge

Bruce, A. and Langdon, K. (2000) *Strategic thinking,* Dorling Kindersley. Excellent pocket-book summary of Strategic Challenge

Clutterbuck, D. and Megginson, D. (1999) *Mentoring executives and directors,* Butterworth Heinemann. A lot of good case studies

Cockman, P., Evans, B. and Reynolds, P. (1992) *Client-centred consulting,* McGraw-Hill. A good summary of the consulting process and skills

Cope, M. (2003) *The three Cs of consulting,* Financial Times/Prentice Hall. Mick Cope provides real wisdom and practical help in understanding the organisational context

Copley, D. and Copley, N. (1978) *Building with bananas: people problems in the local church,* Paternoster Press

Covey, S. (1989) *The seven habits of highly effective people,* Simon & Schuster. Timeless, foundational and practical reading. Helps with Vision, Strategy, Influence, Proactive, Wisdom and Work–Life Balance Challenges

Covey, S. (1992) *Principle-centred leadership,* Simon & Schuster. Good for Strategy, Influence, Managing the Tension Between Holding On and Letting Go and Work–Life Balance Challenges

Covey, S. (1994) *First things first,* Simon & Schuster. Good for Vision, Strategy and Work–Life Balance Challenges

Covey, S. (1995) *The seven habits of highly effective people, Version 2.0,* Covey Leadership Center

Csikszentmihalyi, M. (1990) *Flow,* Harper Perennial. What are the conditions or environment for people to perform to their best?

Downey, M. (2003) *Effective coaching,* 2nd edn, Thomson Texere. A great basic summary

Eaton, J. and Johnson, R. (2001) *Coaching successfully,* Dorling Kindersley. Good summary of key skills

Fisher, R. and Ury, W. (1997) *Getting to yes,* Arrow. Readable research-based favourite on Influence Challenge and adds into 'Bigger and Bigger Challenge' Challenge for those who haven't been trained in influencing and negotiation

Forster, M. (2000) *Get everything done and still have time to play,* Help Yourself. Original content, great tips and techniques explained in entertaining format for Work–Life Balance Challenge

Frankl, V. E. (1984) *Man's search for meaning,* Pocket Books

Freedman, M. with Tregoe, B. B. (2003) *The art and discipline of strategic leadership,* McGraw-Hill. Excellent for the Strategy Challenge

Gallwey, T. (1974) *The inner game of tennis,* Pan. This seminal book introduces the principles

Gallwey, T. (1979) *The inner game of golf,* Pan. Applying the principles and adding more detail

Gallwey, T. (2000) *The inner game of work,* Orion. Applying the inner game to work and introducing some further crucial concepts around performance

Gardner, H. (1997) *Leading minds – an anatomy of leadership,* Harper-Collins. Looks at famous leaders as examples; has an excellent definition of leadership that he works with

Gerber, M. (1986) *The e myth,* Harper Business. Good perspective on the Strategy Challenge

Goldsmith, M., Lyons, L. and Freas, A. (eds) *Coaching for leadership,* Jossey-Bass/Pfeiffer. The 'encyclopaedia' on the subject; comprises 34 essays by different writers

Goleman, D. (1996) *Emotional intelligence,* Bloomsbury. Underpins all the leadership challenges

Goleman, D. (1997) *Vital lies and simple truths*, Bloomsbury. Important thinking for the Pathology Challenge

Goleman, D. (1998a) *Working with emotional intelligence*, Bloomsbury. A good underpinning of the 'Bigger and Bigger Challenge' Challenge

Goleman, D. (1998b) 'What makes a leader', *Harvard Business Review*, November–December, 94–102

Goleman, D., Boyatzis, R. and McKee, A. (2001) 'Primal leadership', *Harvard Business Review*, December, 43–51

Greenleaf, R. K. (2003) *The servant leader*, Paulist Press

Handy, C. (1995) *The age of unreason*, Arrow. Proactive Challenge in action

Handy, C. (1997) *The hungry spirit*, Arrow. An important analysis of the business context for leaders and underlines the importance of Life and Career Transition and Internal Compass Challenges

Harding, F. (1998) *Creating rainmakers*, Adams. Links between Influence, Strategy and 'Bigger and Bigger Challenge' Challenges

Harvard Business Review (2001a) Special issue: 'Breakthrough leadership', December. Full of excellent essays on leadership. Usually each month has an article on leadership

Harvard Business Review (2001b) *Harvard business review on managing diversity*, Harvard Business School Press. Collection of eight articles from the *Harvard Business Reviews* which give good perspectives for the Confusion–Complexity–Chaos Challenge

Heller, R. (2001) *Charles Handy – a reader*, Dorling Kindersley. A good summary of Handy's thinking on leadership into the next century

Holdaway, K. and Saunders, M. (1996) *The in-house trainer as consultant*, Kogan Page. Good on skills and techniques

Hollis, J. (1993) *The middle passage – from misery to meaning in midlife*, Inner City Books. Excellent insight into Life and Career Transition Challenge

Hughes, R., Ginnett, R. and Curphy, G. (1996) *Leadership – enhancing the lessons of experience*, Irwin. Excellent encyclopaedia covering skills and models

Huszczo, G. (1996) *Tools for team excellence*, Davies-Black. Good for applying the leadership challenges to team leadership

Hutcheson, D. and McDonald, B. (1997) *The lemming conspiracy: how to redirect your life from stress to balance*, Longstreet Press

Hyde, D. (1966) *Dedication and leadership*, University of Notre Dame

Press. Fascinating study into why communists were such dedicated and successful leaders

Inamori, K. (1995) *A passion for success,* McGraw-Hill. Developing yourself as a leader: Internal Compass and Wisdom Challenges

Johnson, S. (1998) *Who moved my cheese?* Vermillion. Delightful story on leading change

Kaplan, R. and Norton, D. (2001) *The strategy-focused organization,* Harvard Business School Press. Case-study-based insights into how to implement strategy. Strategy Challenge

Keirsey, D. and Bates, M. (1984) *Please understand me,* Prometheus. Shows how personality affects styles of leadership and management

Kelly, G. A. (1995, 1991) *The psychology of personal constructs, Vols 1 and 2,* Norton (reprinted by Routledge, 2001)

Kets de Vries, M. (1993) *Leaders, fools and impostors,* Jossey-Bass. Looks at 'the profound psychological forces at work in the leader–follower relationship'. Essays in the psychology of leadership. A great writer for the Influence and Pathology Challenges

Kets de Vries, M. (2001) *The leadership mystique,* Financial Times/Prentice Hall. Excellent on Pathology Challenge

Kotter, J. (1996) *Leading change,* Harvard Business School Press. Good for Vision, Strategy and Managing the Tension Between Holding On and Letting Go Challenges

Kouzes, J. and Posner, B. (1995) *The leadership challenge,* Jossey-Bass. Excellent for Influence, Vision and Reality Challenges and much more

Krebs Hirsh, S. and Kummerow, J. M. (1994) *Introduction to type in organisations,* Oxford Psychologists Press

Landsberg, M. (1997) *The tao of coaching,* HarperCollins. Introduces coaching through a business story

Levinson, D. J. (1978) *The seasons of a man's life,* Ballantine. Excellent insight into life transitions and particularly helpful for Life and Career Transition Challenge

Litwin, G. and Stringer, R. (1967) *Motivation and organization climate,* Harvard Business School Research Press

Machiavelli, N. (1979) *The prince,* Oxford University Press. First published in 1532, a historic look at the power of influence underpinning leadership

McBurnie, T. and Clutterbuck, D. (1987) *The marketing edge,* Penguin. Good example of an area of learning in the 'Bigger and Bigger Challenge' Challenge

McCarraher, L. and Daniels, L. (2002) *The book of balanced living*, Spiro Press. Well-defined – it's about facing and moving ahead with the Work–Life Balance Challenge

McClelland, D. C. (1984) *Motives, personality, and society*, Praeger

McFarlin, D. and Sweeney, P. (2002) *Where egos dare*, Kogan Page. Excellent on Pathology Challenge

Mills, H. (2000) *Artful persuasion*, Amacom

Morrell, M. and Capparell, S. (2001) *Shackleton's way*, Nicholas Brearley. Eight excellent lessons from someone regarded as one of the greatest natural leaders of the 20th century

Olivier, R. (2001) *Inspirational leadership*, Industrial Society/Work Foundation. 'Timeless insights from Shakespeare's greatest leader [Henry V]'

Parsons, R. (2002) *The heart of success*, Hodder & Stoughton. 'Before you read one more book about how to climb the corporate ladder read this: it will help you make sure the ladder is up against the right wall,' Kevin Kaiser, INSEAD. Excellent for Work–Life Balance and Internal Compass Challenges

Patenaude, J. (2003) *Too tired to keep running, too scared to stop*, Vega

Pearce, T. (1995), *Leading out loud*, Jossey-Bass. Brings together the Influence, Vision and Internal Compass Challenges

Pearman, R. and Albritton, S. (1997) *I'm not crazy, I'm just not you*, Davies-Black. Good for the Personality and Influence Challenges

Peters, T. (1987) *Thriving on chaos*, Pan. Good for Confusion–Complexity–Chaos Challenge

Pottruck, D. and Pearce, T. (2000) *Clicks and mortar*, Jossey-Bass. Good integration of Wisdom, Strategy, Vision and Internal Compass Challenges through organisation case studies

Richardson, P. T. (1996) *Four spiritualities*, Davies-Black. Personality and Work–Life Balance Challenges

Robbins, H. and Finley, M. (1997) *Why change doesn't work*, Orion Business Books. Good perspective and an illustration of the needs for the Wisdom Challenge

Rosinski, P. (2003) *Coaching across cultures – new tools for leveraging national, corporate and professional differences*, Nicholas Brearley. Excellent perspectives for the Confusion–Complexity–Chaos Challenge

Schoemaker, F. with Schoemaker, P. (1996) *Extraordinary golf*, Perigee. Applies the inner game to golf but is directly relevant to any aspect of life

Schoemaker, P. (2002) *Profiting from uncertainty – strategies for succeeding no matter what the future brings,* Free Press. Excellent for Confusion–Complexity–Chaos Challenge as well as Reality and Strategy Challenges

Scott-Peck, M. (1990) *The different drum,* Arrow

Scott-Peck, M. (1993) *A world waiting to be born,* Rider

Silver, A. D. (1988) *When the bottom drops,* Prima Books. Organisational leadership perspective on Confusion–Complexity–Chaos Challenge

Smart, J. K. (2003) *Real coaching and feedback,* Prentice Hall. Practical help in using coaching in the line management role

Smith, H. W. (2001) *What matters most,* Franklin Covey/Simon & Schuster. Practical help on Internal Compass Challenge

Spencer, L. M. (1986) *Calculating human resource costs and benefits,* Wiley

Spencer, L. M. (1995) *Reengineering human resources,* Wiley

Spencer, L. M. and Spencer, S. M. (1993) *Competence at work: models for superior performance,* Wiley

Thompson, J. (1997) *Lead with vision,* International Thomson Press. Good for the Strategy Challenge

Thurbin, P. (2001) *Playing the strategy game,* Financial Times/Prentice Hall. Practical help on the Strategy and Reality Challenges with help on the Insight and Vision Challenges

Tichy, N. M. with Cohen, E. (1997) *The leadership engine – how winning companies build leaders at every level,* Harper Business. Good for Wisdom, Internal Compass and Reality Challenges

Trout, J. (2000) *Differentiate or die,* Wiley. Good example of an area of learning in the 'Bigger and Bigger Challenge' Challenge

Tuckman, B. (1965) 'Developmental sequence in small groups', *Psychological Bulletin,* 63, 384–99

Urch Druskat, V. and Wolff, S. B. (2001) 'Building the emotional intelligence of groups', *Harvard Business Review,* March, 80–90

van Maurik, J. (2001) *Writers on leadership,* Penguin Business. Essays from 30 of the gurus on leadership, putting theory into practice

Watts, A. (1979) *The wisdom of insecurity,* Rider Books. A 'spiritual' perspective on the Confusion–Complexity–Chaos Challenge

Wellins, R., Byham, W. and Wilson, J. (1991) *Empowered teams,* Jossey-Bass Wiley

Whitmore, T. (1999) *Coaching for performance,* Nicholas Brearley. Still the best place to start

Whitworth, L., Kimsey-House, H. and Sandahl, P. (1998) *Co-active coaching*, Davies-Black. Excellent journey through skills development

Wieand, P. (2002) Article on leadership, 'Drucker's challenge: Communication and the emotional glass ceiling', *www.iveybusinessjournal.com*

Williams, N. (1999) *The work we are born to do: find the work you love, love the work you find*, Element Books

Yalom, I. (1980) *Existential psychotherapy*, Basic Books

Zohar, D. and Marshall, I. (2001) *Spiritual intelligence*, Bloomsbury. Fits in well with Personality, Life and Career Transition and Work–Life Balance Challenges